GARDENER TO GARDENER™

1,001 Greatest Gardening Tips

GARDENER TO GARDENER™

The Best Hints and Techniques
from the Pages of
Organic Gardening Magazine

EDITED BY FERN MARSHALL BRADLEY

RODALE

RODALE

WE INSPIRE AND ENABLE PEOPLE TO IMPROVE
THEIR LIVES AND THE WORLD AROUND THEM

Editor: Fern Marshall Bradley
Project Manager: Christine Bucks
Cover and Interior Book Designer: Patricia Field
Cover and Interior Illustrator: Keith Ward
Front Cover Photographer: Kurt Wilson
Layout Designer: Faith Hague
Copy Editors: Sarah Sacks Dunn, Nancy W. Humes
Product Specialist: Jodi Schaffer
Indexer: Nanette Bendyna

RODALE ORGANIC LIVING BOOKS
Executive Creative Director: Christin Gangi
Executive Editor: Margot Schupf
Art Director: Patricia Field
Content Assembly Manager: Robert V. Anderson Jr.
Copy Manager: Nancy N. Bailey
Editorial Assistant: Sara Sellar

We're always happy to hear from you. For questions or comments concerning the editorial content of this book, please write to

Rodale Book Readers' Service
33 East Minor Street
Emmaus, PA 18098

Look for other Rodale books wherever books are sold. Or call us at (800) 848-4735.

For more information about Rodale Organic Living magazines and books, visit us at

www.organicgardening.com

Library of Congress Cataloging-in-Publication Data

Gardener to gardener : 1,001 greatest gardening tips : the best hints and techniques from the pages of Organic Gardening magazine / edited by Fern Marshall Bradley.
        p.   cm.
Includes bibliographical references and index.
ISBN 0–87596–891–0 (hardcover : alk. paper)
1. Organic gardening—Miscellanea.   I. Bradley, Fern Marshall.
SB453.5 .G328 2002
635'.0484—dc21   2002012248

Distributed in the book trade by St. Martin's Press

2 4 6 8 10 9 7 5 3 1   hardcover

RODALE
Organic Gardening Starts Here!

Here at Rodale, we've been gardening organically for more than 60 years—ever since my grandfather J. I. Rodale learned about composting and decided that healthy living starts with healthy soil. In 1940 J. I. started the Rodale Organic Farm to test his theories, and today the nonprofit Rodale Institute Experimental Farm is still at the forefront of organic gardening and farming research. In 1942 J. I. founded *Organic Gardening* magazine to share his discoveries with gardeners everywhere. His son, my father, Robert Rodale, headed *Organic Gardening* until 1990, and today a third generation of Rodales is growing up with the magazine. Over the years we've shown millions of readers how to grow bountiful crops and beautiful flowers using nature's own techniques.

In this book, you'll find the latest organic methods and the best gardening advice. We know—because all our authors and editors are passionate about gardening! We feel strongly that our gardens should be safe for our children, pets, and the birds and butterflies that add beauty and delight to our lives and landscapes. Our gardens should provide us with fresh, flavorful vegetables, delightful herbs, and gorgeous flowers. And they should be a pleasure to work in as well as to view.

Sharing the secrets of safe, successful gardening is why we publish books. So come visit us at www.organicgardening.com, where you can tour the world of organic gardening all day, every day. And use this book to create your best garden ever.

Happy gardening!

Maria Rodale

Maria Rodale
Rodale Organic Gardening Books

Contents

Your Greatest Garden Ever

What makes a gardening tip great? First and foremost, it has to be a tip that works. After all, if a "hot tip" doesn't produce results, it wastes your time, money, and effort. Some other characteristics of great tips are originality, simplicity, efficiency, ingenuity, and frugality. For example, the best gardening tip you'll ever discover may be a new method for sowing seeds, a simple system for managing mulch, or a time-efficient way to control weeds. And let's not forget that trying out new gardening tips makes gardening more fun!

Separating gardening myths from great gardening tips isn't always easy. It's surprising how long a gardening tip that's just plain wrong can stay in circulation. One famous myth is the fiction that you can use chewing gum to control moles. The myth says that moles love chewing gum. Put chewing gum into mole burrows and the moles will devour it, gumming up their digestive systems so badly that they can't eat, and thus they die. This would be a great tip if it were true—but it just ain't so, no matter where you garden.

Tips for Every Garden

1,001 Greatest Gardening Tips is bound to include a wealth of tips that *will* work in your garden. These tips are mined from the vast stores of gardening wisdom that the staff of *OG* magazine and books has accumulated during 60 years of publishing in-depth stories on organic gardening, from contributors in every corner of the country. Plus, there's a healthy dose of garden-tested tips from magazine readers—gardeners just like you who are applying their down-to-earth ingenuity to improve their gardens. We've even dredged up some old-time gardening wisdom from venerable publications that predate your grandmother's gardening days!

Where you garden *can* make a difference in the efficacy of some gardening tips, especially tips about how to treat particular kinds of plants. For instance, a growing tip for tomatoes that works well in the Northeast may not work at all for a gardener in the Southeast. Keep in mind that factors such as soil conditions may also affect your results, as can the vagaries of the weather in a particular season.

Where should you turn first in this book to seek tips that will fire your gardening imagination? We've organized the book by topic, so you may want to start with the chapter that fits your gardening passion, whether that's making supercharged compost, growing and harvesting succulent berries, or creating intriguing container gardens. Have a more specific problem or interest? Refer to the index to track down tips that will answer your particular question, such as how to stop cutworms from ruining your new transplants or how to make a trellis from natural materials in your garden.

Of course, it never hurts to browse through a book like this one at random. A gem of an idea may be waiting just beyond the next page turn. You may rejoice to find out that planting asparagus doesn't have to be the back-breaking digging ordeal that's always deterred you from starting your own asparagus patch (see page 70—asparagus will do just fine planted only a few inches deep!). You may discover that a new angle on raised beds can allow you to plant extra-early in spring. (See page 137 for directions on how to slope your beds for maximum sun absorption.) Or, you may be delighted with a fellow gardener's suggestion for a low-cost way to find uniquely stylish permanent plant labels for marking perennial beds. (See page 45—flea market silverware is the answer!)

A Never-Ending Story

One of the greatest things about sharing gardening tips and ideas is that the fountain never seems to run dry. Horticulturists, farmers, nursery owners, and everyday gardeners are an amazingly curious and imaginative group of folks, and experience proves that no matter how much you know about gardening, there's always something new to learn. When you try out a tip in your garden, chances are you may discover yet another variation on the technique that makes it easier, faster, or more successful.

If you'd like to be in direct touch with organic gardeners who enjoy sharing their gardening tips and trials, visit the Gardener to Gardener Forum at www.organicgardening.com. Some of the tips in this book had their birth in that forum—as real answers to real questions from gardeners like you. It may lead you to discover yet another 1,001 great gardening tips!

Chapter 1

Sustaining Your Compost Supply

Compost is a constant in an organic garden; you need a supply year in and year out to keep your garden healthy. Compost feeds your plants, and its vast array of beneficial soil microorganisms helps your plants fight disease and insect pests.

The basic process of composting is to pile together organic raw materials—such as shredded leaves, pulled weeds, kitchen wastes, and straw—along with a "starter" dose of rich soil or already-finished compost. The "starter" supplies the bacteria, fungi, earthworms, and other tiny creatures that feed on the raw materials, transforming them into rich humus—a decomposed organic material that supplies nutrients in a form that plant roots can absorb easily.

You'll love the creative ideas in this chapter for finding compost ingredients everywhere from your vacuum cleaner bag to your neighbors' curbside trash. Several tips show you how to ventilate (add air to) a compost pile; others reveal secrets for success with compost tumblers and with specialized insulated setups for winter composting. Plus, you'll find suggestions for using compost, including a super-simple idea for sifting compost with a nursery tray.

Iced Compost

I've had a compost pile for years but never liked keeping the kitchen scraps in the house until I could dump them. Despite using a bucket with a tight-fitting lid, I still occasionally found fruit flies in my kitchen. Then I had an inspiration: I now put all my compost scraps into a used plastic bag that I keep in the freezer. When it's full, I dump the frozen block onto the pile. No muss, no fuss.

Veronica D.
Colchester, Connecticut

3 Signs of a Perfect Pile

How do you know whether your compost pile is working? Check for these features.

Steam. Heat in a newly made pile is a sign that a healthy microbial community is hard at work eating, reproducing, and making more compost.

A sweet, earthy smell. If compost stinks, it needs to be fixed. Likely culprits of the foul odor are not enough oxygen, too much nitrogen, or too much moisture. Fluff the pile and add dry matter to bring it into balance.

Volume. In this case, size matters. To heat up and carry on the decomposition process effectively, a pile needs to be at least 1 cubic yard.

Tablecloth Transport for Leaves

Use an old plastic or vinyl tablecloth or a tarp to speed the chore of collecting leaves. Lay the cloth on the ground near the leaves and use a broom or rake to whisk the leaves into a pile in the middle of the cloth. (On a windy day, use rocks to weight the corners of the cloth).

When you have a large pile, gather the four corners of the cloth together and drag the bundle to your compost pile. You'll cut leaf-gathering time fourfold compared with raking leaves and loading them into baskets or a wheelbarrow. The leaves are so light that you are limited only by the size of your tablecloth or tarp.

Clean for Compost

The contents of your vacuum cleaner bag can be good fodder for your compost pile. A vacuum cleaner typically picks up dust, human and pet hair, lint, and food crumbs (as well as the odd paper clip). If you have wood floors or 100 percent wool carpeting, pretty much everything in the bags will compost. However, if you have synthetic carpeting, the fibers aren't organic material, won't break down, and certainly won't enrich compost.

Avoid adding vacuum bag contents if you've recently used carpet freshener or cleaner or if the rooms you vacuum have flaking paint, which may contain lead.

Hide Compost in the Hedgerow

OK, maybe you don't have an actual hedgerow, but even a cluster of shrubs can help keep your compost pile hidden from view. You can hide a compost pile behind or among trees or shrubs. Some people don't hide compost bins in these shady areas because they think that a pile needs sunlight. However, sunlight isn't necessary for composting; it just helps the materials break down faster. So unless you need compost as soon as possible, go ahead and put your pile where the sun doesn't shine so it will be less of an eyesore. (Shaded compost can take longer to dry out than nonshaded compost, though, so keep a tarp handy to limit the rainfall on compost located under trees.)

Size It Right

It's a basic fact that compost won't really cook unless your pile is at least 3 feet square and 3 feet high. Conversely, if the pile is too large—over 5 feet high—the top-heavy mass packs down, squeezing out air and slowing down decomposition. A well-constructed pile will heat up to at least 130°F within 3 or 4 days.

A Campsite for Compost

When you're deciding where to put your compost pile, pretend you're selecting a campsite on a chilly weekend.

- Seek level, well-drained ground. If you locate your pile on a slope, a heavy rainstorm may wash out your pile, or the runoff that drains downhill could sap valuable nutrients away from your compost.

- Set up in the sun. Full sun provides extra heat, which speeds up the composting process. (You can put your pile in a shady site if you lack a sunny area; the materials will just take longer to decompose.)

- Find a secluded spot. This isn't so you won't be bothered by neighbors; it ensures your pile won't be a nuisance—or an eyesore—to them.

- Look for natural windbreaks. If you're in a windy area, protect the pile from excessive heat loss by siting its windward side behind a windbreak such as a hedge or fence.

Hack Attack

Long, stringy vines and tall weeds in the compost heap can make turning the pile with a fork difficult. While I use a shredder for larger quantities, the shredder is noisy, and it seems silly to start it up for what may be only an armful or two of stringy material. My solution was to buy a machete. Now when I find stringy material matting up the heap, I simply take out my machete, yell, "Take that!" and start hacking. I then turn the pile and hack some more until I have reduced any long, stringy material to lengths that are easily turned.

Wharton S.
Des Plaines, Illinois

Hair Helps Compost

All kinds of hair, including dog hair and human hair, can be added to compost piles. Although hair breaks down slowly, it is rich in nitrogen. Hair is also reported to deter slugs when used as a mulch around susceptible plants. You may want to ask a local barber or stylist to save hair clippings for you to use in your compost pile and garden.

Post-Halloween Treasures

An excellent time to scour your town for free compost and soil-building material is the week after Halloween. Lots of people decorate with bales of straw and corn stalks, and many of them gather leaves in those bright orange pumpkin-face bags. Check on trash collection day. You may find plenty of these materials set out at the curb, just waiting for you to collect them for your compost.

Compost Dipstick

To check the status of your compost pile, use a wooden stake as a "dipstick." Find a stake long enough to penetrate to the bottom of the pile, and thrust it in. Wait a minute, and then pull out the stick. If it's hot and damp, your pile is still "working." When the pile is finished, the stick will be cool and wet. If the stick comes out dry, it means your compost isn't moist enough to stay active.

A Compost Pile Watering Hole

A moist compost pile will break down faster than a dry one, but compost piles sometimes tend to shed water, especially if the outer layer has become dry. To encourage water to soak into your pile, dig a hole in the top of your pile. Pour water into the hole by the bucketful or stick the hose into the hole (use a slow flow of water).

Chicken Wire Compost Ventilator

Ventilation—adding air—speeds the composting process. To make an open "chimney" for air circulation to the center of a compost pile, double a 6-foot section of chicken wire, then roll it up to create a chimney about 1 foot in diameter. Use twist ties or flexible wire to secure the roll. Set the chimney upright in your compost pile and layer compost materials around it.

Compost: It Just Happens

Yet another study has confirmed what we have been reporting for years: Special compost "activators" do not speed up the composting process as they claim. Three different activators were added to compost piles of leaves and food wastes that were turned and watered weekly. After 60 days of composting, the "activated" piles were compared with a control pile with no activator added. The activators had not accelerated the rate of decomposition, nor was the quality of the compost improved compared with the untreated pile. The bottom line: Don't waste your money.

Seed Closed Bins with Soil

If you use a composter that sits above ground or has a solid bottom, be sure to throw in a few shovelfuls of soil or finished compost when you fill the bin. Otherwise, earthworms (who help the decomposition process) won't be able to get in.

Stalk Your Compost

Sunflower stalks can be a great natural aerating tool for a compost heap. When you build a compost heap in fall to overwinter, crisscross several stalks to form the bottom layer. Top it with about 1 foot of other materials, plus a thin layer of soil. Lay more stalks on top of the soil, and keep building the pile in this sequence until it's about 4 feet high. The soft centers of the stalks rot quickly, bringing air right to the middle of the pile.

Chickens on the Compost

If you keep chickens, give your birds first choice of the kitchen wastes after you dump them on the compost pile. Besides adding natural fertilizer to the pile, chickens help aerate the compost as they scratch, and they'll eat fly eggs and maggots, too, reducing fly problems.

Ventilation Stakes

Build your compost pile around one or more upright 2 × 4s (you can use warped or damaged pieces). Once you've piled on materials to the desired height, pull out the 2 × 4s to form ventilating shafts. Building the pile around a perforated plastic pipe produces the same results (and you can leave the pipe in place).

GARDENER TO GARDENER

Homemade Shredder

We wanted to increase our earthworm population and their rich gift of castings. We learned that some worms thrive in shredded corrugated cardboard, so I made a machine to make cardboard worm bedding. I installed a lawn-mower blade and motor in a metal trash can. We have an unlimited source of discarded cardboard, and now there is no end to the bountiful earthworms that thrive in the shredded cardboard that we add to our compost pile.

Gregory G.
Chapel Hill,
North Carolina

A Safe Place for Compost

I produce a lot of compost by using two ComposTumblers. My favorite recipe is a mixture of 10 parts fresh grass clippings, 13 parts shredded maple leaves, and 5 parts coffee grounds, which I get for free from a local coffee shop. To hold the finished compost, I built a raised bin that keeps the compost off the ground and stops plant roots from growing into it. The bin has wire mesh over plastic lattice on the bottom and sides for good air circulation, and a fiberglass-panel roof to keep rain and snow out.

Jim W.
Rochester, Illinois

A Hot-Rot Pile

If you can't wait a year for a slow compost pile to finish cooking, you're ready to make a hot-rot pile—one that heats up and rots quickly, giving you a rich, slow-release fertilizer in as little as 2 to 4 weeks. To have a really hot pile, you need to assemble the right mix of carbon and nitrogen ingredients all at one time, supply moisture, and provide lots of air—and you'll need to do some physical work. Follow these seven steps for successful hot compost.

1. **Save your leaves.** In fall, bag all the leaves you can. Leaves are a great source of dry, brown material for the pile.

2. **Find the "N" stuff.** Green grass clippings supply some nitrogen, but grass clippings can become a problem in some piles because they like to group together and mat down—especially when they are (or get) wet—which greatly restricts the flow of air through the pile. In the past, gardeners used raw manure for hot compost piles, but there are concerns now about virulent strains of bacteria in raw manure that can be very harmful to humans. For health reasons, avoid using raw manure in your home compost pile unless you are certain that it will heat up to higher than 140°F. (And never ever add dog or cat feces to your compost pile.) Instead, try other sources of nitrogen, such as vegetable-type kitchen scraps and alfalfa and soybean meals (available at farm supply stores).

3. **Hold the weed seeds.** Gather all the nonmeat kitchen scraps you can find. If you want to add other organic materials like hay, straw, spent crops, or weeds, be sure you don't add any weed-seedy materials. Some weed seeds will be killed in a hot compost pile, but many will remain viable. When you spread the compost in your garden, you'll be spreading seeds too, creating work for you down the line.

4. **Chop things up.** The finer your ingredients are chopped, the faster they'll decompose. Grass clippings don't need any more chopping, but stalky material does—and even dry leaves will benefit from some chopping. Make a pile of leaves and mow them; then mow them a second and even a third time. If you have a chipper/shredder, now's the time to use it.

5. **Hose it down.** Watering the ingredients will speed their decay. Several days before you plan to construct your hot pile, use your hose to wet all the individual ingredients (but not manure). Then turn everything with a rake or garden fork and wet it all again.

   If you try to wet the materials after you build the pile, you can get a shingle effect—water running down the sides and off the edges of your heap before it can sink into the pile. Also keep in mind that you want a moist—but not soggy—pile.

6. **Build the pile.** If you live in a hot climate, build your pile in a shady spot so it won't dry out too quickly. If it rains a lot where you live, cover the pile with a tarp to keep it from becoming too wet.

   Pick the site that's right for you, and use a rake or hoe to loosen the soil surface. Put down a layer of dry, brown (high-carbon) material about 3 inches thick and 5 to 6 feet square, followed by a layer of high-nitrogen material about 1 inch thick. Keep layering until the pile is at least 4 feet high. After every two layers, stir the materials to mix the nitrogen-rich stuff in with the leaves and stalky materials. You should end up with a four-sided structure with sides that slope out; in other words, each layer is slightly smaller than the one below it.

7. **Turn and turn again.** Turning is the most work you'll have to do with a compost pile, so do it efficiently. Some people use a pitchfork; others like to use a mattock. Whatever tool you use, your goal is to get the materials that are at the outside of the pile to the inside and vice versa. The more you turn the pile, the faster it will break down.

   Your pile will be ready to use when the pile is two-thirds to one-half its original size and the fiery heat of decomposition has subsided.

Double Up on Compost

To double your compost heap output, dig all compost-in-progress into your garden beds in the fall. The partially decomposed materials will finish breaking down right in the soil during the winter months. Start a new compost heap with fresh organic materials. By the time spring arrives, you'll have twice as much finished compost.

Compost in a Bag

I live in an apartment with a small, fenced-in concrete patio. The only effective way I have found to make compost is in a trash bag with some airholes poked in it. Turning it is simple: I just flop the bag around.

Sherla F.
Sparks, Nevada

Turn to Worms

Let a bin full of worms do the work when it comes to composting kitchen wastes. Buy a commercial bin, or make your own: A basic worm bin—1 foot high, 2 feet deep, and 3 feet wide—will handle about 6 pounds of garbage per week (a typical amount for a family of four to six). Fill the bin with about 10 pounds of shredded newspaper, 1 gallon of garden soil, and about 4 gallons of water. Then add about 2 pounds of red worms, the worms best suited to the conditions in your bin. Feed your worm herd with fruit and vegetable trimmings, coffee grounds, plate scrapings, and so forth. Avoid meat scraps, bones, oils, and dairy products, which can make the bin smelly. Start slowly, adding no more than 2 to 3 pounds of trimmings at first, then more later in the week. Once your worms settle in, they'll easily handle 6 to 8 pounds of waste per week. To harvest rich vermicompost from your bin, move the dark, crumbly finished material to one side of the bin and fill the vacant side with new, moistened bedding and some fresh garbage. Give the worms a few weeks to move to the new bedding, then remove the finished material and replenish the bedding as needed.

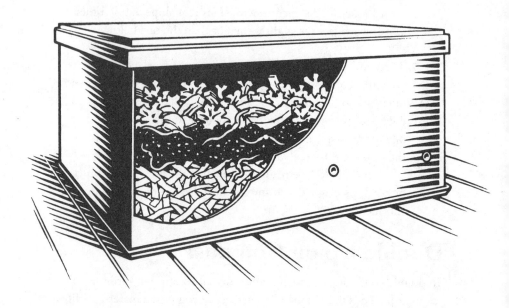

Worms work around the clock making vermicompost in a worm bin like this one. Once the bin is set up, all you do is add kitchen scraps every few days and harvest the rich worm compost.

Green Cone for Kitchen Waste

As you probably know, some types of kitchen waste, such as meat and fish scraps, bones, fats, and oils, shouldn't be added to traditional compost piles. These materials can attract animals and may become infested with maggots—which you definitely don't want in your compost pile. However, you can buy a special composter called the Green Cone that can handle all types of kitchen wastes, including meat and fats, because it is an aboveground, sealed system. The Green Cone consists of an open-mesh bottom basket called the digestion chamber, the cone-shaped top, and an airtight lid.

To use a Green Cone, dig a hole in your yard or garden deep and wide enough to accommodate the basket. (Make sure to dig the hole in an out-of-the-way spot that's not central to your landscape.) Then, attach the conical top so that it sits a couple of inches below soil level. The walls of the cone create a solar heat trap. Inside vents allow warmed air to circulate into the digestion chamber. The airtight lid protects against vermin and insects and forces the composter to "breathe" through the soil. You need to clean out this composter only about once a year.

Keep in mind that this device isn't for garden waste: It doesn't replace traditional yard waste composting.

Animal-Proof Compost Bin

Managing a composting site that borders woods has advantages and disadvantages. The woods provide shelter from wind and a ready source of rough twigs for building a base layer for your pile, but the woods are also home to many kinds of animals that may enjoy rooting through your compost for a midnight snack. If you need to keep animals out of your compost pile, consider buying a sturdy plastic prefabricated composter instead of setting up a free-form pile. These bins have only small openings. A mouse or two may get in or out, but your contained compost will be less likely to attract opossums, raccoons, skunks, or bears.

Another animal-proof option is to try a compost tumbler—a barrel-type container that sits above ground on a frame that allows the barrel to be turned easily with a crank or handle. With this type of bin, it's also easy to turn your compost regularly to add air—which will help the materials decompose faster. For more about compost tumblers, see "Refine Your Rotary Technique" on page 10.

Drum Roll, Please

Last summer I noticed an ad for several used 55-gallon plastic drums, priced at $5 apiece. I purchased three of the drums, two of which had removable lids, and put them to work as compost bins. They have worked great. I fill them halfway with yard and kitchen waste, dampen the mix with water, secure the lids, and place them in direct sunlight. Once a week, I push the barrels onto their sides and roll them back and forth to mix the contents. They are easier to work with and are more portable than my old system. They also take up less space and are better at keeping little critters out.

Robert D.
Fremont, Nebraska

Refine Your Rotary Technique

Using a compost tumbler saves you the heavy physical work of turning compost with a pitchfork, but unless you know how to work with a compost tumbler, you may be disappointed with the results.

The secret to success with rotary composting is to finely shred all the materials you put in the composter. Long stems and clumps of organic debris don't tend to mix as well.

It's also important to have a carbon-to-nitrogen ratio of about 25:1 for fast composting in a drum composter. Examples of mixes that will provide this ratio are equal parts of garden debris, kitchen scraps, and leaves, or equal amounts of straw, grass clippings, and garden refuse (weeds and spent plants).

When you fill the drum, layer the ingredients, wetting them down as you go, until the drum is almost full. The mixture should be as damp as a wrung-out sponge, not dripping wet. Turn the drum five times a day, and add more water if the materials start to dry out.

If you follow these directions, you should have a drumful of dark, crumbly compost in 2 or 3 weeks.

Set Up a Compost Trellis

Move your compost pile into your garden and composting becomes as easy as tossing an overripe tomato. In big gardens there's plenty of space for a bin, but in small ones you'll need to use some ingenuity. One way to save space is by making your compost bin do double duty as a trellis. Set up a bin made with snow fence, then use the fence to support a bumper crop of tomatoes or other vegetables. The fence and tomatoes hide the pile from view, but they don't get in the way of the composting process.

Grow any tall or vining plant up an in-garden bin and you'll have compost close at hand—and easy pickings at harvest time, too. When the growing season is over, pull the plants off the bin and add them to the compost. Don't bother turning the pile—the materials will continue to break down and you can dig finished compost from the bottom of the bin in spring.

Cover Compost with Glory

Morning glories are happy to climb up the sides of a compost bin made of chicken wire, fencing, or boards. If the sides aren't rough enough to provide places for the vines to cling, simply tie strings to the top of the bin, then attach them to the soil with stakes to provide vertical trellises. Your pile will be a blaze of heavenly blue, white, red, purple, pink, or crimson from summer until frost makes its appearance.

Compost Pile Container Garden

No space for pumpkins? If you want to grow large vining plants like pumpkins but don't have the room, turn your compost bin into a tall container garden. In spring, make a simple compost bin by bending a 10-foot piece of 48-inch-tall welded-wire fencing into a circle. Tie the ends of the wire together to hold it closed, and put the bin in a sunny area. Pack the bin with garden waste and top it with an inch or so of topsoil. Punch tiny holes in the sides and bottom of a plastic bucket and sink it into the center of the pile. Around the bucket, sow cucumber, gourd, melon, pumpkin, or squash seeds. Watering and feeding are easy. Add a shovelful of finished compost to the bucket, fill it as needed with water, then let the compost tea slowly leak into the pile. In fall, simply pull the wandering vine stems into the compost bin for a quick cleanup.

Compost in the Trenches

For an easy way to fertilize your garden and save trips to and from the compost pile, try trench composting. You can dig trenches in the footpaths between your garden beds and cover them with straw so they'll still be usable for walking. The trenches can be as deep as you need to accommodate the materials you want to compost. Trenches 6 inches deep may suffice; if you have a lot to compost, you may find yourself digging down 2 feet.

Start trench composting in late spring when you have a lot of material to compost, such as spent flowers, old plants, and fallen vegetables. Dig the trench, fill it up, cover it with straw, and let the compost cook through summer, fall, and winter.

The following spring, when you need some compost, just toss it from the trenches onto your garden bed with a pitchfork. Then plant seeds or transplants right into the freshly composted beds. Refill the trench with new composting materials or, if you don't have material, refill with straw.

If your garden soil is hard to dig, try this technique for easier digging: Shovel out only as much soil as you can with ease, then soak the trench with water. Return 2 days later to shovel more; the water will have loosened up the next 6 to 12 inches of soil.

GARDENER TO GARDENER

A Slow Burn

We always have two compost bins going. Our "active" bin is a 50-gallon plastic drum that we added handles to for turning. Our "passive" one is a wire cage we move around to different areas of our raised-bed vegetable garden. In winter, the heat from the compost cooking in this cage melts the snow around it. In spring, we rake the compost into the soil and then set the cage up in another area. We always harvest plenty of vegetables from our small garden.

Bob and Mary J.
South Milwaukee,
Wisconsin

The New Organic Method

In 1950, J. I. Rodale and his staff decided to move beyond traditional composting, which wasn't yielding enough finished compost for the farm gardens. At the end of the growing season, they spread organic materials such as shredded leaves, weeds, manure, and ground-up corncobs directly onto the garden. They called this technique the "new organic method." It's also called sheet composting, and it's a great method for your garden, too. Not only does it produce rich compost but it also suppresses weeds. You can sheet compost on existing beds or use the technique to start new beds. Just follow these simple steps.

1. Use stakes and string to mark out the shape of your garden bed right on the ground. There's no need to till first.

2. Put a layer of mulch, such as leaves, grass clippings, or pulled weeds, over the entire bed.

3. Place a layer of newspapers—10 to 12 sheets thick—on top of the compost or mulch. Wet down the paper with a hose to keep it from blowing away.

4. Cover the wet paper with a 2- to 3-inch layer of mulch, grass clippings, shredded leaves, or wood chips. Use whatever is available and looks nice to you. Make sure all of the paper is covered.

When the pile is done, wait at least 6 months for the material under the newspaper to break down. Check in spring—like J. I., you'll find earthworms "multiplying prodigiously" under the mulch. You can plant straight into the sheet of compost—no tilling required.

Underground Compost Weathers Winter

When winter freezes come, even the best-managed compost pile can turn to ice. The secret to a compost pile that cooks all winter long is to surround it with the earth's natural heat. The technique is called pit composting, and it uses the insulating properties of the soil to keep the pile from freezing.

You will need a plastic garbage can (the larger the better) and several straw bales or bags of dry leaves.

1. Using a saw or utility knife, cut the bottom out of the plastic garbage can.

2. Drill several 1-inch holes around the top two-thirds of the garbage can for ventilation.

3. Dig a hole at least 6 inches deep and as wide as the diameter of the garbage can. The deeper the hole, the more insulated your pile will be.

4. Set the garbage can into the hole and surround it snugly with straw bales or bags of leaves. Try not to block too many of the vent holes.

5. Add kitchen scraps, mixing them well with dried leaves or shredded newspaper. The mixture should be damp but not wet. The finer the ingredients are chopped, the more rapidly they'll decompose. Keep the lid on the bin.

Pit composting proceeds much more slowly than warm-weather composting, but it should remain above freezing and continue to break down even in sustained below-freezing air temperatures, producing finished compost in 3 to 4 months.

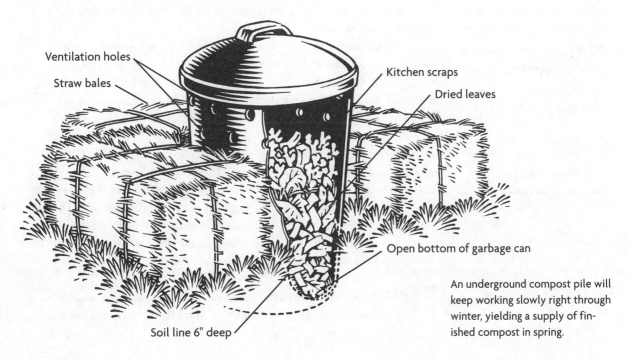

Ventilation holes

Straw bales

Kitchen scraps

Dried leaves

Open bottom of garbage can

Soil line 6" deep

An underground compost pile will keep working slowly right through winter, yielding a supply of finished compost in spring.

Easy Compost Sieve

Last spring I had a nice big pile of compost ready and a big garden screaming to be planted now, *but I still had not gotten around to constructing that sturdy compost sieve I've needed. Then I spied the black 10 × 20-inch plastic trays that garden nurseries use for bedding plants. The sides are solid, but the bottom is an open grid—perfect for sifting compost. I spread the sifted compost in my garden. When I got toward the end of the batch, I emptied the last of the compost into an old pillowcase, tied it shut, and steeped it in a trash can of water. Now I have a barrel of compost tea to tide me over until my next batch of compost is ready.*

*Lynda Gene R.
Quakertown,
Pennsylvania*

How Much Compost?

Home gardeners don't usually have a scale on hand to measure compost by the pound, so how do you know how much to add to garden beds to boost soil fertility? One way is to use the bushel-basket rule of thumb.

Try to make enough compost to spread 2 or 3 bushels per 100 square feet of your garden every year. Depending on your compost's texture, this amount should give you enough to spread compost an inch or more deep over the soil surface. Make sure to spread the compost before planting.

But just how much compost is in a pile, anyway? Here's a good way to estimate how much compost you're creating. A pile that's 4 feet square and 4 feet high (64 cubic feet) should give you enough to spread over a 40 × 50-foot (or 2,000-square-foot) garden.

If all this math seems too complicated, don't worry. Just keep adding to that compost pile. After all, you can *never* have too much compost!

A Home-Garden Compost Spreader

Compost can be hard to spread evenly because it is heavy when damp, hard to dig with a shovel, and not very crumbly. This is especially true if you use it before it's fully decomposed. So why not steal an idea from farmers: Use a spreader.

With a little ingenuity—and an old wheelbarrow—you can build a garden-size spreader that helps you put an even layer of compost on your garden. (If you don't have an old wheelbarrow tucked in your garage or shed, look for one at the local dump, at a garage sale, or on the curb during trash pick-up day in your neighborhood.) Here's how to make the spreader.

1. Use a saw with a metal-cutting blade to carefully cut a "window" at the front end of the wheelbarrow. Make the cuts right where the sides meet the bottom of the wheelbarrow. The opening should be 2½ to 3 inches wide and run from side to side at the front end of the wheelbarrow (the end over the wheel and opposite the handles).

2. Carefully bend the cut edges toward the outside of the wheelbarrow so that you don't cut yourself on them when you use the compost spreader.

This spreader works best if you pull it rather than push it, and shake it from side to side as you go. Compost will trickle out the window as you pull it along. If your load is too clumpy to slide out easily, get a friend to help by using a push broom or garden rake to shove the compost out the opening as you move along.

Screen Out the Lumps

If you've been turning your compost pile through the fall and winter, by spring it should be filled with crumbly black gold. But some of those nuggets may not be ready for the garden—and that's where a compost sieve comes in handy. Placed atop a wheelbarrow, the sieve catches the bulky, uncomposted pieces from the pile while allowing the fine, usable stuff to sift through. The lumps can then be returned to the pile to continue to break down. Here's how to make a simple but effective sieve.

1. Arrange four pieces of 1 × 4-inch lumber into a square or rectangle that is slightly larger than the top of your wheelbarrow. The boards should be positioned on edge to form a box. Secure the four corners with 2½-inch nails or wood screws.

2. Using wire cutters, cut a piece of galvanized hardware cloth (with 1-inch openings in the mesh) to a size that will fit the wood frame.

3. With galvanized U-shaped brads, tack the hardware cloth securely to the underside of the frame every 3 or 4 inches. Place the frame over the wheelbarrow; shovel in the compost. Shake and rock the sieve to sift.

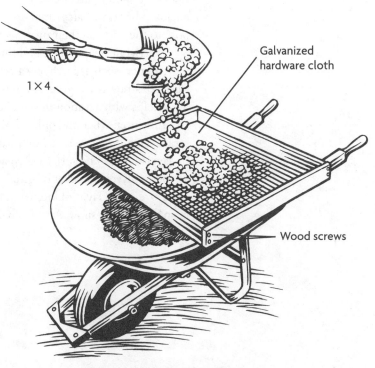

Galvanized hardware cloth

1 × 4

Wood screws

Pouring your compost through a simple sifter screens out lumps and uncomposted material, yielding a fine compost that's perfect for mulching and adding to potting mix.

Keep Compost Warm
in Cold Weather

Insulating a compost heap will help keep the pile active even when outside temperatures drop in fall. To insulate your compost bin, build a second enclosure outside it and fill the space between with leaves, hay, straw, sawdust, or any other insulating material you have on hand.

Straw Bale Bin Works
for Frigid Temps

Another tactic for composting through winter is to build a compost bin in fall out of straw bales. Make a four-sided bin, with an open area in the center at least 3 × 3 × 3 feet. Straw is a great insulator for compost piles because the straw itself is hollow-stemmed and stiff, so it allows air to enter and circulate from all sides and levels. Compost heaps enclosed by straw bales often do not need to be turned; they decompose to the edge on their own.

Start your heap in fall, building the pile in layers. Alternate "active ingredients" such as kitchen wastes or alfalfa hay with "cooler" materials like straw, dried grass clippings, shredded leaves, and cornstalks. This helps with aeration in the pile.

In winter, when the only additions to the pile are moist kitchen scraps, keep a bale of straw or a bag of leaves nearby so you can keep on layering. Also be sure to keep adding some garden soil to the layers as you go: Keep a bucket of sifted garden soil on hand, and sprinkle some over each layer of kitchen scraps. Place a plywood lid over the heap to keep out snow. Attach a handle to the lid so you can lift it easily.

Chapter 2

Renewing Your Soil

Don't you wish you could buy brand-new soil at the garden center along with your plants and tools? Some lucky gardeners can celebrate their yard's naturally rich, easy-to-dig soil. But most of us cope with less-than-lovely soil that's too heavy, too sandy, or too wet to support a bountiful garden.

Before you embark on a soil improvement crusade, you may want to learn more about soil by collecting samples and having them tested. In most states, you can pick up a soil test kit at your local Cooperative Extension office or buy one at a garden center. The instructions in the kit tell you how to collect samples and where to send the samples for analysis. The results will tell you about soil pH, nutrient levels, and possibly the organic matter content.

One common theme in most soil improvement schemes is adding organic matter to enrich the soil, and this chapter has a wide range of tips to help you do just that. You'll discover the role of mulch and cover crops in soil improvement. You can sample several mulch-management systems and learn how to deal with pH problems. And check out the special cover crop mix for maximum results. Your soil will thank you, and so will your garden plants.

Natural Sod Buster

Our community garden is surrounded by grassland. Each year a few gardeners give up because it is almost impossible to break up this heavy sod. A friend and I were offered one of these plots to grow vegetables for our local food bank. We cleared the 20 × 30-foot plot and mowed the grass as short as possible. Next, we covered the entire plot with five layers of newspapers. Then we piled partially rotted leaves about 6 inches deep over the papers. This smothered the grass and killed the roots as well. We placed compost and soil on top of the leaves and planted tomatoes, cucumbers, and zucchini. Later that summer we harvested a bountiful crop. The leaves turned to rich compost, and the grass did not return. The next gardener will have fertile and workable soil.

Bunny L.
Eugene, Oregon

Tame Tough Clay

Stick with raised beds if you have sticky clay soil, and improve it annually with a three-part program of compost, mulch, and cover crops. Apply compost in spring, spreading it thickly. Dig it in gently as long as the soil isn't too wet or dry. Always keep the soil covered with mulch while plants are growing to keep both the soil and the compost moist. Plant a cover crop as soon as a patch of ground has finished for the season, then turn it under 1 week before planting. Plant buckwheat as a cover crop in warm weather; when it's cool, try fava beans interplanted with winter rye.

Clay, Clay, Go Away

You can improve your clay soil's structure and drainage by adding gypsum (calcium sulfate), an effective soil conditioner. It also adds calcium and sulfur to the soil without making the soil more acidic or alkaline. To get the fastest benefits, use pelleted gypsum instead of the ground form—ground gypsum can contain chunks that won't dissolve for 3 years or more. Pelleted gypsum dissolves to a fine powder as soon as it gets wet, so it goes to work rapidly.

Use a fertilizer spreader to apply pelleted gypsum. Try using 20 to 30 pounds per 1,000 square feet of garden. Pelleted gypsum is available at garden centers, nurseries, and hardware stores.

Size Up Alkaline Soil

In the inland West, many soils have a pH higher than 7.0, and that can be a problem for some garden crops. If the soil also contains large amounts of salt or sodium, gardening at all is a struggle. If you live in an area where alkaline (high pH) soil is common and your garden isn't doing well, have your soil tested. Be sure the test results include not just pH but also the percentage of soluble salts and the exchangeable sodium percentage (ESP). If your soil has an ESP of 20 or greater, or if the percentage of total soluble salts is 0.5 or greater, you'll need to take some special steps to remedy the problems. Consult with your local Cooperative Extension agent for suggestions.

One way to combat high pH is to add acid-forming organic material to your soil—the more the better. Try sheet composting with leaves, pine needles, or hardwood sawdust. Growing cover crops will help, too.

Feed Deep for Drought Defense

Dry weather makes plants hungry, not thirsty. When the soil dries out, plants can't absorb nutrients—that's the real cause of drought damage. To protect your plants from drought starvation, build fertility deep in your soil, where soil stays moist longer, allowing plant roots to absorb vital nutrients.

A Soil Amendment from the Sea

Pacific or Atlantic, if you live near the ocean, you can take advantage of a great natural soil amendment: seaweed. Seaweed contains all the trace minerals that plants need for ideal growth. Use seaweed as a mulch or work it into the soil at planting.

Develop Great Soil with Daikons

Break up hardpan soil by planting daikon radishes, which have long taproots that can reach down 18 inches or more. Leave them to rot in the soil for an added soil-building boost.

Let Coffee Make New "Grounds"

Convert terrible soil into great gardens with ease by drinking lots of coffee. Actually, it's not the coffee that helps; it's the coffee grounds. For alkaline soil, such as you'll find in many community gardens or near building foundations, coffee is a great natural soil amendment that will help bring down soil pH.

You probably can't drink enough coffee yourself to generate the grounds you need, so check with local coffee shops and ask them to save leftover coffee-bean burlap bags and used coffee grounds for you. Another acidifying material is sawdust, so see if you can round up some from a local woodworker.

Layer the coffee grounds, sawdust, and burlap bags over your site. The nitrogen in the coffee grounds will help the burlap and sawdust to compost, and the pH should drop during the composting process, too.

For other sources of sawdust, check lumber mills if any are nearby. Before adding sawdust to your garden, check first to make sure the lumber isn't pressure-treated. The chemicals used to make pressure-treated wood are not safe to add to your organic garden.

In the Trenches

I use my tiller's trenching tool to deliver fertility right where my plants need it—at their roots. After tilling my garden 6 inches deep, I dig parallel trenches the length of my plot, about 3 feet apart. (An energetic gardener with a hoe can do the same job.) Into the trenches I shovel compost, shredded leaves, grass clippings, and old rotted straw. Then I run the trencher over the two mounds thrown up beside the trenches. This replaces the soil on top of the trenches, giving me nice, mounded raised beds. On these hills, I plant potatoes, sweet potatoes, tomatoes, peppers, broccoli, and more. When the roots reach all the buried goodies, the plants spring to life.

Max V. E.
Ames, Iowa

Rely on Local Rock Dust

If a soil test indicates your soil is lacking minerals, use rock dust from local sources as a soil amendment. Local rock dust likely contains all the minerals your soil requires. Slow-release rock dust weathers naturally and is gentler on the soil than other mineral fertilizers.

Wood Ash Warning

Until recently, many sources recommended adding wood ashes to garden beds to supply potassium and reduce soil acidity. However, soil scientists have found that wood ashes are highly soluble and can cause dramatic pH changes, which in turn can harm earthworms and beneficial soil microorganisms.

To use wood ashes safely in your garden, try adding a small amount to your compost—about 2 pounds of ashes to a standard compost bin. Allow the ashes to dissolve in the compost for several months before putting the compost on your garden.

Sanitize Your Soil

A promising new organic technique developed in the Netherlands can dramatically reduce problems caused by most soilborne diseases. By incorporating fresh plant residues with soil and then covering the soil tightly with plastic, the researchers created anaerobic (no oxygen) conditions that resulted in the death of various disease organisms. They found that any fresh green crop matter is effective.

Here's how to use this new technique to sanitize your soil: Till in at least 11 pounds of fresh green plant residue per square yard, water well, and keep the area covered with heavy opaque plastic for 15 weeks. It's important to do this during warm summer conditions and to keep all the edges sealed by covering them with soil.

The Ruth Stout Method

Pioneer organic gardener Ruth Stout, who gardened until she was 95 years old, never tilled her garden and seldom had to water. Her secret to no-work gardening was her heavy mulching technique. Stout piled on about three times as much mulch as most gardeners do. Try it yourself: You'll find that the superthick carpet of mulch conditions the soil underneath so beautifully that it is always ready for planting. Just push aside the mulch as needed to make room for seeds or plants.

Mulch Free-for-All

Why bag leaves in fall when you can turn them into instant mulch with a rake and shovel? In fall, open up the fence around your vegetable garden and rake your yard leaves onto the beds to make a layer 3 to 4 inches deep. Then use a shovel to turn the leaves under. There's no need to dig deep—just put enough soil on the leaves to keep them from blowing away in winter. If you don't have time to turn the leaves, lay fencing down over the leaves to hold them in place.

The leaves will decompose somewhat over winter, giving you a nicely mulched garden come spring. Simply stir the soil with a garden fork and rake it smooth before sowing seeds.

Mulch—But Not Too Much

Mulch is important to the success of any landscape, but don't overdo it. Piled up too heavily, mulch can block air from reaching plant roots and may hold too much moisture during rainy periods. In most cases, apply no more than a 2- to 3-inch layer of shredded leaves or bark mulch. And when you mulch around trees, use a "bagel" mulch pattern instead of the typical but incorrect "volcano" style. Keeping the mulch away from tree trunks is important to prevent diseases and discourage rodent damage.

If you like the tidy look of freshly mulched beds but already have old mulch in place, you can fake it (and save some money) by using a garden rake (instead of a lighter-weight leaf rake) to loosen and fluff up layers of the old, packed-down mulch.

Mulching offers many advantages to your soil and your trees, but only when properly applied. Piling mulch around tree trunks *(left)* can lead to rot problems; leave the area around the trunk clear *(right)*, and pile mulch only 2 to 3 inches high.

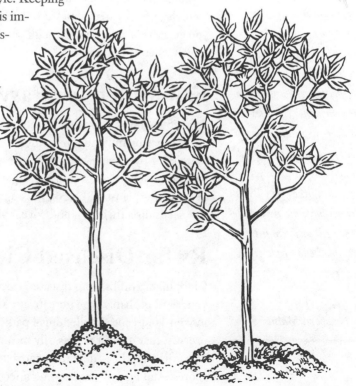

In Love with Leaves

I've composted in my garden for years. Each fall I gather up all the leaves from my yard and any I can get from the neighbors. I store them in a huge pile next to my garden. Around Thanksgiving I till all I can into the garden. The next summer I use the rest as mulch. I put leaves on each side of a row of cucumbers in piles about 6 inches deep and 3 feet wide. The cuke runners go out over the leaves, and in no time the leaves are covered up. No dirty cukes, no weeds, less watering. After my corn gets a foot tall or better, I dump the rest of my leaves between the rows. Sometimes the piles are a foot deep, depending on my supply of leaves. I enjoy good, clean walking in the rows when picking the corn. By fall the leaves have mostly disintegrated. I till any remains into the garden before I plant my winter rye.

Errald T.
Newport, Maine

Leftover Path Liners

Don't waste precious organic mulches on your garden pathways. Line your garden paths with handy leftovers like these, and you can work in the garden in any kind of weather.

Boards
Cardboard
Old wool or cotton carpets or rugs
Wood or slate roofing shingles
Worn-out clothing

Mow Leaves for Mulch

Shredded leaves are an excellent mulch for flower and vegetable beds. But how to shred leaves quickly and easily? Heap them in shallow piles on your lawn and run over the piles with your power mower.

Winter Mulch Bucket Brigade

Winter wind and weather can disturb the mulch blanketing your garden, exposing roots and crowns to damaging cold. To facilitate "mulch repair," carry a bucket of bark mulch or shredded leaves with you every time you walk through your garden in winter. Replenish the mulch wherever it's needed.

Fall Mulch for Easy Spring Planting

Save yourself the effort of clearing out crop residues or turning under cover crops by mulching over them instead. Spread a layer of wet newspaper over the garden debris or cover crop and top the newspaper with shredded leaves or another organic mulch. By spring, the bed will be ready for planting. Just dig through the mulch to set transplants, or sow seeds directly into it and cover them lightly with compost.

Rx for Diseased Chips

Chipping up limbs from diseased trees and shrubs to use as mulch in your yard probably won't create any significant new disease problems in your landscape. While fungal pathogens can survive the chipping process, that doesn't necessarily mean they will infect other plants. Most diseases that infect trees move freely by wind- or waterborne spores. And many trees become infected only when under stress, such as during drought or after injury. Still, it's always better to compost chips in a hot compost pile (one where the pile temperature reaches 140°F) before using them as mulch. Mix the chips with a nitrogen source, such as grass clippings or rotted manure. Compost the chips for 6 weeks if you are using them as a mulch, longer if incorporating them directly into the soil. Keep the pile damp and turn it frequently. The inside of the pile should be hot to the touch. Composting usually destroys any disease organisms and reduces the nitrogen tie-up that occurs in the soil as the cellulose in the wood breaks down.

Shred Leaves with a Rake

To create shredded leaf mulch without using a shredder, start by setting up a large cylinder of chicken wire or wire mesh about 6 feet in diameter and 5 feet high. Pile partly decomposed leaves into the cylinder. Put boards on top of the leaves and use a few rocks to weight the boards.

After a few months, take the boards away and try scratching back and forth over the surface of the compressed leaves with a metal rake. This action should do an excellent job of tearing the leaves into small pieces, which you can use immediately for mulch.

Sow Cover Crops Simply

The great thing about cover crops is that you don't have to till before planting. Just pull any spent vegetables and weeds, and rough up the soil surface by raking it free of clumps. Broadcast the seed, then press seeds into the soil, rake them in, or just walk on them to firm them into place.

If you're planting a legume cover crop in your beds, it's a good idea to inoculate the seeds with friendly bacteria first because the nitrogen fixation process occurs only when these bacteria colonize the roots of your cover crop plants. These bacteria are often already present in your soil, but you should still buy the correct inoculant (ask your seed supplier for it) and follow the application instructions listed on the packet.

A good general sowing rate is 2 cups of cover crop seeds per 100 square feet (although you should use less with crops that have very small seeds). After broadcasting the seeds, water the area if no rain is forecast. If you have it handy, a light mulch of fine straw or dried grass clippings will keep the surface of the soil moist and improve the germination of your crop.

Choose the Right Cover Crop

The best type of cover crop for your garden is the one that is physically easiest for you to manage. If you choose a cover crop that requires heavy work to dig into the soil and you're not equal to the task, then you'll end up with yet another garden problem instead of an improved garden.

The easiest cover crops to manage are the ones that are easy to kill or ones that die off on their own—either from winter cold or summer heat. These "pushovers" include winter and spring wheat, winter and spring barley, spring oats, grain rye, and succulent annual sweet clovers. Buckwheat is easy too, but only if you time your planting so that the buckwheat will die before it can go to seed.

Whether a cover crop will survive your winter or die off depends on how cold your specific winter gets. Crimson clover, for instance, will die a reliable winter death in Maine, but usually survives Zone 6 winters.

It also helps to match the cover crop to the use you're planning for the bed. For example, for beds you want to plant with early spring vegetables, sow a cover crop in the fall that won't survive winter. Annual white sweet clover would be a good choice for gardeners in the northern half of North America.

In spring, you'll have a thick mulch of dead sweet clover on the beds, and you can set your transplants right into a hole punched into the dead clover (a bulb planter is the perfect tool for this), cut strips through the clover to sow seeds, or till in all the clover and plant traditionally.

Crop Choices for Climatic Corners

Here are some specific suggestions for cover crop management in various parts of the country.

Northeast. In spring, plant spring oats and turn them under before planting summer crops. In midseason, plant buckwheat, turn it under before it goes to seed, then plant fall crops. In the fall, plant spring oats to winter-kill, or crimson clover, which you can plant directly into in spring as a living mulch.

Mid-Atlantic and Midwest. In spring, plant spring oats or crimson clover, and turn them under before planting summer crops. In midseason, plant crimson clover as a living mulch between vegetable plantings, and turn it under the following spring. In fall, sow spring oats, berseem, and annual sweet clovers, which will winter-kill.

South. In spring, plant southern peas, marigolds, or millet as early as the soil can be worked; turn them under before planting fall crops. For midsummer, sow buckwheat; turn it under before planting fall crops. In fall, any grain will do. Let it grow through the winter, then mow it down and turn it under before planting spring crops.

North Central. In spring, plant Austrian winter pea (as early as possible), crimson clover, or spring oats, and turn them under before planting fall crops. Sow buckwheat in midseason, and turn it under before planting fall crops. In the fall, sow spring oats to winterkill.

Pacific Northwest. In spring and again at midseason, sow winter wheat or spring oats, and turn them under before seedheads form. You can also plant soybeans at midseason; chop them down and plant a fall crop into the stubble. In fall, plant winter wheat or fava beans. Let them overwinter, then mow and turn them under before planting spring crops.

California. In spring, plant buckwheat and mow or turn it under before it goes to seed. In midseason, plant Sudan grass; keep it mowed and turn it under before planting summer or fall crops. In fall, plant California red oats, which will over-winter. Mow and turn them under before planting spring or summer crops.

Ryegrass Saves Soil

Prevent soil compaction and erosion by planting annual ryegrass among your crops from midsummer until early September. Sow it at a rate of 1 pound per 1,000 square feet. By frost the rye will have grown into a thick stand, creating a protective cover that holds and shelters soil through winter. Till or dig it under in spring before it goes to seed, and it will enrich the soil to boot. If the growth is very heavy, chop it before incorporating it into the soil by running over it with your lawn mower.

4-Greens Blend for Maximum Results

More is better when it comes to planting green manure crops to improve your soil. Sowing more than one green manure crop at the same time provides more balanced nutrition, and it doesn't take any more time than sowing just one type.

A mix of 20 percent Austrian peas, 40 percent fava beans (also called broad beans), 30 percent hairy vetch, and 10 percent oats is a perfect green manure mix that works well for spring planting in most parts of the country.

Mix the seeds together before planting. Sow in the spring, using 3 to 5 pounds of seed per 1,000 square feet of garden space. This green manure blend will also attract a wide variety of beneficial insects if you let it flower.

Once the plants are in full bloom (but before they set seed), till them into the soil.

Top 4 Rules for Easy Cover Cropping

You can experiment with a wide variety of cover crops and cropping techniques. But if you'd rather focus your attention on your garden plants than on growing cover crops, stick with these easy cover-cropping rules to get the best benefits without a lot of work.

- Choose an annual plant (one that grows and dies in a single season) that is easily killed by heat, cold, or you (the gardener).

- In fall, sow legumes 6 to 8 weeks before the first hard frost; sow grasses 4 to 6 weeks before the first hard frost. In spring, sow all types of cover crops 1 to 2 weeks before the last hard frost.

- If a cover crop gets more than 10 inches high, cut it with a lawn mower (set as high as possible), a string trimmer, a scythe, or a hand tool with a sharp blade.

- Chop up your (living or dead) cover crop as finely as possible. If it's still alive, dig it into the top few inches of soil. If it's dead, leave it on the soil's surface.

Chapter 3

Designing Your Landscape and Gardens

Designing a garden or home landscape is a creative work-in-progress. There's always room for improvement or for a change in a garden bed. Over time, your needs and interests change, too. For instance, gardeners with young children landscape to create play spaces and to keep precious garden plants from being trampled in the heat of lively games. But when children grow up, those gardeners may want to reduce the lawn area and create more beds and borders—or an "outdoor room" they can enjoy in peace.

Making your yard work better, finding the right location for plants, creating privacy, and choosing plants that will grow well and look beautiful together are all part of design. In this chapter, you'll find lots of plain talk and helpful garden-tested design tips, such as ways to add interest to your entry garden, suggestions for privacy screens, and ideas for using bulbs in a home landscape.

You'll also appreciate the advice on how to use self-sowing plants without regret, and which tough plants can take a beating in high-traffic areas and still look good.

Gardening for Grandchildren

I have a 1-year-old grand-daughter. Seeing her in my garden picking up pinecones and leaves, with those tiny hands that go so regularly to her mouth, makes me so glad that no traces of chemicals could be hiding there—and I don't need to curb her explorations. I did take down some of my fencing I use to keep the rabbits out of my garden, in deference to her. I know I won't be growing datura and I may have to reconsider some of my clematis and other showy but poisonous ornamental vines that I've always enjoyed growing. But I've already cleared a space to plunk down a playhouse in the center of my cottage garden. A child in an organic garden is a perfect addition.

Linda P.
Shamokin, Pennsylvania

Landscape with the Locals

A little research pays off big when choosing landscape plants for your yard, especially if you've moved to a new area where you're not familiar with the local climate. Find out which plants are well suited for your conditions, and then build your landscape around them. If you've moved to southern California, for example, pick plants that do well in a Mediterranean climate, where winters are mild and there's little rainfall. Try palm trees, fig trees, and oleanders, and consider planting succulent groundcovers such as sedums instead of lawn grass.

A Bird's-Eye View of Your Garden

Seeing your yard and gardens in a new light may be all you need to improve their design. But how? One way to get a new perspective is to climb on your roof to survey your yard.

If you decide to give this a try, *be careful.* And expect to experience a completely new garden view. You'll see how plants or structures that seem important from the ground may not make sense in the overall picture. For example, you may notice that a huge shrub you thought was a garden focal point may actually be blocking a gorgeous view of a neighboring skyline. You'll be able to note subtle changes in soil types by how similar plants are growing differently—better in one area than another. You may find ways to improve your mowing patterns, see opportunities for new paths, or identify where problem areas are or where there's wasted space. This bird's-eye view may or may not change your garden style, but it's the fastest way to evaluate your garden layout.

Snow—A Cool Garden Design Tool

Use the materials you've got on hand to help you visualize your landscape, and you'll get the design you want without a lot of expense or bother. One (free) tool on hand in many yards during winter is snow. Take your snowplow or shovel and pile the white stuff into makeshift hedges, walls, and beds, or reshape your normally straight walk into a curve.

Try out different plant sizes and planting styles. Build dwarf- and standard-size snow shrubs to see which fit best in your landscape, then keep adding snow to find out what they'll look like as they grow. Or see what your yard will look like with an informal planting like an island bed, or a formal garden with neatly clipped plants of snow. The possibilities are endless.

If you want a more realistic look, spray your "snowplants" with a plastic squirt bottle filled with water and several drops of green food coloring. Spray a snow pathway with other colors, and you can decide if you want your future walkway to be red brick, brown wood chips, or gray slate.

Before your creations melt away, draw them on paper or photograph them so by the time spring arrives you've got a landscape plan and are ready to go.

Manage Your Microclimate to Foil Frost

The lay of your land can greatly affect whether you get frost and how heavy it hits. If your garden is situated in a valley, it will most likely be frosted more often than your uphill neighbor's bed. Also, the first frost in fall will occur earlier than it would if your garden were on the side of a hill. That's because cold air flows down hills and settles in low areas at night. You may want to consider moving your garden uphill, if possible. Or, put a fence on the uphill side of the garden to force some of the cold air that's moving down the hill to go around your garden. Make sure there's no obstruction on the downhill side; it could block cold air from flowing down the hill and effectively stall that cold stuff right in your garden.

Accent with Herbs

Culinary herbs are also versatile landscaping plants that you can dress up or down to include in formal or informal gardens. Use herbs with unusual colors and forms as accent plants in a perennial garden. Try out chives, as well as ornamental sages such as 'Tricolor' and 'Purpurascens'. For a restful garden, combine gold and purple sages with pink, yellow, lavender, and purple flowers. If you like something more intense, mix the yellow, orange, and red flowers of purple sages with neutral herbs.

Create a Fragrant Outdoor Room

How about designing an outdoor room with a theme of fragrant plants? If you have a patio with a seating area, create an L-shaped bed around it with lower-growing flowers in the foreground backed by shrubs. Use a small flowering tree as a focal point. If your patio is bordered by a fence, you could even include a fragrant vine such as sweet autumn clematis. Your annual choices include standards such as sweet alyssum (*Lobularia maritima*), sweet peas (*Lathyrus odoratus*), and heliotrope (*Heliotropium arborescens*). Fragrant perennials range from groundcovers such as creeping phlox (*Phlox stolonifera*) and lily of the valley (*Convallaria majalis*) to favorites such as lilies, pinks, and lavenders. Many native azaleas are fragrant; other fragrant shrubs include lilacs, daphnes, and viburnums. These are just a fraction of the fragrant choices you can try; ask a knowledgeable gardening friend or nursery owner for more suggestions. And as always, be sure to choose plants that suit your site and conditions.

Make a Grand Entrance

The garden at the entryway to your house is your most public garden, so it should always look good. It sets your style and tells who you are. So put your best foot forward and create a wonderful garden to your door. Keep these ideas in mind as you do.

Plan for long-lasting color. Select plants so that something will be in bloom each season. For example, pansies or tulips could light up your walkways in spring, while asters and mums shine in fall. For summer, the sky's the limit—hundreds of plants bloom in midseason. And don't forget plants with colorful foliage, such as purple heuchera, painted ferns, or chartreuse hostas.

Choose pretty perennials. Plant perennials that bloom over a long period and look good even when they are not in flower. Mix in annuals to help fill the gaps between the perennials in bloom.

Develop your design. Choose plants that complement the color of your home. For example, blue oats or blue fescue ornamental grasses are always winners paired with red brick walls. Also consider the size of the plants: Small grasses are a good choice for an entryway garden because they are not invasive. Low groundcovers like lamium and liriope roll out the green carpet, too.

Dress up your foundation. Evergreen foundation plantings are beautiful on their own in winter, and they also provide the perfect backdrop for color in summer. Look for dwarf or compact varieties that don't need to be trimmed.

Look at the big picture. Don't forget to include walks and patios in your design; they're perfect locations for container plantings, a bench, or a table and chairs. People love sitting in a garden, so make your entryway part of your living space.

Plants decorate an entryway the way paintings and objets d'art decorate the interior of your home. Container gardens and foundation plantings can set the style for your entryway.

Casual Garden Design

*In my rather casual peren-
nial flower garden, a large
bed of reseeding oriental poppies seems to be happy interplanting itself in an equally
large bed of tall, dark pink
phlox. In the same bed, toward
the front, are some free-
seeding purple columbines
(perennial), a couple of sedate
'Nora Barlow' pink double
columbines, and a spreading
patch of mixed pink yarrows.
Last year, I noticed that some
white campanulas, free-seeded
from another area of my
garden, had sprouted in with
the columbines. In the same
bed, next to the poppies and
phlox, is a large bed of
lavender flags (tall bearded
iris), and in front of them an
assorted mix of Harlequin and
McKana hybrid columbines.
This basically self-sufficient
perennial garden, which runs
along the south wall of my
house, always has something
in bloom, and several times a
year provides a dramatic
splash of color.*

*Marie S.
Shandaken, New York*

Grow a Fruitful Landscape

If your yard seems too small to grow both food crops and ornamentals, try landscaping with edibles, especially fruit. Blueberries and gooseber- ries are handsome shrubs that can stand alone or form a hedge. Straw- berries serve well as groundcovers. Dwarf fruit trees fit nicely along a driveway or a property line. Grapevines on an arbor provide inviting shade over a patio; they also grow well against a wall.

Go Native but Not Wild

There's no such thing as a *no*-maintenance landscape, but the wise use of native plants can help create a *low*-maintenance one. Native plants often have the advantage of being disease- and insect-resistant. Some are widely adapted or tolerant of difficult landscape conditions.

However, there are as many poor-choice native plants as there are good ones. Natives, like other plants, may need fertilizing, watering, and weeding to become established. They may have occasional pest problems and require some pruning.

Keep in mind that "going native" in your landscaping doesn't mean taking plants from the wild. Even if you remove a common plant from the wild, you may unknowingly be disturbing other species that might not grow there again for a century. When you dig a plant from the wild, you may also bring problems, such as poison ivy roots, into your garden in the soil around the wild plant's roots.

Instead of digging plants from the wild, find out how you can buy nursery-propagated native plants. One good way to get information is to contact your state native plant or wildflower society.

Bright Spots for Bulbs

Even the smallest yard has plenty of room for bulbs. Most spring-flow- ering bulbs don't compete with trees, shrubs, or perennials—the bulbs emerge long before anything else is stirring, then fade away as other plants come into their own. Here are some suggestions of likely loca- tions for bulbs.

■ Many spring-flowering bulbs will flourish and bloom beneath deciduous trees such as oaks, maples, dogwoods, and redbuds. Keep in mind that bulbs planted in light shade bloom later than bulbs in full sun, so you can extend the bloom season by planting in varying degrees of shade.

■ A picket fence, the clapboarded side of a garage, or a brick wall will help frame your designs and shelter bulbs from the wind.

■ A bed of tulips along the foundation of your house is easy to plant, and it will look like a stroke of genius in spring. Choose a color that will stand out against the foundation, or choose colors to complement the blossoms of spring-flowering shrubs in your yard. You can even plant bulbs among existing foundation shrubs. Choose lower-growing bulbs that will peek out from the twiggy growth of deciduous shrubs.

■ Add interesting detail to your front yard by planting pools of bulbs along walkways or drifts in the lawn.

■ Drifts of bulbs work well down the middle of perennial and mixed beds. The perennials will nicely disguise the fading bulb foliage. Any pocket of a flowerbed reserved for annuals can also be planted with spring-flowering bulbs. The foliage of the bulbs will be fading by the time you're ready to plant tender annuals.

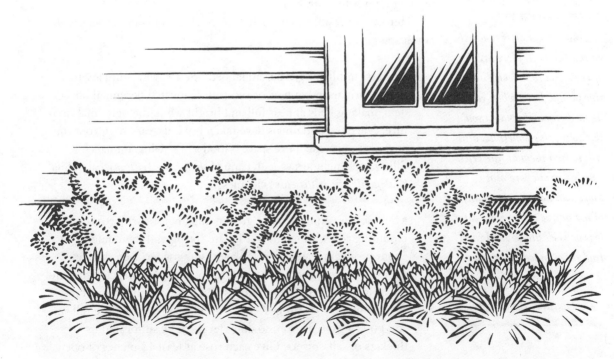

Planting crocuses and other small spring-blooming bulbs around foundation shrubs is just one way to use bulbs to add early spring color to your landscape.

Finding Natives

*I am a landscape architect
and ecologist in central Pennsylvania and I specialize in designing with native plants and
natural processes. Unfortunately, I've found that most of
the people working at garden
centers and nurseries are not
familiar with which plants are
native. To gardeners looking
for information on native
plants, I recommend checking
a university library for books
on natives or contacting the
ecology department of a university in your state.*

*Another option is to search
on the Internet; there are lots
of Web sites that deal with native plants. Even when you've
decided on native plants you'd
like to try, it's sometimes difficult to find them at nurseries
locally—exotics are much
more common. I order many
of my native plants from catalogs or Web sites when I can't
find them in local nurseries.*

*Cheryl J. L.
Howard, Pennsylvania*

Flowers That Plant Themselves

Self-seeding plants are a wonderful surprise in a flower border. These annuals and perennials drop their seeds after they bloom, and when those seeds flower the following season, they create unexpected, in-triguing new partnerships with other plants in the garden. Self-seeders are also useful because they sprout and fill open areas of the landscape that would otherwise be prone to a weed takeover. And, because self-seeders emerge where conditions suit them best, they perform as well or better than painstakingly nurtured plants.

Before adding self-sowing flowers to any bed or border, make sure the seeds are hardy enough for your area. The seeds must survive your winter conditions to germinate the next year, or there won't be any self-sowing. For example, butterfly bushes (*Buddleia* spp.) self-sow in warm climates, but not farther north.

At the other extreme, some self-sowers shouldn't be allowed to scatter their seed because their seedlings come up everywhere, be-coming worse pests than dandelions and chickweed. Different plants are invasive in different regions, so check with fellow gardeners, local horticulturists, and your County Extension agent to identify self-seeding tyrants in your area.

Here are four ways to use self-sowing plants in your gardens and landscape.

■ Let them fill gaps in perennial beds. Self-sowing annuals are particularly useful in new or recently renovated perennial bor-ders, making beds appear full and bright while the perennials ma-ture. Once the perennials have taken hold, it's easy to uproot the annuals to provide more space. Good self-sowing annuals for filling gaps include sweet alyssum (*Lobularia maritima*), calendula (*Calendula officinalis*), and cleomes.

■ Self-sowing annuals make great company for shrub roses. Once-blooming roses, which flower in late spring and then quietly go about producing seed hips, look appealing when seen through a veil of pink, red, and white cosmos, rocket larkspurs, cleomes, and flowering tobacco. These annuals make good companions for everblooming roses, too. Keep in mind that roses require full sun and good air circulation, so don't let them be suffocated by thickets of self-sowers. Give each rose at least 12 inches of open space all around.

■ If your landscape has mature shade trees—especially deep-rooted species, such as oaks and hickories—you have the perfect place for a self-sowing pretty woodland garden. Try wild cranesbill (*Geranium maculatum)* and jewelweed (*Impatiens capensis*), as well as Virginia bluebells, celandine poppies, violets, and cardinal flower (*Lobelia cardinalis*). These plants will fill in slowly; they do best in rich, moist soil heavily amended with lots of compost.

■ Self-sowers that bravely arise between stones in a walkway stand out as they never could in a crowd of other blooms. These hardy plants thrive in hardscape growing conditions. You'll find plants such as moss rose (*Portulaca grandiflora*), moss verbena (*Verbena tenuisecta*), pot marigolds, and forget-me-nots. To keep paths and other areas from being overwhelmed by self-seeders, rake gravelly areas and uproot unwanted seedlings once a week in spring and early summer.

Fruitful Vines Produce Privacy Fast

Privacy is a problem for many of us, as more and more houses are built on smaller and smaller lots in planned communities. All the fencing solutions seem to have drawbacks—a solid wood or masonry fence is expensive, wire fences are unsightly, and hedges take forever to grow. What can you do? Solve your privacy problems with prolific fruiting vines!

Hardy kiwi vines are legendary for fast, luxuriant growth, with glossy, dark green leaves and fragrant white flowers. And recent research shows that, gram for gram, kiwis are the most nutritious fruits of all. Hardy kiwis are smaller and smoother than their fuzzy cousins, but they'll take winter lows of –20°F to 25°F, making them hardy from Zones 5 to 9. Plant them 8 feet apart on a sturdy wire fence or a wood-and-wire trellis for beauty and bounty. Plant one male kiwi vine for every two or three females for good pollination.

Grapevines, with their beautiful foliage and delicious fruit, are also great for privacy and productivity. Choose a variety that's trouble-free in your area—for example, 'Concord', 'Niagara', and 'Canadice' are three of the best for the northeastern United States. Or try maypops (*Passiflora incarnata*), a cold-hardy species of passionflower. This perennial vine has roots that are hardy from Zones 5 to 10, and it climbs readily on a fence or trellis.

GARDENER TO GARDENER

Designing for Dogs

We have five dogs on our farm (used to be seven) and there is a walkway through the yard that they love to use. The two puppies especially love to tear through there. I planted chocolate mint there, and it is running rampant along the walkway. It is heavenly to smell. (Warning: You get hungry for chocolate when you smell it.) I also planted Roman chamomile along the walkway. Both plants seem to stand up well to foot and paw traffic, and even to the dogs wallowing in it.

Ann Y.
Columbus,
North Carolina

GARDENER TO GARDENER

Redesigning a Bed

Four years ago, I planted butterfly bushes in a large triangle in one of my borders. At the time, all I was thinking about was how they would look, all in bloom at the same time, with the different-colored blossoms overlapping. That worked, but I discovered that the lower two-thirds of the plants really look better hidden by other perennials (butterfly bushes aren't really that pretty when not in bloom).

So I redesigned that border, opening 60 square feet in front of them to plant a screen of perennials that are attractive all season long. And now, each year in late February, I cut every branch of my butterfly bushes back to 5-inch stubs. A great design idea for Buddleia *is to underplant closely around them with spring bulbs because crocuses, daffodils, and tulips have time to bloom before the butterfly bushes take off.*

Linda P.
Shamokin, Pennsylvania

Design with Textures

We love the beauty and variety of perennial flowers, but if truth be told, most perennial plants bloom for only a few weeks. However, their foliage is present for the whole growing season. To get the most from a perennial flower garden, do your best to include in the mix plants with interesting leaf textures and colors, such as artemisias, heucheras, and hostas.

Color Strategies

The most successful perennial gardens are often based on a wise use of color. There are three basic approaches to effective color use: color grouping, color theme, and concentrated color. All three strategies are effective and satisfying. The point is to choose the one that suits you and your yard.

Color grouping. Think of your garden as distinct patches of color separated by shrubs, rocks, paths, foliage, or plants with cream-colored flowers. You could cluster plants that offer wonderful pastel spring color in front of a shrub or beside a rock. Another group of plants nearby will bloom in mid-June, and yet another group of hot-colored flowers will bloom in late summer. A garden like this one always has spots of floral interest and also has lots of places where plants are about to bloom or have just bloomed. Choosing plants that have interesting and pleasing foliage is key to this strategy, since most of the garden will be only foliage the majority of the time. The colors of the garden may shift dramatically from season to season as one group of plants comes into bloom and another group goes out.

Color theme. You can choose a single color to plan around, or work with a combination of colors. For example, you may be a fan of the color lavender and wish to see it from spring to fall in your garden. Thus, you'll seek out perennial species and cultivars with lavender flowers that suit the conditions of your site. You may want to include some flowers with related colors, too, such as blue, pinkish blue, purple, violet, and pale red-violet. There are plenty of plants that can take you all through the seasons, sticking close to the chosen hue but varying its effect. You may want to add a few spots of a complementary color, too, such as yellow.

You can achieve the same striking effect with any color. A spring-to-fall garden based on one color avoids the awkward moments that may occur when the dominant color changes in your beds from season to season.

Concentrated color. If there's a time of year you like best or when you're frequently outside and would like to see a mass of blossoms, this strategy may be for you. It involves devoting a garden to a spectacular display for a specific length of time each year. For instance, you may find that you spend a lot of time outside—eating, relaxing, gardening, or playing games—in mid- to late June. So you plant a garden that's visible and close at hand with plants that all bloom in late June, massing them close together in drifts and pools, for an absolutely spectacular display at that time of year. In a garden like this, there really is no room for plants that may bloom earlier or later. When this garden stops blooming in July, it remains mostly foliage with no flowers for the rest of the season.

Gardens with concentrated color are beautiful, dramatic, and lush—but only for a short time.

Antique Roses: Great Garden Companions

When designing your landscape, think about how to include roses in any and all of your gardens instead of creating a garden for only roses. Interplanting roses with other types of ornamentals creates a more pleasing garden, and the plants will be less prone to pest problems than they would be in a traditional rose garden.

In particular, antique garden roses (roses introduced before 1867) enjoy the company of other plants. Their graceful, arched, sprawling, or rambling forms can highlight fences, trellises, and walls. Or they can be trained as a living fountain, showering sprays of fragrant blossoms from eye level to the ground. A smaller variety can serve as a focal shrub in mixed plantings with irises, daylilies, peonies, or other shrubs and bordered with geraniums, dianthus, a plethora of other perennials, and herbs. Some varieties can even be grown in containers to accent walkways, where their scent of myrrh, cloves, or tea will entice visitors.

Plants to Brighten Shady Areas

Perk up a drab, shady foundation bed with bedding plants suited to shade. Among them are balsam, lobelia, pansies, browallia, begonias, calendulas, torenia, nicotiana, coleus, forget-me-nots, and impatiens.

Plant a Tree, Cut Your Energy Bill

Strategically placed trees and shrubs in your landscape can reduce your heating and cooling bills—by as much as 25 percent! If you live in the North, plant deciduous trees on the south and west sides of your home. In summer, the trees' foliage blocks sunlight, helping to keep your home shaded and cool; in winter, after the leaves fall, the warming sun will shine through. Evergreen trees on the north side of your home act as a winter windbreak. Southern gardeners, try planting evergreens to the south and west of your house to create year-round cooling shade.

When you plant a tree in your yard, choose a location that will help save on energy costs. For example, evergreens planted on the south side of a house provide year-round shade, which is helpful in the warm South.

Decorate Your Gardens with Stone

If you live in an area where rocks seem to "hatch" out of the soil on a regular basis, use the stones ornamentally around your gardens. Designing rocks into your landscape will save you the trouble of hauling them away. Set the stones in and around your gardens, at the base of rose bushes, even under fruit trees. The rocks will trap and radiate heat, and they help conserve soil moisture. Over time, you'll notice that plants growing closest to the stones will mature earlier, continue growing later in the season, and stand up better in tough weather.

Peak Perennials

What the Eiffel Tower is to Paris, a few well-placed towering plants can be to your garden—soaring landmarks that add drama, contrast, and three-dimensional interest. A common mistake of many novice gardeners is to ignore the importance of height. Tall-growing perennials are an easy, beautiful solution. Don't assume that extra size means extra work. Here's a list of 12 sturdy perennials—all of which grow taller than 4 feet—that are virtually trouble-free. They thrive in a wide range of conditions and rarely suffer from pest problems. Take your landscape to dizzying new heights this spring by planting some of these statuesque beauties.

White mugwort (*Artemisia lactiflora*)

Tatarian aster (*Aster tataricus*)

'Karl Foerster' feather reed grass (*Calamagrostis* × *acutiflora* 'Karl Foerster')

Bugbanes (*Cimicifuga* spp.)

Joe Pye weed (*Eupatorium maculatum*)

Bronze fennel (*Foeniculum vulgare* var. *azoricum* 'Rubrum')

Maximillian sunflower (*Helianthus maximilliani*)

'The Rocket' ligularia (*Ligularia stenocephala* 'The Rocket')

Porcupine grass (*Miscanthus sinensis* 'Strictus')

Coneflowers (*Rudbeckia maxima, R. laciniata* 'Herbstsonne')

Cup plant (*Silphium perfoliatum*)

New York ironweed (*Vernonia noveboracensis*)

Naturally Clean Birdbaths

Last summer I created my first "water garden"—a 7-gallon tub for toads—after reading about it in an old issue of OG. I put in oxygenating plants and floaters, such as water hyacinths, azolla, water lettuce, and waterweed. Within a short time I had more plants than pond surface, so I put in another pond; this one was 22 gallons. Finally, I added fish.

I noticed that the water in my ponds remained clear, and the only maintenance I performed was to add water to replace what evaporated. I also noticed birds drinking out of my ponds. Oddly, I had continued to maintain a birdbath, which sat in full sun and required cleaning once a week. The idea occurred to me that I wouldn't have to clean my birdbath so much if I put plants in the water. Now the bath requires cleaning just once a month.

*Jeanne D.
Cicero, Illinois*

Dress Up Concrete

Concrete wall systems are reasonably priced and weekend warrior–friendly when it comes to construction. The wall blocks fit together easily, and it's only a matter of putting a good base of gravel (from 6 to 12 inches, depending on how deep the ground freezes in your region) under the wall and leveling the first set of blocks. But concrete is concrete, and if you don't like the man-made look, you're stuck. Or are you?

For a little more money, you can cap (add a finishing layer to) the wall and steps with a natural material like bluestone. Use 1½-inch-thick pieces cut at the quarry to the desired width and length. Bond the bluestone or slate to the last layer of blocks with a wet concrete slurry so that it doesn't move. The gray-blue color of the bluestone blends well with the color of the concrete. If you use stone that is slightly wider than the concrete blocks and project it over the edge of the blocks, you'll have your guests thinking the concrete is as natural as the bluestone!

Beds with an Edge

You can install brick, plastic, or metal barriers to block aggressive lawn grasses from spreading into your ornamental beds, but these products are easily damaged by lawn mowers and don't often stay in place. Instead, here's a simple edging technique that will hold back the grass and help your beds to look sharp. Use it in spring before the perennials fully emerge.

1. Use a sharp spade or shovel to cut straight down several inches into the sod all along the edge of the bed. (If the bed has been mulched, rake back the mulch before you start cutting.)

2. Make 45-degree cuts back toward the first cuts, and lift out the wedge-shaped sections of sod and topsoil, leaving a shallow trench. Shake as much soil as possible out of the sod and back into the bed, but don't refill the trench. Let the remaining sod dry out for a few days to kill it, then add it to your compost pile.

3. Apply mulch along the edge of the bed, being careful not to let it fill the trench. When grass roots grow toward the bed, they will stop at the straight side of the trench. You can mow the grass cleanly by guiding the mower so that it straddles the

trench and two wheels roll along the mulched edge of the bed. (It's important to site your plants back from the edge just far enough to leave room for the mower.)

Simple Screens for Ugly Utilities

You can hide utility poles and other modern necessities from sight if you know a few landscaping tricks with trees. Try these easy and effective ways to camouflage tall eyesores. Keep trees at least 10 feet away from the objects you're hiding so utility workers have easy access.

Hide tall poles with a single tree. Plant a basswood (*Tilia americana*), oak, pine, or other tall, spreading tree between the pole and your main viewing point. The upright line of the trunk will block the unsightly view of the pole.

Block eyesores with narrow trees. In a tiny yard, there's no space for large, spreading trees. Instead, plant narrow upright trees or shrubs such as American arborvitae (*Thuja occidentalis*). Cultivars like 'Nigra' and 'Wintergreen' grow 20 to 30 feet tall but only 5 to 10 feet wide. They're so narrow that they won't take up all your yard space, even if you set them 10 feet away from telephone poles.

Screen utilities with a grove. Hide wide eyesores with a cluster of trees like hemlocks (*Tsuga* spp.) or poplars (*Populus* spp.). If you don't have room for a large grove, group two or three multi-stemmed trees like birches (*Betula* spp.) together.

Natural Trellises

Instead of buying an arched trellis, why not make your own with supplies from your backyard? The supple wood from willows, apple trees, and grapevines makes natural, attractive trellises. It's best to make your trellises in spring, when the new growth is green and flexible. Figure out how high you want your trellis to be, double that number, then allow for the width of the arch. (For example, for a 4-foot-high, 2-foot-wide trellis, cut 10-foot sections of branch.) Bend some of the branches into an arch. Twist other branches around the arch and weave or twist the branches to form a structure. When the branches dry, they'll hold their shape. You can insert small trellises in containers to support climbing ivy and other vines, and use larger trellises right in the garden as props for drooping delphiniums, peonies, and other lazy perennials.

A Whole New Walkway

Dress up a boring walkway that's still in good shape (and that you don't want to remove) by installing precast concrete pavers on each side. It's easiest to install a double row of brick-shaped pavers. On each side of the existing walkway, dig a trench about 8 inches wide and 6 to 12 inches deep. The depth depends on how deep the ground freezes in your region—the colder it is, the deeper the trench should be. Fill the trench with ¾-inch plant mix (a gravel with mixed sizes ranging from stone dust to ¾-inch stone) to make a base for the pavers, leaving room for the thickness of the pavers and 1 inch of coarse bedding sand. Compact the gravel, then top it with a 1-inch-deep layer of coarse sand. Bed the pavers in the sand and arrange them in a staggered pattern so that the joints don't overlap.

Grow a Fence with Flavor

Need more space for gardening? Take advantage of fences along the boundaries of your yard for planting food crops or ornamentals that can grow vertically. Bramble fruits, tomatoes, beans, asparagus, dwarf pears, bush cherries, and climbing roses perform better when staked, and you'll free up the valuable garden space that these plants would fill if left to sprawl.

Chapter 4

Filling Your Yard with Flowers

Color, fragrance, cooling shade, and the freshness of tender foliage are your rewards when you grow flowering annuals, bulbs, perennials, shrubs, trees, and vines. Whether you're content to dabble with flowers in your foundation bed and a few containers or are passionate about filling every possible space on your property with ornamentals, you can look to this chapter for new and unique ideas to inspire your flower gardening.

While flowers are the most obvious characteristic of ornamentals, many perennials also offer long-lasting foliage for garden interest. Trees and shrubs provide four-season structure and color in the landscape.

This chapter begins with tips about annuals—so satisfying to grow because of their long season of bloom. Read about underused annuals you may want to try, and a turbo-planting method for setting out annual bedding plants. Look on to find an efficient bulb-planting technique, and suggestions for bulbs to plant in lawns. Follow the recommendations for flowering shrubs that attract beneficial insects, and learn how to use a flowering vine as a groundcover. With ornamentals, there's always a way to find room for just one more!

Buy Buds, Not Blooms

When shopping for annuals or perennials in the spring, look for plants with lots of new growth and tight buds, not open flowers. If you plant a perennial that's already in full bloom in the pot, it may not bloom again in your garden until next year.

Coax Kids with a Floral Clubhouse

An age-old way of fostering a love of gardening in kids is to provide them their own garden space. For an ingenious new twist, let them build an easy tepee frame and grow annual vines to cover it.

Start with a dozen 7-foot-long bamboo poles. Space the poles evenly in a 3-foot-wide circle, then insert one end of each pole about 6 inches into the ground at an angle. Tie the tops together with wire or twine to pull the poles into a tepee shape.

Have the children plant seeds at the base of the tepee—good choices of some quick-growing vines are scarlet runner beans, morning glories, or black-eyed Susan vine.

No-Fuss Zinnias

When the weather turns cool and humid, zinnia foliage often turns ugly with powdery mildew. To avoid mildew mess, try hybrids like 'Profusion Cherry' and 'Profusion Orange'. These mildew-tolerant charmers grow about 1 foot tall and bear single 2-inch-wide flowers.

Underused Annuals

Try some of these less-than-usual annuals, which work doubly well in organic gardens because they attract hummingbirds, butterflies, and beneficial insects.

Angelonica. This heat-tolerant beauty is a cousin of the garden snapdragon. Angelonica flowers look like small orchids and are available in purple or pink. It likes at least 6 hours of sun and will bloom until hard frost.

Annual monarda. 'Lambada' annual monarda is a real workhorse of a flower that can provide the perfect touch of purple for the back of a border. It grows 4 feet tall, reseeds, and may be hardy to Zone 7. Plant it in full sun or part shade.

Calibrachoa. Picture a cascading petunia with flowers all the way down its stems, and you're picturing calibrachoa. These annuals will do well in sun or shade if you feed them monthly and prune when they get shaggy.

'Cosmic Orange' cosmos. An All-America selections winner, 'Cosmic Orange' produces compact plants covered with bright orange, 2-inch double flowers. It thrives in poor soil and is drought-tolerant. It does best in full sun but will flower well in sites with half-day sun.

Flowering tobacco. The large crowns of broad, lime green leaves are striking even before flowering tobacco (*Nicotiana sylvestris*) produces its clusters of tubular white flowers atop 4-foot-tall stems. The highly fragrant blossoms droop during the day but stand up at night. Night fragrance is the forte of this flower, which grows in partial shade or full sun and almost always reseeds if given the chance.

Heliotrope. Why don't more gardeners grow this old-fashioned flower with potent vanilla fragrance, rich purple color, and great heat tolerance? Perhaps it's a misunderstanding. While heliotrope is perennial in its native Peru, in most of North America it should be grown as a warm-season annual.

Texas sage. Try brilliant scarlet 'Lady in Red' and salmon-and-white 'Coral Nymph'. Both of these cultivars of Texas sage (*Salvia coccinea*) are drought-tolerant, tough plants. They're strong reseeders, and occasional casual snipping will keep them in constant bloom.

No-Pick Peppers for Fall Color

Why grow peppers that you won't eat? Because they offer dramatic fall garden interest, rivaling chrysanthemums for vivid color. Ornamental peppers such as 'NuMex Twilight' have abundant, dark green foliage on dense, branching stems. The peppers are tiny (1-inch) firecracker-like fruits that start out purple, then turn, yellow, orange, and finally red. All of these colors may appear on the plant simultaneously. You can grow them in pots or in the ground in full sun. Try them as a low hedge. You may have some luck overwintering them in a warm greenhouse or a very bright room indoors.

Great Blooming Groundcovers

Use annuals as bright groundcovers! It's easy to give your garden a whole new look from year to year just by changing the color scheme of the flowers you select. Try spreading colorful annuals around other flowers in a sunny border, using them to brighten the base of shrubs and trees or cascade out of containers. Any of these terrific annual groundcovers will fill the bill.

- Cascading petunias, such as 'Misty Lilac Wave', 'Pink Wave', 'Purple Wave', and 'Rose Wave'.

- Tapien verbena hybrids, such as 'Blue-Violet', 'Lavender', 'Powder Blue', and 'Soft Pink'.

- Temari verbena hybrids, including 'Bright Pink', 'Bright Red', and 'Violet'.

Homegrown Bouquets

Making your own arrangements of fresh flowers is one of the great pleasures of home gardens. Keep these recommendations in mind when creating garden-fresh bouquets.

- Don't limit your bouquets to traditional annual and perennial flowers. Add some flowering herbs such as oregano.

- Give each bouquet a focal point by including showy flowers that everyone notices, such as small sunflowers or delphiniums.

- Bulk out bouquets with fillers such as strawflowers, statice, bee balm, cockscomb, bluebeard, ageratum, or helenium.

- Include a few delicate flowers such as baby's breath or Queen Anne's lace for an airy feel.

- Don't place cut flowers on the ground—dirt on the stalks can clog the stems. If possible, carry a bucket of water with you, and put flowers directly into the water as you pick.

- Strip flower stems of all leaves below the water line, and recut the stems before adding flowers to an arrangement.

As Easy as Poppies

For rich texture and luminous color with little effort, try growing annual poppies. The secret to growing annual poppies such as corn poppy (*Papaver rhoeas*), Iceland poppy (*P. nudicaule*), and breadseed poppy (*P. somniferum*) is to sow the seeds thinly. Crowded plants will be straggly and produce few flowers. Poppy seeds are tiny, and the oil in the seeds can cause them to clump. The most efficient way to sow the seeds is to mix them with sand so that they disperse evenly. Use a garden trowel to scoop the poppy seeds and sand out of the container, and gently shake the mixture over the seedbed. Thin seedlings while they are still very small, leaving about 8 inches between plants.

A disclaimer: Breadseed poppy is also known as the opium poppy, from which codeine, heroin, and morphine are made. While selling and eating this poppy's seeds are legal, growing the opium poppy is against U.S. law. Although you're unlikely to find the police knocking at your garden gate, grow these at your own risk.

Turbo-Plant for Professional Results

Make planting annuals simple and speedy with "turbo-planting," and you'll have plenty of time for other garden tasks. Here's how.

1. Remove all the transplants from their pots and lay the plants on their sides in a diamond pattern.

2. Select a spot for the transplant, and use the following technique so you don't have to remove the soil for the hole. Stick your trowel into the soil up to the handle. Don't pull the trowel out of the ground; just draw it to the side to create a hole.

3. While holding the soil back with the trowel, use your free hand to gently slip the plant into the hole. Then pull out the trowel, let the soil slide back into the hole, and firm the soil with your free hand.

As you plant, your hands will develop a fast, natural planting rhythm, to the point that you can plant as many as 80 plants in 1 hour. And the system works just as well for a dozen transplants as it does for a large planting.

old-time wisdom

SELF-SOWN VERBENAS

If one does not care to go to the trouble of sowing verbena seed in the spring, the last year's bed may be cleared of the old plants in early spring, the surface soil containing the self-sown seeds may be removed, and the bed spaded with a coating of old manure when the surface soil is to be spread on again and watered. The seedlings will come up too thick to remain, but they can be thinned out, and the surplus transplanted when a couple of inches high.

P. S. Lord
American Agriculturist,
1893

**GARDENER TO
GARDENER**

Bags for Bulbs

I have had very good luck storing canna and calla rhizomes and dahlia tubers in the lined bags that dry dog food comes in. I dig up my summer bulbs and tubers and spread them to dry, but only enough so that I can shake off most of the soil. Then I simply drop them into a dog-food bag, roll the top down, and set it in a cool corner of my basement. I do not need to mist the tubers after storage because the dog-food bags have a waxed inner lining that retains the natural root moisture.

*Harold J. D.
Montpelier, Idaho*

Speedy Sunflower Seed Collection

Sunflowers belong in every garden because of their bright, dramatic flower heads and the tasty seeds they produce. When your sunflower heads mature, harvest the seeds for yourself or to fill your bird feeders. To make this task easier, fashion a simple harvesting device from wire mesh. Cut a piece of ½-inch wire mesh large enough to span the opening of a metal tub (one about 3 feet in diameter is a good choice). To hold the mesh rigid, make a wooden frame of 1 × 2s, then use a staple gun to fasten the mesh to the frame.

Place the mesh frame over the tub. Holding a sunflower head by the stem, press the head against the mesh and vigorously rub it back and forth. The seeds will come loose and fall through the mesh into the tub.

Early Bulbs for Lawns

These bulbs will provide a rich tapestry of vivid color in your yard a full 2 months before the peak of the spring blooming season. When the show is over and your grass begins to green up, simply mow the bulbs down with the grass. For the first few cuts, put your lawn-mower blade on the highest setting to allow the bulb foliage to photosynthesize and store energy for next year's blooms.

Crocuses. Shaped like minitulips, crocuses come in myriad solid colors and combinations ranging from white to yellow to purples. Showy favorites for lawn planting include Dutch crocus (*Crocus vernus*), golden bunch crocus (*C. ancyrensis*), and lilac-colored *C. tommasinianus* and *C. minimus*.

Dwarf irises. These minis bloom in an array of colors. Some of the best for lawn plantings are sky blue and gold 'Joyce' and blue 'Harmony' (both *Iris reticulata*), yellow *I. danfordiae*, and plum *I.* 'George'.

Glory of the snow. Small, starlike blossoms grace your lawn when glory of the snow (*Chionodoxa* spp.) blooms in late winter. These bulbs come in shades of white, pink, or blue.

Grape hyacinths. The flowers of these bulbs look like tiny clusters of grapes. Grape hyacinths (*Muscari* spp.) are available in purple, blue, or white.

Siberian squill. Each Siberian squill (*Scilla siberica*) plant bears four or five true blue or white bowl-shaped flowers atop 4- to 6-inch stems in early spring.

Snowdrops. These diminutive bulbs have three-lobed nodding bells of pure white that stand out in the late winter lawn. Snowdrops (*Galanthus* spp.) prefer partial to full shade.

Spring starflower. Because of its grasslike foliage, spring starflower (*Ipheion uniflorum*) is perfect for lawn plantings. Its lovely little star-shaped flowers come in shades of white, blue, or lilac.

Transplant Timing for Bulbs

Thinking of rearranging the bulbs that are already part of your home landscape? Timing of transplanting is important. Dig bulbs when the foliage is about half-yellowed. By then, the bulbs have ripened but are still easy to find. The dying leaves are a convenient handle for lifting the clumps out of the ground. Separate the bulbs and replant immediately.

Living Bulb Marker

When planting new tulips, daffodils, and other bulbs in fall, it's easy to forget where existing bulbs are planted and, as a result, dig or slice into them. To avoid this, include grape hyacinths—which send up new leaves in fall—in each new planting of bulbs. In subsequent falls, the grape hyacinth foliage marks the area where bulbs are already planted.

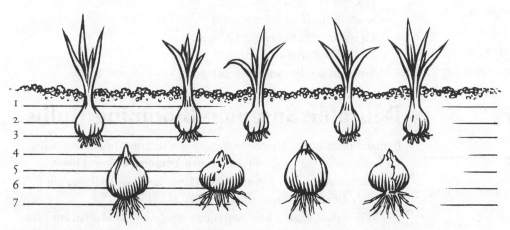

Plant grape hyacinths along with other bulbs so the grape hyacinth foliage, which emerges in fall, will alert you where *not* to dig in spring when planting annuals and perennials.

Recycling Bulbs

For a large spring bulb display on a limited budget, contact florists who sell potted
bulbs or who use the blooms in
arrangements. Florists usually
throw away bulbs after they
harvest the blooms or if the
blooms fade before the potted
plants are sold. In spring I
arrange to pick up the discarded bulbs. I store them
until fall and then plant them
into my garden. I have found
that about half of them will
bloom for me the first spring
after planting, and those that
don't will usually bloom the
second year. You can also ask
your church members if they
will give you their spent
Easter lily plants rather than
throwing them away. Just
plant the lilies into your
garden, and these hardy plants
will continue to bloom for
many years.

Fred A. R.
Springfield, Ohio

Better Bulb Planting

Digging individual planting holes for bulbs is time-consuming and
tedious. Try this motion-saving approach instead.

1. Take a narrow-blade trowel and plunge the blade about 4 inches
   into the ground, as if it were a dagger. Pull the trowel handle
   toward you, making a planting slot.

2. Remove the trowel and place a bulb into the slot with the root
   end pointing down. (If you're in doubt about which is the root
   end, plant the bulb on its side.)

3. Stab the trowel into the ground about 2 inches away from the
   first bulb and pull toward you again. This pushes the first hole
   closed and opens up a second hole for another bulb. Repeat
   until all the bulbs are planted.

4. Water your new planting thoroughly to get it off to a good
   start. Sit back and wait for the show next spring.

Natural Choices for Naturalizing

Get the most from the money you spend on bulbs by choosing types
that will naturalize in your landscape. These bulbs will rebloom year
after year in most parts of the country—and in ideal conditions will
even spread.

Crocuses (*Crocus* spp.)
Snowdrops (*Galanthus nivalis*)
Grape hyacinths (*Muscari armeniacum*)
Daffodils (*Narcissus* hybrids)
Siberian squills (*Scilla sibirica*)

Reusable Summer-Blooming Bulbs

In many parts of the United States, tender summer-blooming bulbs
such as cannas, gladioli, and dahlias won't survive winter. However,
you can get more than 1 year's bloom from these bulbs if you dig them
up in fall, store them indoors, and replant in spring.

When the bulbs' foliage starts turning yellow or brown, cut back
any foliage to 6 inches above the ground. Use a garden fork to loosen
the soil around the bulb. Lift the bulbs from the ground and shake off

excess soil. Lay the bulbs on newspaper to dry (allow 3 to 4 hours in direct sun or a few days in a shady spot or indoors).

To protect against disease, dust the bulbs with sulfur. Clearly label the bulbs, and store them in mesh onion bags or brown paper bags perforated with holes (to ensure air circulation). You can also lay the bulbs in a flat or pot and cover with slightly damp wood shavings, peat moss, or sand. Place the bulbs in a dark, cool spot that stays above freezing (40°F to 55°F is ideal). Check the bulbs monthly and throw out any rotten ones.

Cut and They'll Come Again

Perennial flowers are beautiful in the garden, and many of them are beautiful indoors in arrangements, too. Don't hesitate to cut your perennials whenever you need a bouquet. Many cut varieties will bloom *more* profusely and for a longer period than their uncut counterparts. That's because flowering plants complete their life cycles after they have bloomed and produced seed. When you interrupt this cycle by cutting the flowers, the plants will try again by sending up new flowers. (This is also why deadheading—removing spent flowers before the seeds mature—is recommended as a way to produce more blooms.)

If you want to get really sophisticated, you can even prune your perennials before they flower in order to produce more or better blooms. Snipping back some perennials to half their height before they flower will delay their bloom by several weeks, so they are just getting started when unpruned plants have finished blooming. Plants that respond well to this season-extending technique include speedwell, sunflower heliopsis, purple coneflower, stonecrop, goldenrod, and garden phlox. Cutting back some of these plants before flowering also encourages them to be bushier and shorter overall.

Prevent Perennial Heaving

Alternate freezing and thawing of the soil in winter or early spring can heave your perennials out of the ground, which may result in damage or death. Mulching is the answer, but you need to get the technique and the timing right. In the fall, wait until the ground freezes hard. Then place an inverted plastic flowerpot over each of your perennials. The pot should be larger than the plant's crown. Spread a layer of mulch 2 to 4 inches deep all around the root zone, and up to—but not covering—the pot. The pot protects the crown from being buried by mulch (mulching crowns directly can lead to rot).

Reviving Potbound Perennials

I often buy discounted flowering perennials (potted delphiniums, columbines, etc.) at the end of the nursery season. They are usually rootbound, but I've discovered that if I prune the roots carefully and then plant them into my raised-bed vegetable garden, they will recover. In the spring, I transplant them by scooping them out with a good portion of their surrounding soil. Their new root system is hardly disturbed, and they adjust to their new, permanent homes with neither wilt nor whimper.

Marie S.
Shandaken, New York

Moving Irises

I live in Zone 7 and have been moving and replanting irises throughout winter. My experience is that you can move irises at any time of year. During the active growing season, it's important that you dig up some of the small feeder roots along with the corms. Otherwise, they take longer to reestablish themselves after transplanting. I have very poor soil and add nothing to it, and irises still do fine. A top-dressing of compost seems to perk them up even more. I bury the corms with only ½ inch of soil on top, and since I live in an area with lots of heat and wind, I add a thin layer of leaf mulch, too. I also water them weekly during the growing season.

Jacki W.
Kernville, California

Bring Home Groundcover Bargains

Large-scale plantings of perennial groundcovers can set you back big bucks. Try these tips to squeeze your groundcover dollars.

■ Dig your own groundcovers from a friend's overgrown garden. Offer to remulch the bed in return.

■ Buy plants in flats instead of individual pots.

■ Buy large (gallon-size) plants and divide them into smaller sections.

■ Watch for end-of-the-season bargains.

■ Buy from companies that sell bareroot groundcovers, which are much cheaper to produce and ship than potted plants. You may have to search a little for bareroot plants—most nurseries carry potted groundcovers.

A Groundcover for the Birds

Plant bearberry to feed garden birds. Bearberry's leathery, deep green leaves form a mat with a 1- to 6-inch-high canopy that offers protection for birds as well. The foliage turns bronze in fall and winter. Delicate, rosy white flowers appear on the branches in early summer and are replaced by waxy, nutritious berries that will attract songbirds and game birds. Ruby-throated hummingbirds will occasionally visit the flowers to sip nectar.

Depending on the variety, bearberry (*Arctostaphylos uva-ursi*) can be grown from Zones 2 to 6. It prefers well-drained, acid soil.

Sow a Wildflower Sod

Wildflower meadows can be tricky to start from seed, but one method that works well is to start wildflower "sods," which are basically flats of mixed wildflower seedlings. The sod method works best for perennials that grow in colonies; avoid wildflower mixtures. Sow during the time of year when the flowers would seed themselves in nature. A mix of black-eyed Susan, yarrow, and blanketflowers (*Gaillardia* spp.) survives well with this method. It's important to prepare your site in advance (in spring a year before planting). Use a shovel or spade to remove surface weeds and grass from the planting site and a 2-foot radius around it, leaving the adjoining areas undisturbed. Avoid tilling the area, as it may turn up many unwanted weed seeds, which can hinder young wildflower growth.

Here's how to start a wildflower sod.

1. Line a flat with one thickness of cheesecloth overlapping the sides. Fill with 1 inch of potting soil, then add another layer of cheesecloth and more soil.

2. Broadcast seeds evenly over the soil. After sowing, sprinkle a fine layer of soil, and firm gently. Maximum soil contact is desired. If soil is dry, water lightly.

3. Set the prepared flat outdoors in the shade. This will expose the wildflowers to appropriate temperature and light. Most wildflowers will sprout within 20 days.

4. When you're ready to transplant about 3 months later (or after the seedlings have five leaves), lift the sod out of the flat by the bottom layer of cheesecloth. The roots will be entwined with the cheesecloth, so plant with it attached—the cloth will decompose. Be careful when handling wildflower transplants to avoid damaging roots.

A "sod" of wildflowers started in a flat has a better chance of getting established in your garden than direct-seeded wildflower seed.

GARDENER TO GARDENER

Jolly Hollyhocks

Hollyhocks can be a joy—or a sad-looking mess. I always grow them because they are such old-fashioned traditional cottage garden types, long bloomers with a real presence in the garden. As for soil, I have grown them in clay as well as in sandy loam: Hollyhocks are adaptable. They do like full sun and most important, they do not like stagnant air. The more air movement, the less chance that they will develop rust. Some hollyhocks reach up to 12 feet tall, and growing them with some support (against a fence or hedge) is useful. The seedpods are easy to collect, so you can save your own seeds.

John H. I.
Victoria,
British Columbia

Best Regional Perennials for Shade

There are scores of uniquely beautiful perennials that grow well in shade. What's important to know is which perennials will do best not only in shade but also in your regional growing conditions. Here's a region-by-region breakdown of good shade perennials.

Southeast. Most southern ornamental gardens are shade gardens by necessity—in this sultry climate, large shade trees protect plants and people from the long, hot summers. Try these perennials in southern shade gardens.

- Christmas rose (*Helleborus niger*)
- Lenten rose (*H. orientalis*)
- Heucheras (especially hybrids of *Heuchera americana*)
- Hostas, especially August lily (*Hosta plantaginea*)
- 'Goldsturm' black-eyed Susan (*Rudbeckia fulgida* var. *sullivantii*)
- Foamflowers (*Tiarella* spp.)
- 'Georgia Blue' veronica (*Veronica peduncularis*)

Texas. Texas shade gardeners are often challenged with massive tree roots and alkaline soil. Perennials will thrive in shade gardens in Texas, but they must have extra water if there is competition from tree roots. These plants grow well in Texas shade.

- Mist flower (*Eupatorium coelestinum*)
- Gaura (*Gaura lindheimeri*)
- Mexican petunia (*Ruellia brittoniana*)
- Scarlet sage (*Salvia coccinea*)

Northwest. If you've visited public gardens in the Pacific Northwest, you might have gotten the idea that gardeners here have it easy. However, root competition can be a problem, and summers can be very dry. Try these drought-tolerant shade perennials in this region.

- Corydalis (*Corydalis ochroleuca* and *C. flexuosa*)
- Pacific bleeding heart (*Dicentra formosa*)
- Heucheras (especially cultivars with metallic-looking leaves)
- Fringe-cup (*Tellima grandiflora*)
- Foamflowers (*Tiarella* spp.)
- Toad lilies (*Tricyrtis* spp.)

Upper Midwest. In the upper reaches of Zone 4, choose durable woodland flowers that can handle the rigors of winter. These plants will survive harsh winters.

- Goat's beard (*Aruncus dioicus*)
- Siberian bugloss (*Brunnera macrophylla*)
- Bugbane (*Cimicifuga simplex*)
- Barrenworts (*Epimedium* spp.)
- Virginia bluebells (*Mertensia virginica*)
- Creeping phlox (*Phlox stolonifera*)

Northeast. In the Northeast, shade is often year-round, thanks to numerous white pines and evergreen shrubs such as rhododendrons, azaleas, mountain laurels, and Japanese andromedas. These landscape staples provide greenery during the long winters. Choose shade-loving perennials that will look good against these dark foliage backdrops.

- Bishop's goutweed (*Aegopodium podagraria*)
- Ajugas (*Ajuga* spp., especially variegated cultivars)
- 'Sulphureum' barrenwort (*Epimedium* × *versicolor*)
- Heucheras
- Hostas
- Bethlehem sages (*Pulmonaria* spp.)
- Periwinkle (*Vinca minor*)

Peonies on the 4th of July

Almost everyone knows that peonies are excellent cut flowers that tend to be in bloom by Memorial Day. But did you know that the buds can be cut and kept refrigerated for 4 weeks or more and still open beautifully? That means you can enjoy peony blooms from Memorial Day to Independence Day. Here's how.

1. Harvest the flowers when the green sepals have separated on the buds and color is showing. The peony buds should be marshmallow soft.

2. Strip all the leaves from the bottom third of the stems, wrap the stems and buds in plastic bags, and seal all openings with rubber bands or twist ties. Store the stems horizontally in the refrigerator. (Make sure you place them where they won't get mashed.)

3. The day before you want the flowers to open, remove them from the refrigerator and place the stems into a vase of tepid water.

Ring around the Asters

Asters are hardy perennials that are great for cut flowers, meadow gardens, mass plantings, and attracting butterflies. But after a few years, the center of an aster clump can die out, leaving you with a ring of new growth around an empty center. To fix this odd-looking growth pattern, just dig up and slice the living sections away from the dead with a sharp spade. Compost the dead material; replant the smaller sections or share them with friends.

Peony Pals

I live in my grandma's old farmhouse, and although most of her flowers fell by the wayside in her later years, her large bed of peonies and lilies of the valley are still coexisting peacefully. The peonies and lilies of the valley have been growing together in the same bed since I was a kid—probably even longer than that. The lilies of the valley sprout and grow all among the peony shoots, and neither one has diminished the other. They both continue to be incredible bloomers!

*Janet D.
Alma, Michigan*

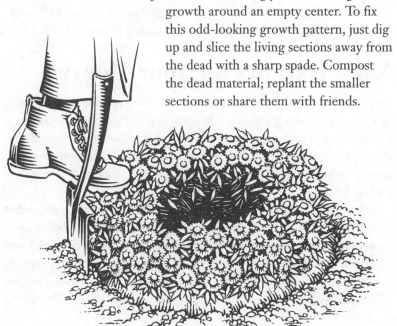

Dig, divide, and replant the young, outer sections of a mature aster plant to rejuvenate the planting. Compost the worn-out center section.

*Portable Shade
for Young Plants*

*When I transplant peren-
nials to a sunny location, I
find that giving them shade
for up to a week makes a big
difference in the young plants'
survival rate. I tried all sorts
of makeshift devices for temporary shade, but they fell
over and squashed the plants.
Finally, I invented my own
sturdy, easy-to-build
"transplant shader."*

*I made mine out of 1 × 2
pieces of wood. To start, cut
eight pieces of wood to 21
inches long. Nail four pieces
of wood together to form a
rectangle. Repeat with the remaining pieces to form a
second rectangle.*

*Attach the two frames at
one end with small hinges and
wood screws. Fold the frames
flat together and use a staple
gun to fasten green shade cloth
over the two frames. Trim the
excess fabric. Place the frame
over young transplants in the
garden.*

*Mary Ann O.
Wilmington, Vermont*

Division Yields More Blooms

Are some of your perennials growing lushly but flowering poorly? To
restore their flowering potential, dig and divide. Most perennials need
dividing every 3 to 5 years, but a drop in flower production is the best
indicator. Some popular perennials—hollyhocks, columbines, delphiniums, and lupines—are so short-lived that dividing won't help.
Your best bet is to replace these perennials every few years with new
plants grown from seed.

Save Time with Hedge Shears

Use handheld hedge shears for fast and easy trims of bushy plants like
asters and mums. The long blades can do the job in just a couple of
cuts instead of the 10 to 20 required by shorter pruning shears. Most
perennials benefit from pinching, shearing, or cutting back to keep the
rest of the plant looking nice during spring, summer, and fall. Use
hedge shears for the following jobs.

- Shearing back the tips of mums, asters, and sedums in spring to
encourage bushier, self-supporting plants.

- Cutting off old flowers on pinks, thrifts, rock cresses, and others
after they bloom.

- Removing old foliage from ornamental grasses and coneflowers
in spring, or old leaves of peonies and other perennials in fall.

More Daylilies for Your Money

While conscientious deadheading keeps daylilies looking neat, it eliminates a propagation possibility. On some daylily cultivars, the old
flower stems produce proliferations (miniature plants that emerge on
the stem below a faded flower). If you use these proliferations to propagate expensive cultivars, you won't have to buy new plants at the
garden center.

Watch for proliferations in late summer. They arise from a bud that
grows into a little cluster of leaves and, by August or September, also
sprouts tiny roots. Cut them free, roots and all, and move them to a separate pot. Or plant them beside the mother plant for easy identification.

Some of the daylily cultivars that may sprout proliferations include
'Coral Crab', 'Fairy Tale Pink', 'Lullaby Baby', and 'Prairie Blue Eyes.'

Grow Beneficial Shrubs

Shrubs can be much more than just "green meatballs" dotting your landscape. Some are flowering beauties that also serve as sources of food and shelter for beneficial insects and pest-eating birds.

Almost any shrub will provide shelter for beneficial beetles and bugs, but certain shrubs, such as spirea, also produce pollen and nectar for beneficial flies and wasps. Other nectar-producers include New Jersey tea (*Ceanothus americanus*) and summersweet (*Clethra alnifolia*). Ninebark (*Physocarpus opulifolius* and *P. capitatus*) and almost any type of rose are great habitats for beneficial insects, too. Another insect attractor is bluebeard (*Caryopteris clandonensis*), which blooms in late summer, drawing thousands of bees, beneficial flies, and tiny parasitic wasps.

Some shrubs score triple points as attractors for beneficials because they produce flowers and berries, so they feed not only beneficial insects but also birds. Hollies (*Ilex* spp.), serviceberries (*Amelanchier* spp.), native viburnums, and junipers are a few examples; see page 58 for more.

These shrubs won't do well in the arid Southwest, though. Gardeners in that part of the country may want to try fairy duster (*Calliandra* spp.), a nitrogen-fixing flowering native shrub that bears seeds loved by quail and doves; algerita, a southwestern cousin to Oregon grape holly; or red bird of paradise (*Caesalpinia* spp.), a favorite of hummingbirds.

One thing to keep in mind when you grow shrubs for birds is that some berries don't become bird breakfast until they have hung on the bushes for many months. For example, juniper and holly berries may not be palatable to birds until they've gone through several freezes and thaws. Birds who eat these late-winter fruits will switch and eat pest insects in spring, when they crave protein for growing new feathers or feeding a nestful of chicks.

Blanket the Soil to Prevent Black Spot

A thick mulch of compost can save your roses from the ravages of black spot, which can cause leaves to become sickly and drop prematurely. The fungus that causes black spot lives in the soil. Raindrops can splash fungal spores from the soil surface onto rose leaves, starting the infection. Mulch breaks the disease cycle.

GARDENER TO GARDENER

Corny Rose Cure

To help fight fungal problems on my rose bushes, I sprinkle a cup of whole ground cornmeal on the soil surface around each rose bush. The cornmeal is a host for a beneficial fungus that attacks other fungi. Last year I had no rose fungus problems until about late December. Coincidently, I also had zero aphids for the first time ever.

*David H.
San Antonio, Texas*

Summer-Prune Roses for More Bloom

Removing spent rose blossoms is always worth doing unless the hips—round seedpods that form on roses after blooms—are part of a particular variety's appeal. Cutting off old blossoms diverts the plant's nutrients and energy from seed production back into more leaves and flower buds. In varieties that bloom repeatedly all summer, removing old blossoms is especially important for abundant bloom—and a spectacular show.

Summer pruning of rosebushes isn't complicated or scary. In general, cut back to a strong bud without removing any more leaves than you have to. The leaves are essential to power regrowth. But on types like floribundas, which produce many small blossoms, don't just snip off individual flowers. Instead, cut to a strong bud just below the entire flower cluster.

Top 10 Shrubs and Trees

Ready to try something new? Here are 10 outstanding ornamental trees and shrubs that were identified in trials by the USDA. The USDA trials are among the largest and longest-running evaluations of landscape plants.

'Cardinal' red osier dogwood

'Emerald Triumph' viburnum

'Fox Valley' river birch, or black birch

'Indigo' silky dogwood

Kentucky wisteria

'Konza' fragrant sumac

'Nugget' ninebark

'Sakajawea' silver buffaloberry

Western larch

'White Knight' weigela

To read descriptions of these outstanding ornamentals and determine if they're right for your conditions, go to www.organicgardening.com/library/ornamentals.html.

'Betsy Ross' Lilac Beats Mildew

Gardeners have long cherished lilacs for their fragrant blooms, but growing lilacs can be a challenge—particularly in the humid South—because of their susceptibility to powdery mildew. Southern lilac lovers should try early-blooming 'Betsy Ross', a new hybrid lilac with increased resistance to mildew. 'Betsy Ross' was also bred to flower without needing cold winters and to tolerate heat and humidity. 'Betsy Ross' bears abundant, fragrant white flowers and has lush, dark green foliage. It's been grown successfully as far north as Zone 4.

2-for-1 Trellises

Get double-duty from your trellises by having them bear an early-summer-blooming climbing rose as well as a later-blooming clematis. Train an old-fashioned climbing rose such as 'Honorine de Brabany' on a trellis or pillar for flowers in early summer. Once the blooms are past, the rose provides quiet greenery through fall. To keep the color coming later in the season, plant a summer- or fall-blooming clematis on the same trellis. The clematis will twine up, over, and around the rose and provide a second floral show for late summer.

Revive That Lilac!

Got an old lilac that you want to rejuvenate? Use a pruning saw to cut out about one-third of the old growth each winter, then spread an inch or two of composted manure and some bonemeal over the root zone. It will come back beautifully.

Passionflowers for Cold Conditions

Exotic passionflowers usually can't survive winters outdoors north of Zone 9, but there are two exceptions. Common passionflower (*Passiflora caerulea*) and maypops (*P. incarnata*) will survive to Zone 6. The secret is to find a site with a protected southern exposure and provide a thick blanket of winter mulch. These beautiful vines need full sun and a strong support to climb. Common passionflower has evergreen foliage; maypop vines die back to the ground in winter. Passionflowers are an important larval host for some butterflies, and hummingbirds will visit the unusual flowers to sip nectar.

GARDENER TO GARDENER

Tree Guards

To protect my trees against marauding mowing machines and wild weed and grass trimmers, I used to place colored plastic bottles with the tops and bottoms removed around the trunks. These tree guards worked well, but eventually the plastic became brittle and the bottles shattered. Now I use black corrugated plastic drainpipe, which is heavier, more durable, and often of a larger diameter so it can protect bigger trees. I often pick up discarded lengths of pipe for free around new-home construction sites. I simply slice them open lengthwise and fit them around the trunks.

Carita B.
Morehead, Kentucky

Firecracker in the Shade

A unique vine for shade is the Brazilian firecracker (Manettia luteorubra). My sister sent me one of these tender vines from her shade garden in Florida. Since I live in Zone 6, I grow the vine in a large pot and bring it indoors in winter. It keeps right on growing in the dim light of my laundry room all winter long. The vine has pretty oval foliage and red tubular flowers with a yellow lip. They really do look like firecrackers.

Dee M.
Springdale, Arkansas

Pruning Pointers for Pussy Willows

Pussy willows are rather plain shrubs, but they have a standout season. In late winter, this humble shrub becomes as treasured as the rarest tree peony. When you grow your own pussy willows, you can enjoy the sight of their catkins daily, both outdoors and inside.

Pussy willows can be problematic, though, because they grow *so* energetically. Pruning them properly goes a long way toward keeping them under control. Remember these pointers.

- Every year, prune out one-third of the oldest wood to shape the plants.

- If you prune when the catkins are emerging, you'll have plenty of stems for decorating, and the plant will throw new branches later in spring.

- Shrub willows can stand hard pruning about every third year.

- For best catkin production and to control the shrub's free-wheeling growth habit, always cut branches back all the way to the main trunk; don't just "head" them back partway.

Perfect Planting Times

The best time to plant trees and shrubs depends on what type you are planting. For balled-and-burlapped and container-grown trees and shrubs, conditions in fall are perfect for maximum root growth. But for bareroot plants, avoid fall planting. Instead, time planting to take place just before the plant breaks bud in spring. Take your cue from other plants of the same species around your neighborhood. When you see the slightest swelling of their buds, it's time to plant.

Major Plant Moves

If a small tree or shrub isn't doing well where it's planted, or if it just doesn't suit your design, you can move it successfully. The biggest concerns when you transplant a large woody plant are to handle the root system with care and to work in accord with seasonal dormancy. You can move most trees and shrubs in early spring, before any bud growth resumes, or during fall, when the plants are dormant. In southern regions, the dormant period may last only 4 to 6 weeks during late winter.

Disrupting the root system is the major cause of transplant stress. If a shrub or tree is more than 8 feet tall, you will probably need professional help to move it.

If you're doing the job on your own, follow these steps.

1. Dig the new hole the day before transplanting, saving the soil on a tarp. Make the hole twice the estimated diameter of the rootball and no more than its depth. Estimate the rootball diameter by measuring the distance from the trunk to the tips of the limbs on each side, adding them together, and then doubling that number—approximately 1 foot for each inch of trunk diameter. The depth of the rootball should be 18 to 24 inches. Test drainage by filling the hole with water. If most of it is not gone the next day, find a better-draining site.

2. Dig a trench around the tree and save all the soil. Fill the trench with water to soften the soil and loosen the roots. When most of the water has drained, dig the trench 6 inches deeper, then finish digging underneath the tree roots, making a pedestal beneath the soil ball around the roots. Avoid pruning roots or tree branches except to remove broken or damaged ones. Slide burlap under and around the rootball and tie tightly with twine. Keep the ball moist and shaded, especially if you have to finish digging the new hole.

3. Don't pull on the trunk. Prop a board or piece of plywood under the rootball and, with a friend helping if it's heavy, slide the tree up and out of the hole by pulling on the burlap and slipping the rootball onto a handcart or another board with rollers under it. Wheel to the new site and transplant immediately.

Handle the rootball of a large shrub or tree with care and you can successfully transplant it to a new location in your yard.

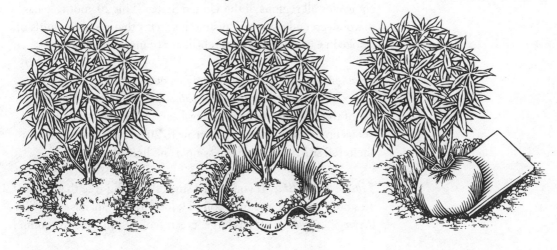

Cover the Ground with Clematis

When you've got lots of ground to cover, forget about slow-growing perennials and let a clematis vine do the job. Many clematis vines are happy to crawl through a perennial border or spread out as an unusual groundcover.

Plant summer-blooming types for a groundcover because they ramble the best. Good candidates include those in the Viticella group—they have smaller blossoms than the ever-popular Jackman clematis (*Clematis × jackmanii*) but bloom profusely and come in a wider color range, including white, violet-purple, red, purple-blue, and white with purple veins.

Clematis are healthy plants, so you'll probably never have to worry about diseases. But if clematis wilt is a problem for you, avoid the large-flowered early-spring bloomers. Susceptible cultivars include 'Henryi', 'Nelly Moser', and 'Ramona'. Instead, choose a clematis that blooms later in the summer—Jackman and other late bloomers are re-sistant. Or pick a cultivar or variety of the small-flowered spring-bloomers like anemone clematis (*C. montana*), which are also wilt-resistant.

Trees for Small Spaces

Many yards don't have the space for a towering shade tree but offer choice locations for a small landscape tree. Here are some great possi-bilities for growing small trees.

American smoke tree. Drought tolerant and pest- and disease-resistant, American smoke tree (*Cotinus americanus*) is a great choice for all regions of the United States. This 20-foot tree has maroon-green leaves with distinctive stems that resemble puffs of smoke in early summer. It has brilliant orange fall color.

Japanese maple. Distinguished by its deeply cut purple (or green) leaves, the Japanese maple (*Acer palmatum*) is near the top of the list of trees for small spaces. It has beautiful fall colors and gor-geous branch structure. It will grow to 20 feet tall and requires a sheltered site (away from hot winds) and light shade.

Japanese tree lilac. If you need a small flowering tree that toler-ates both drought and high soil pH, look to the Japanese tree lilac (*Syringa reticulata*). It has large, cream-colored flowers in summer and glossy cherry tree–like bark that shows to good advantage during winter months.

Parsley hawthorn. For cramped quarters in the Deep South, a great tree choice is parsley hawthorn (*Crataegus marshallii*). It tops out at around 25 feet, has showy white flower clusters in early spring, sports scarlet fruits in late summer, and has attractive peeling bark when mature. Its finely textured leaves really do resemble parsley and are a bright chartreuse when they emerge in early spring.

Strawberry tree. Bright red "berries" and attractive peeling bark are the best features of the strawberry tree (*Arbutus unedo*). It is evergreen and grows 15 to 30 feet tall.

Moderate Mulch for Trees

Go easy on mulch when you plant an ornamental tree or shrub. Don't mimic the mulch mountains you see around trees in many public plantings—2 inches of mulch is plenty. The best mulch to use is leaf litter, perhaps mixed with some shredded twigs and bark. (Let fresh wood chips rot for a year before you use them.)

Turn a Shrub into a Trellis

Plant a clematis vine near a small ornamental shrub like a viburnum or spirea, and you'll have an instant trellis for the vine—and waves of flowers, too. Just train the vine on a short stake at the base of the shrub, and the clematis will grow up into the shrub. This pairing works best with a hybrid clematis that won't get big and that you can cut back to a couple of bud sets each year in early spring before growth begins.

Low-Tech Irrigation

Newly planted trees, shrubs, and perennials appreciate a gentle and thorough watering, but watering slowly by hand takes time. Instead, create a low-tech drip irrigation system using gallon-size plastic juice jugs. (They're sturdier than plastic milk jugs.) Fill a jug with water and carry it to a planting. Poke a small hole into the bottom of the jug and set it beside a newly planted plant. Then loosen the lid slightly to release the pressure so the water drips out slowly toward the plant's roots, right where it's needed.

old-time wisdom

SHRUBS FOR POOR SOIL

We often hear people say their soil is so poor they cannot raise anything. This is a common excuse for bleak surroundings. The following shrubs will grow well in poor, dry soil: beach plum (*Prunus maritima*), sumac, Japanese rose (*Rosa rugosa*), woad wax (*Genista tinctoria*), sea buckthorn (*Hippophae rhamnoides*), groundsel shrub (*Baccharis halimifolia*), and laurel-leaf willow (*Salix pentandra*).

*Loring Underwood
A Garden Diary and
Country Home Guide,
1908*

Preventable Tree Problems

The two most common tree problems are mechanical damage (from care, bicycles, lawn mowers, etc.) and soil compaction. You can prevent and/or remedy both problems the same way: with barriers like mulch, landscape plantings, or edgings. Mulch also discourages foot traffic, prevents competitive weeds from growing near the tree, keeps the ground around the tree porous, and retains soil moisture. For information on the correct way to mulch a tree, see page 21.

Root Wars

When you want to plant perennials or groundcovers under large, shallow-rooted trees, such as maples, birches, or poplars, you'll need to build up soil rather than dig among the roots. Dump a mixture of clay soil, compost, and bagged topsoil or humus to create a 2-inch-deep bed. This will not harm the tree's roots, but be sure to keep the mix 6 inches away from the tree's trunk to prevent bark rot.

Quick Trellises from Trees

Pick up sticks when you want a trellis in a hurry. It's very easy to do: Just stick an interesting-looking forked branch in the ground or rest it against a wall. Sticks and small branches make great trellises for lightweight vines like clematis or passionflower. Found objects such as old rakes and rickety ladders also make unique trellises. Use a few guy wires to steady your trellises if they can't support themselves.

Go Glossy for Mildew Resistance

Rose bushes with glossy foliage are the most resistant to mildew because the thick, waxy coating that creates the sheen on the foliage forms a physical barrier between the leaves and the fungus. Try planting hybrid musk roses in your garden for both attractive foliage and resistance to diseases.

Chapter 5

Growing Vegetables Galore

Taste and freshness are the vegetable gardener's goals. Quantity can be important, too, but never as a substitute for the delight of savoring just-picked sweet corn and tomatoes or preparing a salad from greens that are crisper and fresher than any you could find at the supermarket.

In this chapter, you'll find hints on every aspect of vegetable gardening, from timing of spring planting and preventing transplant shock to methods for shading plants from too much sun. You'll discover how succession planting can increase your total harvest. Check out the bounty of ideas for boosting bean growth, as well as intriguing tips on growing sweet corn to perfection. Find out how to harvest more broccoli from both spring and fall plantings. Ponder the tips for picking peas at their prime and supporting pumpkins on a supersturdy trellis. Learn how to set up a Japanese tomato ring, and follow the sage advice for avoiding the zucchini blues.

The tips don't stop with picking time, either. You'll find good ideas for keeping the harvest, including fast ways to freeze chopped peppers and dry chopped garlic, plus a smashing technique for opening tough-hide squashes.

Bird Benefits

I've had nary a tomato hornworm or cabbage looper—and relatively few destructive beetles—in my veggies ever since I started placing bird feeders around the periphery of my garden. I actually started feeding the birds because I enjoyed observing and keeping records of different varieties. (I'm right in one of the "birdie rest stops" along their migratory superhighway.) In my garden, we get birds who stay all season, plus many of those transitory, one-night-standers just stopping by for a quick meal and a bath!

Sure, the birds love the sunflower seeds, but their favorite delicacies are the above-mentioned buggies. Cardinals love hornworms, and a catbird will pass up feeder food for a tasty, plump cabbage looper any day! If you notice birds setting up housekeeping around your home, cherish and protect them. They've been my best garden cops!

*Linda F.
Jackson, New Jersey*

Suit-Yourself Bed Size

The accepted wisdom for most organic vegetable gardens is that planting in raised beds beats conventional row planting. How wide to make your beds depends on you. Beds can be as narrow as 18 inches across—but the wider the beds, the fewer walkways you'll need and the more space you'll save. When beds are over 5 feet wide, though, it's hard to reach into the center for planting, weeding, and picking. Beds that are 3 or 4 feet wide offer a comfortable range for reaching; the length of your reach should be the determining factor.

Custom Care for Minibeds

Fine-tuning the soil in your vegetable garden for a particular crop is easy when you garden in minibeds. Rather than making beds that run the full length or width of your garden, set up beds about 4 feet long and 3 feet wide. In a small bed such as this, it's easy to specially prepare for growing carrots, for instance, by adding a wheelbarrow full of sand to lighten the soil before planting.

Nature's Planting Schedule

Synchronize planting your garden with bloom times of landscape and native plants in your local area. This lets you coordinate your planting to match the specific climate conditions of your site. For example, when skunk cabbages bloom, it's time to set out asparagus and rhubarb crowns. Plant beets, cabbages, onions, parsley, peas, spinach, candytuft, and snapdragons when yellow forsythia blossoms open. When daffodils and flowering quince are in full bloom, it's time to plant broccoli, potatoes, calendula, cleome, pinks, and zinnias. Hold off on sowing corn, cucumbers, melons, snap beans, zucchini, and sunflowers until dogwoods and lilacs are in bloom.

Succeed with Succession

You can double or even triple the yield from your vegetable garden simply by using the strategy of planting in succession. Succession cropping means planting one short-term crop after another from early spring through fall. For example, start a bed with fast-growing leaf lettuce. After harvesting the lettuce, plant cabbage for fall harvest. Or, plant carrots in early spring; after digging the carrots, plant a late crop of snap beans. Gardeners in warm climates will choose different crop combinations and different timing. For example, in fall, southern gardeners might set out broccoli transplants under row covers after clearing tomato plants out of a bed.

One other tip to remember: Crops planted in succession should be from different families so disease and insect problems won't carry over from one crop to the next. For example, mildew on peas may reappear on the second crop when peas follow peas.

A Shady Setup

As spring warms into summer, cool-weather crops such as lettuce and cabbage will grow better and be less likely to bolt if you provide some protection from the hot sun. You can use shade cloth or ordinary cheesecloth for this purpose. Sew curtain rings or eyelets on the corners of the fabric. Pound four wooden stakes into the corners of the bed where cool-weather crops are planted. Slip the rings over nails or hooks driven into the stakes. Put the cloth up at noon, and be sure to remove it on cooler afternoons. On very hot days, lightly sprinkle the top of the cloth with water to help bring down temperatures underneath even more. Or, you can space the stakes more closely to support a piece of lightweight lattice or a thin layer of brush instead.

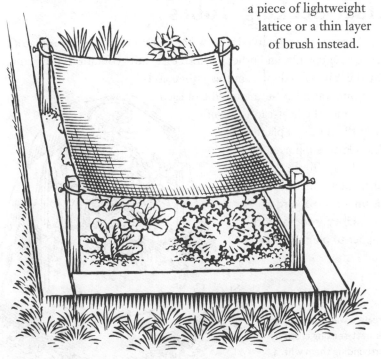

A temporary "arbor" of shade cloth or cheesecloth protects cool-weather crops from sun damage on a hot, sunny day.

Tea Strainer

Compost tea offers many benefits for vegetable crops and other plants. But the tea usually has particles in it that can clog garden sprayers. To make an easy filter, cut a 2-foot-square section of nylon bridal-veil material (available at fabric stores), wad it up in your hands, and stuff it into the neck of a 6- or 8-inch funnel. Place the funnel in the opening of your garden sprayer and pour the compost tea through it. The mesh allows only the liquid to pour into the sprayer. Afterward, rinse the mesh in water and lay it out to dry. It can be reused many times.

William M. K. Matthews, North Carolina

Double-Duty Garden Planting

Slow-growing crops such as tomatoes and cauliflower need plenty of elbow room for expansion over time. While the slow crops are still young, put that open space to best use by interplanting. Plant small patches of fast-growing crops such as beets, peas, and salad greens around the slow growers. You'll harvest the quick crops by the time the tomato plants are ready to fill the space.

Starter Solution Stops Transplant Shock

Transplanting can stress plants because of root disturbance, wind, and dramatic changes in light and temperatures. Help your transplants bounce back more quickly by setting them out with a starter solution made of 2 parts water and 1 part sifted compost. Pour some solution into the transplant hole and let it soak in. Then set the plant in place, fill the hole with soil, and water with starter solution again.

Heat-Seeking Tubes

An old tire inner tube filled with water will trap heat, giving tomatoes, peppers, eggplants, and other warmth lovers the conditions they crave. Lay the water-filled tubes in the garden and plant one transplant in the middle of each. To enhance the heat-capturing effect, cover the tube and plant with clear plastic supported by a metal hoop. To fill the inner tube, cut a 1-inch slit in the top and insert a garden hose. Use a wood or cork stopper to plug the hole.

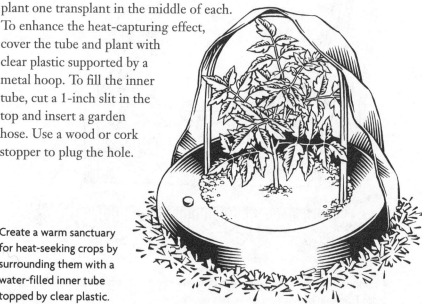

Create a warm sanctuary for heat-seeking crops by surrounding them with a water-filled inner tube topped by clear plastic.

Even Tomatoes Can Overheat

Although tomatoes, peppers, and eggplant are called "heat-loving" vegetables, they can still suffer heat stress in the ultrahigh heat of summer in places like the Southwest, where temperatures can top 110°F. To save plants from getting too much sun, keep shading materials on hand, such as sheets of corrugated aluminum, shingles, boards, house screens, old bed sheets or curtains, or pieces of cardboard. Let plants enjoy the morning sun, then set up the shading materials to shield the plants during the sizzling afternoons. (Be sure to collect all your shading materials early in the summer so you're not looking for things to use while your garden wilts on a blistering August afternoon.)

Sideline Tall Crops

Tall vegetable crops such as sweet corn, pole beans, and vine crops (on trellises) can cast shade on neighboring crops. This can be a strategic advantage in nursing cool-weather crops like lettuce and kale through hot summers, but it can also hinder the growth of crops in cool-summer areas. So plan the placement of tall crops depending on your climate needs. To minimize the shade cast within your garden, plant tall crops along the eastern and northern sides of your garden.

Trouble-Saving, Self-Sown Vegetables

Take it easy in fall and you'll be amazed at the bounty of young vegetable plants that sprout voluntarily in your garden in spring. All you have to do is let your spent crops go to seed and hold off on turning your garden soil until late spring. Many vegetables will reseed to give you another season's harvest. (Some ornamentals, such as sunflowers, also reseed themselves.) Here's a quick list of crops that reliably reseed themselves.

Amaranth
Beets
Cherry tomatoes
Chinese greens
Fava beans
Lettuce
Rustic arugula

Don't Wait for Asparagus

Why wait to start harvesting your asparagus? Ignore the recommendations that say you have to wait until the second or third year after planting before you begin cutting spears. Research studies have found that a light harvest the first year had no effect on second-year spear production—or actually even increased the harvest. In the first year, harvest over about a 4-week period (unless you're gardening in more northern locations, when harvesting for a shorter period the first year is safer).

Asparagus Grows Best When You Dig Less

Now you can skip deep-digging your asparagus bed with good conscience. Asparagus plants grow best at the depth they're happiest, and that's just a few. You'll get just as good results—or better—planting asparagus 4 inches deep as you'd get setting them at the recommended depth of 8 to 12 inches.

Studies show that asparagus crowns originally planted at depths ranging from 4 to 12 inches all ended up at 4 inches after 10 years. The crowns may actually work themselves deeper into the soil or closer to the surface until they find the soil conditions they like best. In sandy soil, the crowns may grow a little deeper than 4 inches, while in a clay soil they'll be a little shallower.

Good Reasons to Grow Dry Beans

Perhaps you buy standard dry beans such as kidney beans and pinto beans at the supermarket, but even so, there are great reasons to grow some in your vegetable garden, too.

Your variety selection will be much larger, allowing you to choose from a multitude of shapes (round, kidney-shaped), sizes (as small as a grain of rice, as big as a jawbreaker), and colors (red-striped, blue-spotted, maroon-splotched).

Dry beans from your home garden will also cook up in about half the time that supermarket dry beans take. And that means you'll get more of those nutrients that beans are famous for: copper, folic acid, iron, magnesium phosphorus, thiamin, and—important for vegetarians—protein. Beans are also a major source of dietary fiber.

A final reason to grow your own dry beans: You're much less likely to suffer from intestinal gas when you eat homegrown dry beans.

Despite being dried and stored, the beans you grow in your own garden are *fresh*. Store-bought beans are anywhere from 6 months to 1 year older than homegrown. And as those beans age they get harder, so they are less likely to soak up water and soften when cooked. The result is starch that doesn't cook no matter how long you leave your beans on the stove. The starch goes through your stomach undigested, passes into the large intestine, and causes gas. Fresh homegrown dried beans cook much more fully and so are easier for your stomach to digest.

Double-Cropping Beans

Southern California gardeners can easily harvest two and sometimes three pole bean crops per season from one planting of vines. The trick is administering a "shock treatment" when the vines seem to be declining. Start the treatment by pulling off dead foliage, watering deeply, and gently loosening the soil around the base of the plants. The following day water with compost tea and apply a thin layer of mulch. The plants should send out a burst of new leaves and flower buds, which in turn will produce a crop of bean pods.

Jump-Start Your Beans

To give your beans an extra advantage, give your seeds a shot in the arm. A powder known as *inoculant* is brimming with the living bacteria that beans need to capture their own nitrogen. Just before planting, simply moisten the seeds and mix them with the inoculant, which is available at most garden centers. Be sure to buy the inoculant specifically for beans and peas.

Stay Ahead of Bean Mosaic

Mottled leaves that curl downward at the edges are a classic symptom of bean mosaic. There's no cure for this viral disease, and infected plants may have very poor yields.

There are two things you can do to stay ahead of mosaic problems in your garden. One is to seed your crop heavily so that you can pull and discard infected plants as soon as you spot them. This will help stop the disease from spreading. Also try covering your plants with floating row covers to keep out aphids (they transmit the virus) as long as possible. You'll need to remove the covers for at least part of the day to allow pollination when the plants begin to flower.

Happy Bean Harvest

Harvesting dry beans is simple. When at least 90 percent of the plants' leaves have dried and the beans rattle in their pods, pull out all the plants by the roots. (Keep an eye on the forecast and yank the plants before rain hits; otherwise your almost-dry beans may become moldy in their pods.)

Hang the plants in a sheltered location to dry completely before you shell them, or shell the beans first and spread the beans to dry on a screen (not in direct sun). The beans are totally dry when you can't make a mark in them with your fingernail.

There are several neat ways to shell beans. Take them with you to an outdoor concert and shell them while you listen to the music. (Perhaps you'll even receive help from your fellow concertgoers!) Another approach is to have a shelling party at home. Put the beans in a big wooden box or an old child's wading pool (no water) and let your helpers step in and act like grape crushers—basically doing the twist while standing on the beans! Afterward, you can separate the beans from the pods by pouring the material on the ground while a breeze or a fan blows away everything but the beans.

If you're feeling aggressive, try beating your bean plants. Spread out the vines on a tarp, and hit them with a tool called a *flail*. A flail is a piece of hardwood loosely attached to a handle with twine. A variation on this method is to put all the bean plants in a burlap sack, hang it from a tree, and play "piñata" with the sack by striking it with a broom handle.

Before you store your beans for fall and winter eating, pick out some of the largest, best-looking ones as seed for next year's crop. Pack the rest into airtight storage containers such as self-sealing bags, jars, or plastic tubs, and then stow the containers in the freezer for 3 days. This prevents bean weevils from hatching out of your beans while they are in storage. After you remove them from the freezer, stash the containers in a cool, dark place.

Bean Boosters

These simple steps can make a big difference in whether or not you harvest a bounty of beans from your bed.

- Southern gardeners should spread a ½-inch layer of well-aged compost over their bean bed and dig it in a week or two before planting. (Southern heat tends to burn up organic matter in the soil quickly.)

■ Buy some bean inoculant (available at most garden centers) when you get your seeds. The inoculant contains the soil-dwelling bacteria that help beans "manufacture" their own plant-feeding nitrogen from the air.

■ Wet the seedbed *before* you plant. Planting into moist soil is very important for beans, and will help them get off to a good start. In a hot climate, spread a thin layer of loose mulch—straw or dried, shredded leaves—over the newly planted bed to retain moisture for germination.

■ Water weekly once bean seedlings emerge, but let the soil dry out between waterings.

■ Watch closely for outbreaks of yellowish brown beetles with black spots. These nasty fellows are Mexican bean beetles. Hand-pick the beetles and larvae daily, dumping them into a can of soapy water.

■ To extend your harvest as long as possible in fall, cover the plants with fabric or plastic if nighttime temperatures threaten to dip below freezing. An old fitted sheet is perfect for protecting bush beans from frost.

The Bean Itch

Bean leaf allergy is not uncommon, and if you've got it, you'll know it. When you pick beans, your skin will become inflamed and itchy, and the irritation may last for days. There's a simple solution: Just wear gloves and a long-sleeved shirt when you pick beans. (As added protection, wash your hands and arms well with soap and water after you've finished picking.)

Grit-Free Beet Greens

Beet greens make a tasty addition to mesclun-type salads. But beet greens are notorious for holding sand and soil. To ensure grit-free greens, pick them before they reach 4 inches in height. Plunge them into a sink or tub of cold water, agitate them, then let them sit for about 5 minutes. The greens will float on the top; the dirt will sink to the bottom. To make certain that your leaves are clean, change the water and repeat two or three times.

Don't Give Up on Broccoli

In warm weather, broccoli can quickly get out of hand if you miss a day or two of harvesting. The uncut heads or sideshoots will suddenly develop into a bouquet of yellow flowers. If this happens, all is not lost; cutting off the flowers before they have a chance to produce seeds will signal the plants to grow more sideshoots.

Let Beans Nurse Fall Broccoli

Broccoli is a great fall crop because you harvest it when the weather is more cool and consistent than in spring or summer, just the way broccoli likes it. The trick is to get the young broccoli plants established during the heat of summer. One way to do this is to plant a "nurse crop" of bush beans or field peas 3 weeks before you plan to plant your broccoli (you'll want to plant broccoli seeds in your garden 12 to 14 weeks before your first expected fall frost date). When it's time to sow the broccoli seeds, thin the peas or beans to about 6 inches apart. Sow the broccoli seeds ½ inch deep between the beans or peas, and water the bed daily until the broccoli sprouts—about 1 week later.

Continue to thin back the nurse crop so that the broccoli seedlings gradually get more and more direct sunlight. Then, about 3 weeks after planting the broccoli, pull out the last of the legumes and compost them. Pulling out the nurse crops helps break up any crust that might tend to form on your soil in hot weather. Once you pull out the

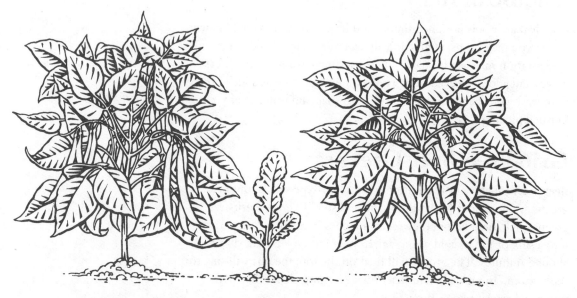

Summer-planted broccoli seedlings benefit from the shade of a "nurse crop" of beans.

nurse crop, it's a good idea to mulch around the broccoli plants with compost or grass clippings.

Feeding Program for Broccoli

Broccoli does best in rich, moist soil and cool conditions. You can't control the weather, but you can make sure your broccoli gets the moisture and nutrition it needs. Start by lavishing the planting bed with compost before you plant. Then, 2 to 3 weeks after transplanting, water the young plants with compost tea or a fish emulsion solution, and also spray the leaves with liquid kelp. Mulch around the plants and weed regularly if weeds get through the mulch so the broccoli plants don't have competition for moisture and nutrients. Feed the plants with compost tea or fish emulsion again when the heads first begin to form, even if they are growing in rich soil.

Broccoli: Harvest Bonanza or Steady Supply?

Before you plant broccoli, decide what sort of broccoli crop you want: a sustained harvest of both central heads and sideshoots, or a single-shot, high-yield crop. The sustained harvest is usually provided by nonhybrid (open-pollinated) varieties, which have less uniform maturity rates and growth habits than hybrids. Pick varieties that promise good sideshoot production, and space plants 24 inches apart. After each central head is harvested, continued sideshoot production will keep you in broccoli for weeks. To extend the season even more, plant a mix of varieties with differing days to maturity. If you prefer an all-at-once harvest, choose hybrid varieties.

Let Frost Sweeten the Harvest

To enjoy an especially sweet flavor from cabbage, brussels sprouts, and kale, delay harvest until after a good fall frost. The cold snap will induce starch stored in the leaves to change to sugar.

Three Sisters

Plant corn, pole beans or peas, and squash or melons together. This arrangement not only saves space but also lets the plants enjoy each other's benefits. The corn supports the climbing beans, the beans fix nitrogen in the soil, and the squash or melon vines act as a living mulch to cool the soil and keep weeds down. Native Americans called this companion planting system "Three Sisters."

---

old-time wisdom

PROTECT BROCCOLI FROM COLD

Sometimes broccoli does not head before there is danger of frosts, especially if growing vigorously. If taken up with small balls of earth, and set in a damp cellar, they will still perfect themselves.

The Gardener's Monthly, 1871

GARDENER TO GARDENER

Brassica Bonus

In climates with mild winters, leave your brassica crops, such as cabbage, broccoli, brussels sprouts, and collards, in the garden to overwinter. They will form seedheads in spring and provide a long harvest of tasty flower buds that can be eaten raw or cooked like other vegetables.

*Lloyd O. S.
Portland, Oregon*

Special Mix for Streamlined Carrots

If your carrots always look like the prongs of a pitchfork instead of streamlined and smooth, take some advice from English gardeners. After heavily fertilizing their soil, they take an iron bar and punch holes 6 inches apart and 12 inches deep in a row. They fill each hole with a half-and-half mixture of sand and rich soil (compost added). Sow several seeds over every filled hole and later thin to one plant per hole. Exhibition-quality carrots are the happy result!

Tiny Carrots for Timely Crops

For a faster crop of sweet homegrown carrots, make your first planting of the season a short-rooted selection. Short carrots mature faster than longer ones, so you'll be eating carrots sooner. In addition to shaving as much as 15 days off the time it takes to put carrots on your table, short-rooted carrots can produce a crop in heavy soil. These carrots are often dubbed "baby" or "mini" and may be rounded or ball-shaped. Look for 'Thumbelina', a ball-shaped cultivar that's widely available.

Color-Coordinated Cauliflower

One easy way to blanch cauliflower is to gather the leaves around the developing head and use string to tie them in place. The head should be ready to harvest about 1 week after tying. Trouble is, if you have several cauliflower plants developing at different rates, how do you keep track of when you tied which head? Use string of various colors. Just keep track in your gardening journal or on your garden calendar which color you used on what day. You can do the same thing by using rubber bands of different colors. Just stretch a rubber band around the leaves of a cauliflower plant and then let it draw the leaves together over the head.

Tag-Team Corn Cropping

Even if you didn't remember to cover-crop your corn bed before the season, you can still help build the bed's fertility for the future while your corn is growing. The trick is to sow a legume cover crop between the rows of sweet corn after the corn is up and growing. Plant the corn rows 3 feet apart, and sow a crop such as hairy vetch or red clover in July or August. Be sure to cut off the corn stalks as soon as you harvest all the ears so the cover crop can get that extra sun. Keep in mind that some crops will die over winter while others will need to be cut back in spring and then turned into the soil.

The fast-growing cover crop captures nitrogen from the air and "holds" it in its tissues. In winter, the crop also prevents soil erosion. When it's turned under in the spring, the crop releases all that wonderful nitrogen into the soil for the benefit of the next corn crop.

Pick the Perfect Ear

Not sure when corn is truly ripe? Follow these guidelines for judging when you can pick the perfect ear.

- Your first ears of homegrown corn will be ready to pick 20 to 24 days after the silks are 1 to 2 inches longer than the tip of the ear.

- Your ears are ready to eat when the ends of the silks are dried to within ½ inch of the tips of the ears.

- When the silks look right, pull back a husk slightly and pierce a couple of kernels from the second or third full row with your fingernail. If the juice is milky, pick and eat! Clear, watery juice means the corn still needs a few days on the stalk. (To keep insects and birds out of those opened ears, secure the husks back in place with a clothespin or rubber band.)

Remember that corn tastes sweetest when cooked immediately after picking. The longer the time between picking and cooking, the more time the corn's sugar will have to convert to starch.

Special Soil Care for Corn

It pays to prepare in advance the bed where you plan to plant corn next year. Corn is a heavy nitrogen feeder, and the stalks will grow spindly and yields will be low if the plants can't get enough nitrogen. A great way to ensure fertility for corn is to plant a nitrogen-fixing cover crop, such as hairy vetch, alfalfa, or clover, in the fall. Let the cover crop overwinter and then dig it into the bed a couple of weeks before planting corn in the spring.

For extra nitrogen insurance, you can also feed the plants with diluted fish emulsion or a fish-and-seaweed blend when the stalks are about knee-high.

Storing Garlic

I braid most of the 200 to 300 bulbs of garlic that I harvest each year and hang them in a cool, dry shed or garage. (The bulbs will keep for up to 6 months this way, as long as it doesn't get too hot in the storage area.) My family eats a lotta garlic!

I've never been satisfied with freezing garlic. My Italian grandmother always said that once you put garlic in the freezer or the refrigerator, it starts losing its "bite." So any garlic that I don't braid, I dry in the oven. I mince the garlic up real fine, spread it on cookie sheets, and leave it in the oven (set at its lowest setting) overnight. That's the best way. It keeps almost forever.

Linda F.
Jackson, New Jersey

Early Corn Saves Space

Some gardeners erroneously believe they need a lot of room to grow corn. Not so.

It is true that you have to plant corn in blocks for good pollination. But if you have rich organic soil, you can plant corn fairly close together, allowing you to reap a generous harvest from a small area. And if you put in early varieties that mature in 70 days or less, the resulting stalks won't be so big and cumbersome. Early maturing corn plants stand, on average, 1 to 2 feet shorter than later varieties, which reach 7 feet or taller.

You can also consider taking corn out of the vegetable garden altogether. This native grass makes an attractive living screen in the landscape. If you want to harvest ears, though, be sure your screen of cornstalks consists of blocks of four single rows or two double rows.

Good Neighbor for Cucumbers

Problems with cucumber beetles could be a thing of the past if you plant flowering vetch near your cucumbers. A research study showed dramatic increases in cucumber yields when the crop was planted into a living mulch of rye and vetch (mowed to control height) between "habitat strips" of flowering vetch, compared with the yield from cucumbers grown using black plastic mulch and insecticide treatments. The flowering vetch attracts Pennsylvania leatherwings, pest-munching insects that feed on cucumber beetles. You may not be able to reproduce the conditions of the research study precisely, but you can try maintaining a border of flowering vetch along one side of your vegetable garden.

Eggplant Thrives with Mulch and Cover

To achieve true success with your next crop of eggplant, try a special system that protects the young plants from flea beetle damage and gives them the warm soil they prefer. Spread black plastic mulch over the bed where you plan to plant eggplant, and then set the eggplant transplants directly through holes in the mulch. Cover the entire planting with a double width of row cover stapled together. Bury one side of the cover along the length of the bed and drape it over the plants. Roll up the excess and anchor the rolled fabric with bricks, stones, or lengths of scrap lumber. As the transplants grow, keep un-rolling the fabric to cover the plants as they ramble.

Once the plants begin to flower, open the cover for a couple of hours in the morning if you're not getting fruit set or if fungus mold develops on the blossoms. Eggplant flowers don't need insects for pollination, but air movement helps. You can also remove the cover when the plants start to bloom.

Treat Garlic Like a Tulip

In all but the longest growing seasons, plant garlic in the fall so that the bulb can develop strong roots that will anchor it through the heaving frosts and thaws of winter.

Once you've planted your garlic cloves, tuck them in with a thick layer of organic mulch to further protect them from winter heaving. Or, sow a cover crop of oats over the area you've planted in garlic at a rate of 2 to 3 pounds per 1,000 square feet. You could use other cover crops, but oats works well because it puts on some growth in fall and then dies from winter cold, creating a nice mulch for the garlic. The garlic will emerge through the mulch in late winter, but the dead oats will keep out the weeds for quite some time.

Garlic Greens Are Tops

No garlic heads to dig, no cloves to peel. You can enjoy fresh garlic flavor earlier in the growing season and with much less effort by harvesting the leaves of your garlic instead of the heads.

You can begin harvesting garlic greens as early as late April or when the foliage is about 8 inches tall. Cut it back nearly to the ground. You can make three to five cuttings each spring before letting the plants rest and rejuvenate until the next year, much as you'd do with asparagus or rhubarb.

To grow garlic greens, plant individual garlic cloves or entire small heads in the fall. Space the cloves much closer than standard spacing for producing leaves. This makes it easier to harvest quickly because you cut along a solid row of greens.

The garlic you grow for greens will do best with two doses of fertilizer per year. Feed once at planting time with bonemeal or a good organic bulb fertilizer. Feed again in spring with compost.

Garlic doesn't compete well with weeds. If you don't keep the patch well mulched and weeded, you'll probably need to dig it up every 3 years or so to clean out the weeds.

GARDENER TO GARDENER

Garlic Fights Bugs

Here in the Sierra Nevada foothills, deerflies can be brutal. One summer I was in the garlic bed slapping myself silly, and in desperation I crushed a fresh garlic bulb and smeared it on the backs of my legs. (I know, I know—nothing else would come near me either!) But it worked—not just on the deerflies, but on the mosquitoes, too.

Lené B.
Mariposa, California

Shallots vs. Onions

I usually plant shallots in the spring and harvest them in July. They are a lot easier to grow than onions, but in the kitchen the shallot itself is a bigger pain to work with because it's so small and has a thick skin. But shallots taste wonderful; they are exquisite raw in salads. And for some French dishes, there is no substitute for shallots.

On the onion front, this is the second year we have direct-seeded 'Walla Walla' in the fall. We keep the beds weeded regularly, and they do well from seed. 'Alisa Craig' is a nice heirloom onion that I like to grow; the bulbs can grow to over 5 pounds if given enough room.

Lucy G.
New Paris, Ohio

Hold Off on Horseradish Harvest

Horseradish is easy to grow and is famous for its pungent, sinus-clearing root, which is grated to serve as a condiment or add to sauces. For best horseradish flavor, wait until October or November to dig the roots. Digging any earlier will yield watery, weak-tasting roots.

Dig small batches as needed and store the roots in a plastic bag in the refrigerator. The flavor will be strongest if you grate horseradish with a food processor or hand grater, rather than a blender, and use it right away.

Clip Kale for a Super Crop

For a bumper crop of kale that is easier to harvest and is not riddled with flea beetle damage, keep clipping the leaves. As the plants develop, harvest every leaf that is more than 8 inches long. This has a shocking effect on the kale, encouraging the plants to grow really fast. After the first harvest, leave the plants alone for 2 weeks, then return and again harvest all the leaves that are more than 7 to 8 inches long.

This method promotes rapid growth that seems to diminish the effects of flea beetle feeding. As a result, your kale will have fewer holes in the leaves. At the same time, this method encourages the plants to grow tall and upright, making them easier to harvest with less bending.

Just Enough Lettuce

The average packet of lettuce contains about 2,000 seeds. No wonder it's so easy to overplant this crop! To keep your lettuce supply steady and moderate, try sowing a few lettuce seeds in pots once a week. You can provide ideal conditions for the seedlings, producing strong transplants that are free of insect damage and don't need thinning. The weekly potting up—10 to 12 seeds and some rich, well-drained potting soil—takes less than 15 minutes. In summer you can keep the pots outdoors in filtered light, but be aware that direct sun can be fatal. A plastic cover will help prevent moisture loss and protect against sudden cloudbursts, which can wash out the seed.

From sowing time to transplanting out into the garden takes roughly 3 to 4 weeks (in cool weather). That's a month of space saved for other vegetables. To save more space, plant the lettuces among vegetables that take longer to mature. The plants will fit well among young tomatoes, eggplants, cucumbers, corn, melons, squash, and beans.

Sand Your Lettuce

Lower leaves of lettuce may rot in the garden before harvest, especially if the plants are closely spaced, which traps moisture. To encourage drier conditions and prevent rot, spread a layer of clean sand around lettuce plants when they're young. The sand helps wick moisture away from the leaves.

Seeds, Not Sets

Onions are biennials; they grow a bulb the first year and produce seed the second. That's why planting sets (small 1-year-old bulbs) often results in plants that quickly flower and set seed. When you start onions from seed, you can avoid the checks in growth followed by good conditions that fool the plants into believing they have entered another growing season. Also, when you start onions from seed, you'll have a much greater choice of varieties and can pick ones that will grow best in your local conditions. (To get the best choice of onion varieties, check out specialty seed catalogs.)

Cure First, Then Keep Onions Dry

The trick to having onions that last a long time in storage is to cure them properly and keep them dry. To prepare onions for curing, once they reach mature size push over the tops to encourage the stalks to dry, which helps prevent neck rot. A couple of weeks later, pull the onions out of the ground and lay them in the sun to dry. If you live in an area with strong sun, you should probably cure your onions in partial shade (or in a shed) rather than full sun. Spread the onions on wire mesh held up off the ground (to prevent them from rotting) until the papery outer skins are completely dry and brittle and the tops are withered-looking.

To keep stored onions dry, hang them up if possible. You can cut the tops off, put the onions in a mesh bag, and hang the bag from a hook. Or leave the tops attached and braid them. Tie loops of string to the braids, slip a pole through the loops, and lay the poles across the rafters in an attic, or hang them from hooks in the ceiling of a garage or shed.

The colder the room where you store your onions, the better—32°F is ideal. Also, keep your stored onions away from stored apples. Apples give off ethylene gas, which can trigger early sprouting of onions.

GARDENER TO GARDENER

Mesclun in a Box

I grow my mesclun in boxes on a table outside. The table's height makes it easy to harvest the greens without a lot of bending over. I have three boxes, and by staggering the planting dates of the mesclun I always have two boxes ready for harvest. To keep the ants and earwigs from getting to my plants, I place the table legs into 5-quart plastic ice-cream buckets filled with water. A drop or two of oil in the water controls mosquitoes.

Thompson M.
San Jose, California

Pick Every Last Pea

A productive planting of peas can yield a bumper crop, and it's easy to let them slip past prime for fresh eating. If this happens to you, don't give up on your crop. Let excess pea pods remain on the vine to dry. When the peas are ripe, the vines will begin to die, and the pods will turn hard and brown. Harvest as the pods begin to split. To finish the drying and to kill insect eggs, place the peas in a pan in a 125°F oven for 3 hours. Then store them in an airtight container. Whenever you make homemade soup or stew, throw in a handful of dried peas—delicious!

Productive Pea Picking

Knowing just when to pick peas is essential for maximizing your enjoyment of their flavor and texture. Cues for harvest vary with the type of pea you're growing. Pick shelling peas when pods are full and swollen but young. Sugar snap peas are best when the pods just start to fatten but before the peas grow very large. Snow peas are best when pods are young and tender and the peas are just developing. Peas low on the vine mature earlier and should be picked first.

Picking peas should always be a two-handed operation: Hold the upper stem with one hand and pinch off the pod with the other. Yanking pods off with one hand may be quicker, but you'll almost certainly damage the plants, sacrificing later production.

Keep the Crunch in Snow Peas

Fresh snow peas and sugar snap peas are the highlight of vegetable stir-fries, but add frozen pea pods to stir-fry and the result is a mushy disappointment. Although frozen sugar snap and snow peas will never keep the crispy texture of freshly picked pods, you can get darn close by blanching them in the oven *before* freezing.

Warm a dry baking sheet in a 500° F oven for 2 minutes; then quickly spread a single layer of trimmed pea pods on it. Place the sheet onto the top shelf of the hot oven. Cook sugar snap peas for exactly 2 minutes; snow peas for exactly 1 minute. Transfer the peas to a cool tray, and spread them out evenly. Put the tray of peas into the freezer, uncovered, for 1 hour; then transfer the frozen peas to plastic freezer bags. Seal tightly, label, and date.

When stir-frying the peas, do not thaw first. Cook the frozen peas no more than 2 minutes during the final moments of the stir-fry—they were cooked before freezing.

Early Picking Means More Peppers

You'll get a bigger, more bountiful harvest if you pluck off any peppers that are forming before you get your pepper transplants in the ground. Otherwise, your plants will put their energy into producing the fruit rather than establishing strong roots and stems. You might get a few small, early peppers from those first little fruits, but they'll come at the expense of a later, bigger harvest from healthier plants.

Staggered Picking Spurs Pepper Success

Get the most out of your bell pepper plants by picking some fruit in the green immature stage, then leaving the rest of it on the plant to color up and mature. Here are three good reasons to stagger your pepper picking.

- Peppers commonly form their first fruits in a center cluster. If you leave all of these fruits to ripen, they may rot from moisture trapped between them.

- Leaving the first flush of fruit untouched will discourage the plant from setting a second flush of fruit.

- Picking the first fruits is a bonus for green pepper lovers since they're larger than later ones.

Store green peppers in a cool, dark area of your house, and they'll finish ripening naturally in a couple of days.

Potatoes under Grass (Clippings)

Instead of digging trenches for planting potatoes, simply press seed potatoes into the soil and cover them with a 6-inch blanket of dried grass clippings. Trials conducted at the Rodale research farm show potatoes grown by this method produced at least 40 percent more tubers than those grown without an organic mulch.

An added benefit of this method is no-dig potato harvests. And you can raid your potato stash early by simply reaching beneath the grass clippings to sneak out a few baby potatoes with absolutely no harm to the plant.

Super-Easy Spud Save

Don't feel bad—it's practically impossible to harvest your home-grown potatoes without slicing and dicing a few. But you don't have to heave those carved-up cuties. You can keep them for weeks by using this simple trick. Just fill some clean wide-mouth jars with washed spud chunks (you may have to cut up large chunks so they'll fit into the jar), top off with fresh water right to the brim of the jar, and put the lid on tightly. Stored in the refrigerator, these jarred chunks won't turn brown or get soggy. They'll stay in perfect shape for several weeks. Use them to make mashed, boiled, browned, or fried potatoes.

Dirt and Darkness for Stored Spuds

Two important rules to remember for storing potatoes: Keep them out of the light, and don't wash them before storage. You can put them in barrels, bags, or anywhere completely dark; light stimulates "greening," which is due to formation of poisonous compounds called alkaloids. Store potatoes in a cool, dark place with fairly high humidity, but not below 40°F. At temperatures below that, potatoes start converting starches to sugar, which will affect their flavor.

If there is a lot of soil on your potatoes, let them dry, and then gently brush the soil off before storing them—but resist the urge to wash them with water. Potatoes are very susceptible to bacterial disease that can spread from one diseased spud to the whole crop if the potatoes are washed.

Strong Trellis Supports Pumpkins

Pumpkins take more space than many gardeners can afford to give, but not when they're grown on a trellis. It's critical to create a trellis that will support the sprawling vines and enlarging fruit, and this simple design is equal to the job.

1. Cut four 2 × 2s, each 8 feet long; these will form the vertical supports of the trellis.

2. Fasten the 2 × 2s together in pairs by drilling a hole 14 inches from one end of each support and bolting the pairs together with ¼-inch carriage bolts.

3. Spread the supports apart to measure 4 feet at the base.

4. Cut eight 1 × 3s, each 4 feet long, to serve as cross supports for the trellis.

5. Nail cross supports to each pair of vertical supports, starting about 1 foot up from the bottom. Space them equally.

6. Drive 12-inch stakes (scrap lumber will do) into the ground where you want the trellis to be. Secure the four legs of the trellis to the stakes with baling wire or twine.

7. Secure the trellis with baling wire or twine where the two sets of vertical supports meet at the top.

8. Apply two or more coats of linseed oil, which will help extend the life of the trellis.

If you're growing very large-fruited pumpkins, support individual pumpkins with a sling made of panty hose or strong cloth. Most, however, need only the support of their tough vines and stems.

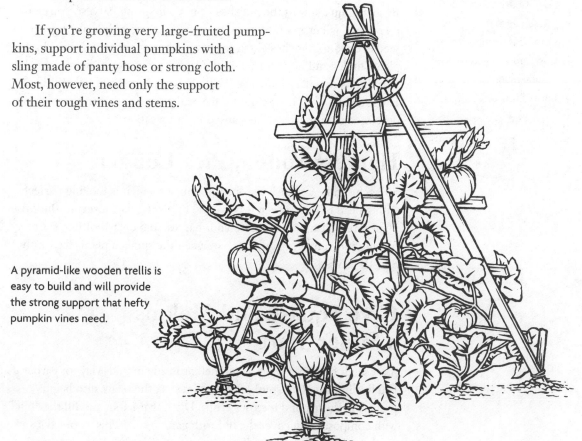

A pyramid-like wooden trellis is easy to build and will provide the strong support that hefty pumpkin vines need.

A Trick for Ripe Treats

Pumpkins that aren't turning orange in time for Halloween display are a problem, but the remedy may be to withhold water for several days. Dryness will stress the plants and hasten ripening.

Radical Radishes

Want the zinginess of radishes without having to get your knees dirty? 'Rattail' is a unique heirloom radish (*R. sativus* var. *caudatus*) grown for its edible foot-long seedpods. Those pods can be used to add zip to stir-fries, and they make a great substitute for beer nuts. (Honest—sliced and salted, the colorful pods are a favorite snack in Europe!) Rattails grow 4 to 5 feet tall and produce a plethora of pods in 50 days.

Free Fall Radishes

By giving up a few of the radishes from your spring harvest, you can reap a free fall crop of the crunchy roots. Let one radish plant go to seed every 5 to 6 inches along the row. When the seedpods dry, dig the plants under and hope for fall rain. Or you can water to help ensure that the seeds will sprout. You'll end up with a carpet of fall radishes. Fall radishes often have a milder flavor than spring radishes, which can develop a strong, spicy taste caused by hot weather.

Harvest Young, Pick Longer

Spinach can be an elusive crop. You notice the plants looking perfect, with a head of deep green leaves. The following day, it seems, the plants are bolting! To increase your harvest and delay bolting, start picking individual expanded leaves when the spinach plants have only 8 to 10 leaves.

Give Squash and Melons a Super Start

Start seeds of winter squash and melons inside in mid-May (or earlier if you live in Zone 6 or south). When you start the seeds, also begin preparing the ground for your crops. Dig down 1 foot and fill the "hill" with compost, then cover the hill with garden soil. This warms the soil nicely and gets the plants off to a good start. Set the plants out 2 to 3 weeks after seeding. One final advantage you can give your vine crops: Surround melons and squash with hairy vetch or another low-growing cover crop. Sow the cover crop seed at transplanting time or shortly afterward. The vetch controls weeds throughout the growing season, and in the fall you can till or dig it under to enrich the soil for future crops.

Squirrel Away Squash

Harvest winter squash long before frost for best storage quality. The ideal storage temperature is about 50°F. Place the squash on the floor on top of thick pads of newspaper and check them regularly. Every so often, a squash will have an imperceptible nick where rot begins, and the next thing you know, the squash dissolves into mush.

Butternut squash will store for 4 months and is a great substitute for pumpkin in pumpkin pie. Another great winter squash for storage is 'Delicata'. Buttercup and Hubbard squash also do well in storage, lasting up to 6 months.

Store Sweet Potatoes Wisely

Few things are more frustrating than harvesting a bumper crop from your garden only to have it quickly deteriorate in storage. Unfortunately, this happens all too often with sweet potatoes because the average American home lacks the proper conditions for storing sweet potatoes.

The only safe place to store sweet potatoes for any length of time is in your freezer. Coat each root with vegetable oil and bake in a conventional oven—not a microwave—at 375°F for 90 minutes. Once the sweet potatoes have cooled, wrap them individually in aluminum foil and put them in your freezer.

Swiss Chard Cocktail

If you go overboard sowing Swiss chard, solve your problem by brewing up a Swiss chard tea, then feed it to the other plants in your garden. Applied as a soil drench, it's a great pick-me-up for plants that are lagging a bit. To make the brew, place 2 cups of coarsely chopped Swiss chard leaves in a blender. Add hot water to the top and blend thoroughly. Strain the mixture through cheesecloth or a colander. After the liquid cools, use it to water the plants of your choice. You can also lay cooked leaves around the base of plants as a soil-enriching, weed-suppressing mulch.

GARDENER TO GARDENER

Smashing Squash

We like to grow winter squash, and our cool spare bedroom is the perfect place to store them. But getting the large Hubbard squash upstairs into the bedroom used to be a challenge. The big ones (some varieties can weigh up to 45 pounds) had to be moved by two people using a canvas tarp.

Our home has a deck on three sides of the second story, so we decided to train the rambling squash vines up wire mesh onto the deck. Now the squash can grow right on the deck, and we can just roll them through a sliding door into the bedroom.

We discovered another benefit of this unusual technique. The squash can be very hard to cut up for cooking. But now I simply roll a big one out the door and over the side of the deck. It smashes into pieces when it hits the ground; we cook the pieces in the microwave, scrape out the meat into containers, and freeze it.

Philip and Phyllis K. Horseheads, New York

Urging Early Tomatoes

To push ripening of the first fruits on a tomato plant, take an old butcher knife and cut (carefully!) a 6-inch-deep arc into the soil about halfway around the plant about 4 inches out from the base. This won't hurt the plant in the long run, but it severs some of the plant roots, which will stress the plant and cause the green tomatoes that are already on the plant to ripen faster. You can use a shovel instead of a knife; just push the blade straight down into the soil and pull it out carefully, without turning over any soil. I usually use this technique on smaller-variety tomatoes, because they ripen more quickly anyway.

Robert D. G. Hermiston, Oregon

Store Tomatoes in Eating Order

Frost doesn't have to mean the end of your tomato harvest. Before frost comes, harvest fully developed, unripe tomatoes, and bring them indoors to ripen. Separating them into groups by stage of ripeness makes it easy to find those that are ready to eat and any that are too green. You can store the tomatoes wrapped individually in newspaper and placed about three layers deep in open crates or boxes. Try using three boxes and designate them "Green," "Partly Green," and "Almost Ripe." Use up the boxes in that order.

Timely Mulch for Top Tomato Crops

Be a "late bird" when it comes to mulching tomato plants. Tomato plants need thoroughly warmed soil for best growth, and mulching around plants too early can delay soil warming. You may want to try a two-part mulching strategy with tomatoes. Leave some tomato plants unmulched until they are flowering profusely, then mulch to seal in the heat, which will encourage the earliest possible ripening. Mulch other plants right at transplanting time to slow down their fruit development. This approach pays off with a sizable crop of very early fruit while spreading your total harvest over a longer season. This strategy also works well with sweet corn and melons.

Build a Japanese Tomato Ring

Looking for a way to grow tomatoes in limited space while conserving water? The Japanese tomato ring may be just what you're seeking. The tomatoes are tied to a cylinder of wire mesh that encloses a supply of rich organic matter. To build a Japanese tomato ring, clear an area in your garden about 7 feet in diameter. Then, make a wire mesh cylinder about 5 feet high and 5 feet in diameter (you'll need a section of wire mesh about 16 feet long for this). You can use chicken wire or welded wire. Use wire screening to line the inside of the cylinder to a height of 18 inches. Set the cylinder in place and secure it with stakes or pins made from pieces of metal coat hangers.

Fill the cylinder with organic matter to about 6 inches, then plant your tomatoes around the outside of the cylinder at 2½-foot intervals. As the plants grow, tie them to the wire mesh with strips of yarn or cloth. Train each plant to two main branches. After the tomatoes have been growing for a few weeks, put another 6 to 12 inches of soil and compost into the ring. You can also add some granite dust and phosphate meal each time you increase the material. The tomatoes will send their roots into the ring, searching out the excellent source of nourishment there.

Because the ring is so compact, it's easy to protect the plants from frost by covering the entire structure with a blanket or tarp on threatening nights.

Tomatoes in the Pits

Deep planting is the secret to success with tomatoes if you have sandy soil. Dig down as much as 2 feet, and set your tomato transplant into the hole. Add compost and loose soil to cover the roots; water thoroughly. As the vine grows, keep adding soil and compost until you've filled the hole. This method encourages the tomato to send out roots all along its stem as well as deep into the soil, where conditions will stay moister than the fast-drying surface layers in the summer. And the added compost supplies nutrients that may be deficient in the sandy soil.

Set tomato plants in a sizable hole if you have sandy soil. Add compost to the hole as the plants grow to supply nutrients and steady moisture.

Tomato Favorites

'Cherokee Purple' and 'Sungold' are my favorite tomatoes. Try them—once you have grown them, you will never not plant them. 'Sungold' seems to be more heat-resistant than other cherry tomatoes and keeps producing long after the other tomatoes have given up. As I write this (in April), temperatures are in the high 80s. Last year, my 'Sungolds' survived into July when nothing else did!

Lisa A.
Homestead, Florida

Stop Cherry Tomato Splits

Cherry tomatoes have a nasty habit of splitting. Sometimes even fruits that are perfect on the vine will inexplicably split after picking. Is there a way to prevent this problem? Not completely, but you can lessen splits by using mulch and watering regularly—hot weather and uneven watering are the biggest causes of splits.

Don't Sing the Zucchini Blues

Zucchini is an easy, rewarding crop to grow, but it has some quirks that are important to understand for a successful harvest.

- All zucchini are not created equal. Fruits can be round, cylindrical, or bulbous, with speckled, striped, or solid skin, and colors ranging from light yellow to nearly black. Flavors range from mild and buttery to full and nutty. So don't assume that any packet of zucchini seed you buy will produce regular green fruits like those in the grocery store. Research varieties before you buy, and don't be afraid to experiment!

- Avoiding being inundated with zukes is as simple as not over-planting. Many people think that they'll harvest six or seven zucchinis per plant when, in fact, a zucchini plant typically produces 6 to 10 *pounds* of fruit per plant.

- If your fruits are growing in the shape of an hourglass, that's a sure sign of inconsistent watering. Fruits swell when they get plenty of water, then shrink when they don't get enough.

- Cold weather can hamper zucchini production and fruit quality. Wait until the weather has warmed and the soil temperature has reached at least 60°F before sowing seed or setting out transplants. Chilly weather can also damage the surface of zucchini. Fruit that's been exposed to cold temperatures (32°F to 40°F) for several days can wind up with pitting on the skin surface.

- Zucchini can suffer from blossom-end rot just as tomatoes can, which is the result of irregular watering, poor water uptake, or calcium deficiency. To avoid calcium deficiency, add a calcium-rich natural amendment, such as oyster shells, to under-nourished soil.

Chapter 6

Enjoying the Pleasures of Herbs

Herbs in the garden smell so fragrant, taste so delicious, and look so beautiful. Plus, herbs are easy to grow—and when they're properly preserved, their wonderful aromas and flavors can be yours for months after the gardening season ends.

Some gardeners plant fewer herbs than they would really like—many don't realize that you don't have to limit herbs to a single herb garden. In this chapter, you'll find some great ideas for using herbs in a variety of landscape settings, such as a fragrant herbal pathway and a patio-side planting (that also helps repel mosquitoes).

Read on for tried-and-true tips for pruning and propagating lavender, as well as how to plant herbs so they'll serve as a natural flea repellent. There are strategies for growing herbs in the hot South and instructions for quick-drying herbs in the oven, preparing herbal oils, and preserving herbs in ice-cube form.

To round out the chapter, you'll find tips for growing specific herbs, including favorites like basil, mint, and thyme. In particular, check out the tips that tell you how to select the right species and varieties of herbs for maximum flavor.

Mix Herbs with Ornamentals

A sunny ornamental garden can be the perfect spot for a few herbs. Edgings of herbs such as rosemary, santolina, and sage help visually to unify mixed plantings. Other attractive edgers are lamb's-ears and lavender, which also work well in arrangements of fresh flowers.

Take Your Herbs to the Beach

All it takes is sand to make your herb garden thrive and look great for months—a 1-inch layer of large-grain sand, to be precise. Light-colored sand reflects sunlight and gives Mediterranean herbs such as lavender and rosemary the intense sunlight they need. Sand mulch also helps moderate temperature swings, just as an organic mulch would. But unlike organic mulches, sand doesn't hold moisture, so it won't encourage the root and crown rots that can cause a quick end to herbs.

Sand mulch will help prevent weeds from coming up, and it's easy to pull out any weeds that do emerge through the loose sand. And when you mulch with sand, less soil splashes back up on herbs when it rains or when you water. Your herbs stay clean, so you can harvest without having to wash them—and that saves time and essential oils.

Beach sand is too fine to give your plants the drainage they crave, so look for a coarse version—like mason's sand—at building supply centers. Put a ½-inch layer of sand on top of potting soil for container herbs, too.

Southern Seed-Sowing Strategies for Herbs

Many herbs have an affinity for the South. The long, hot summers and mild winters are similar to the Mediterranean, where many herbs originated. However, the southern herb grower may face problems right from the start when sowing seeds of annual herbs. A surprise 90°F day in April will halt germination or fry tender seedlings. One way to avoid this problem is to sow seeds indoors in flats and plant them in the garden once they are established. Or plant seeds in a small outdoor seedbed that you can tend carefully as the seedlings emerge, and then transplant them to a larger garden.

In the South, it's easy to start basil from seed in the spring, and it will bloom prolifically all summer. Pinch the seedpods back continually to encourage new growth. Black spot may be a problem on basil during spells of high heat and humidity, but picking off the diseased leaves helps control the spread of this disease.

With cilantro, the best strategy for southern gardeners is to start the seeds in early fall and let them overwinter. You'll have healthy plants throughout spring. (Spring-planted cilantro tends to bolt prematurely, robbing you of the harvest.)

Early fall planting also works well for dill and fennel in the South because summer's heat is hard on these plants.

Fragrant Herbal Pathways

Drooling over photographs of garden pathways lined with thyme and chamomile, but worried that walkways are too much work to achieve? It's actually not that difficult to install one; you can have one started in a weekend.

To begin your pathway, but down a weed barrier such as cardboard or thick layers of newspaper. Then lay cement pavers in the pattern you desire, and spread fine sand between them. Sow seeds of creeping thyme between the pavers. Keep the area well watered, and by summer's end you should have a well-established herbal carpet. Maintenance is simple—just mow once a year!

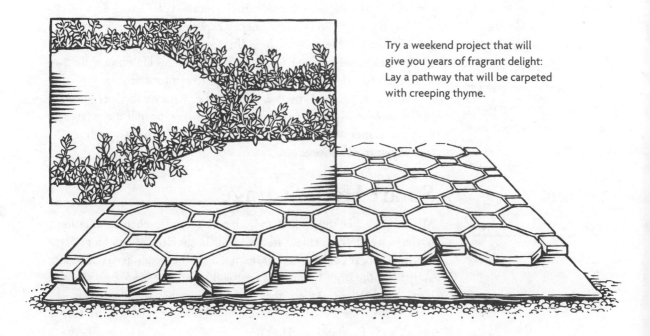

Try a weekend project that will give you years of fragrant delight: Lay a pathway that will be carpeted with creeping thyme.

*Beating Fleas
the Natural Way*

   *I grow large amounts of
aromatic herbs—in all shapes
and sizes—to repel fleas. I
plant herbs everywhere, especially near walkways and en-
tranceways to my house. As
the cats roam freely in and
out among the herbs, the oils
in the herb leaves rub on the
cats' fur and naturally repel
fleas. My house has been surrounded by herbs for the past
8 years, and none of my four
cats has ever had a flea problem. Specific herb varieties
planted near the house (and
close to the cats' entrances) are
tansy, sage, catmint, lavender,
bee balm, thyme (several varieties), and garlic chives.
Dozens and dozens of other
varieties carpet the property,
and the cats play freely in all
of them, coating their fur
with herbal flea repellent.*

   *Jill W.
Lykens, Pennsylvania*

Snip Herbs Early and Often

As soon as leafy annual herbs reach 6 inches tall, start snipping them
for kitchen use. You'll have fresh herbs for cooking all season long, and
frequent trimming produces compact, bushy plants.

   With perennial herbs, give them one hard pruning in early spring,
just when they begin growing. Pruning rejuvenates herbs and saves
you from having to replace them. As a rule of thumb, cut the plant
back to one-third its original size as soon as you see new growth begin
to develop. This applies to English lavender, French tarragon, thyme,
and winter savory. Of course, you can also cut stems from these plants
as needed through the season for cooking or crafts.

   One exception to the perennial pruning rule is sage, which you
can leave unpruned in spring and then cut back lightly after the plants
bloom. Keep harvesting several times until late summer arrives.

Quick-Dry Your Herbs

To shortcut the process of drying herbs, try drying them in your oven.
Spread harvested flowers or leafy stems onto cookie sheets, set the
oven at its lowest setting (if you have a gas oven, simply use the pilot
light), and dry them with the oven door open for circulation, turning
the herbs twice daily. Once the leaves or flower petals crumble when
pinched or rubbed, they're ready; this typically takes 1 to 3 days.

   If you're really in a hurry, you can experiment with drying small
quantities in your microwave in as little as 3 minutes. Lay herbs in a
single layer between paper towels and zap them on high power for 2 to
3 minutes. Check every 30 seconds to guard against burning.

   Whatever method you use, after drying, separate the leaves from
the stems by rubbing them onto a piece of paper, or pull the petals
from the center of the flower heads. Store dried herbs in airtight containers out of direct sunlight.

Smart Herb Storage

Many people like the look of an herb rack on the kitchen counter next
to the stove. It's convenient to have your herbs close at hand for
cooking, too. If you're smart, though, you'll keep your herb collection
away from the stove because its heat will hasten the evaporation of the
herbs' essential oils. Don't store herbs in the cupboard above your
kitchen stove for the same reason. They'll do best in a cool, dry cupboard, away from heat and light.

Yarrow First-Aid Tincture

It's great to feel the warm earth between your toes while you garden. But it's no fun when your bare feet meet with sharp or hard objects in the soil. Keep a simple yarrow tincture on hand for times when your feet (or other parts) need a little first aid.

To make the tincture, fill a 1-quart glass jar loosely with fresh yarrow flowers, then add vodka (the cheapest you can buy) to the jar to cover them, allowing room to top it off with 2 inches of clear alcohol at the top. Let the jar sit for 2 to 3 weeks at room temperature, then strain out the yarrow. Fill a quart-size spray bottle with the yarrow tincture and add 20 drops of lavender essential oil. To use, shake the bottle well and spray directly on bruises, cuts, and scrapes. Repeat every several hours until healing is evident. This tincture will keep for at least 5 years.

A Sacred Ritual

The motions of boiling water, filling a tea ball, and spooning honey can be as cherished as the drink itself. There's no right or wrong way to make a cup of tea; it's more art than science, more meditation than method. Start with this sequence, then experiment.

1. *Measure.* Most herbalists recommend 1 teaspoon of dried, or 2 tablespoons of fresh, herbs for each cup of tea.

2. *Steep.* If you're drinking purely for pleasure, you'll achieve the best flavor by letting your tea steep for 3 to 5 minutes. For medicinal purposes, steep the herbs for 10 to 15 minutes. Some herbalists recommend an overnight steep.

3. *Mix.* One of the great rewards of growing herbs is the ability to custom-blend your teas. You can do this according to taste (mint plus lemon balm—yum!) or medicinal needs (chamomile plus valerian—off to sleep you go).

Put Herbs in a Vacuum

In a vacuum cleaner, that is! Vacuuming becomes less of a chore when you sprinkle ½ cup of fresh-smelling dried herb leaves, like lemon verbena or rosemary, on the carpet. Run the vacuum cleaner over the leaves, and then continue vacuuming the rest of the room. The pleasant fragrance will travel with you as you work.

GARDENER TO GARDENER

Invite These Ladies In

When fall comes, I pot up several herbs from my garden and place them in the basement under fluorescent lights. Some of the plants inevitably show signs of insect infestation—and that's where my personal army of friendly Asian lady beetles comes in. Most of my neighbors complain about the Asian lady beetles that flock into our homes each fall, but I happily gather up a few dozen or more, bring them downstairs, and set them loose on the plants. Not all stay, but most do. They patrol my herbs, gobbling up any fungus gnats, whiteflies, and spider mites that appear. They must be finding enough to eat because late in winter I see their larvae on patrol, as well.

Carol K.
Saltsburg, Pennsylvania

Herbal Disinfectant

To make housecleaning more enjoyable, use a natural herbal disinfectant instead of chemical cleaners. First, make an herbal infusion of lavender, rosemary, mint, or thyme: Steep the herbs in boiling water for 15 minutes (this releases the herbs' water-soluble components). To make the disinfectant, combine 2 cups of the infusion with 3½ quarts of hot water and 1 cup of vinegar (either white or apple cider) in a bucket. Clean as usual with your sweet-smelling concoction!

Herbal Ice Cubes

Herbs can hold their flavor better if you freeze them into herbal ice cubes. If you make a lot of soups, stews, or sauces, ice cubes may be the most convenient for you. You can simply toss whole cubes into the pot when you cook. (Beware of thawing cubes for other types of dishes since some of the flavor will be lost in the water that drains off.) Remove leaves from the stems of fresh herbs, chop, and pack into ice cube trays. Cover with cold water and place in the freezer. Once frozen, remove the cubes from the trays and store in freezer bags.

Beyond Ordinary Basil

If you'd like to experiment with other types of basil, try some of the following.

- 'Spicy Globe' basil works well as a minihedge to edge a garden or along a path. It's also fantastic for growing in containers.

- Lemon basil really does have lemony flavor and is widely used in Vietnamese and Thai cooking. Enjoy its subtlety in delicate-flavored main courses, iced teas, baked goods, fruity salad dressings, fruit sauces, ice creams, and sorbets.

- Purple-leaved basils such as 'Dark Opal' and 'Red Rubin' are sensational for salads. The stunning dark purple, ruffled leaves contrast beautifully with leaf lettuces.

- Thai basil has a robust flavor that is essential to cooking in Southeast Asia. The plants are beautiful, too, with unusual blooms that appear in pale lavender clumps. They make an impressive show in containers.

Basic Basil for Pesto

Although there's a dazzling choice of basils available for home gardeners, plain old sweet basil (*Ocimum basilicum*) is *the* choice for making pesto. That's because sweet basil usually has the sweetest flavor and best yield among basil varieties, without the strong aftertaste of licorice that some basils impart.

Sweet Bay Basics

Growing your own sweet bay (*Laurus nobilis*) plant isn't hard to do, and it provides you with the freshest possible source of bay leaves for seasoning roasts, soups, and sauces. In its native Mediterranean climate, sweet bay grows as a large shrub, but it's hardy only to Zone 8. Most gardeners in the United States and Canada will need to grow bay in a pot and bring it indoors during winter.

Outdoors, bay plants prefer partly shaded areas. Indoors, keep them in a bright window and feed them with a topdressing of ½ inch of well-aged compost when new growth appears in spring. Harvest the leaves to use fresh or dried in the kitchen. Because potted bay plants are prone to developing scale insect infestations, move them outdoors in summer so beneficial insects can feed on the scale.

Easy-Sow Chamomile

Chamomile is one of the easiest herbs to grow. When danger of frost is past, just throw some seeds onto prepared soil and pat them down. The seeds don't even need to be covered. Water the plants occasionally if the weather is dry. They will grow to about 8 inches tall, and you can clip off the flowers any time after their petals appear and dry them for a calming tea.

Fast-Track Chives

Create a hearty clump of chives for your kitchen garden quickly by sowing seed en masse. Sow 20 or so seeds together in a 4-inch pot. When the chives are several inches high, set the whole clump into your garden as one plant. You can plant as early as a week or two before your frost-free date.

Remember that chives have the best flavor when the leaves are young, narrow, and tender—*before* the plant flowers. To harvest leaves, cut them off in clumps about ½ inch from the ground.

Controlling Chamomile

If German chamomile is spreading like wildfire through your garden, do not let any flowers remain on the plant to set seed. To begin dealing with the excess plants, dig them up, pot them, and give them as gifts with a card about how to make tea from the flowers.

*David H.
Snohomish, Washington*

Losing Lavender

Here where I garden in Ontario (Zone 4), nature can throw some nasty pieces of weather at a garden in early spring. I have learned the hard way never to prune lavender plants in fall. Without the protection of their own stems and foliage, the plants didn't survive the winter. I lost most of my lavenders by pruning in fall. I replaced them and although I didn't repeat the mistake of fall pruning, I lost more the next year due to rodent damage because I mulched with straw (instant mouse house). This year, however, I believe my persistence will pay off. Last summer I planted thyme around the baby lavender plants. Thyme's low, bushy growth provided winter protection. Although still dormant, the lavender plants are healthy. As the plants become well established, I intend to move the thyme away from the lavender.

Judy B.
Ontario, Canada

Succession-Sow Cilantro

Young cilantro leaves add that special zing to salsa and other Mexican and Asian dishes. But once plants form flower stalks, the leaves turn very acrid, hot, and inedible. To make sure you always have tender, tasty leaves for cooking, make successive sowings of cilantro through the season. Start some seeds indoors a month or more before your last frost, and then sow some more outside as soon as all danger of frost has passed. Cover the seeds with ½ inch of soil, and keep them moist until the seedlings appear.

When your cilantro does form its round, flat flowers, don't pull the plants—they are just beginning to take on their second identity as "coriander." These spicy, aromatic seeds are used in baking and pickling, in Asian and Indian recipes, and in Caribbean spice mixes. And even if you don't use them in cooking, you can save them for sowing next year's cilantro crop!

Harvest seeds when they turn brown and hard but before they turn fully ripe and fall off the stalks. Cut the heads from the plants and hang them to dry in a protected spot; when everything turns crisp and dry, rub the seedheads between your hands to separate the seeds from the stalks.

Grow Gorgeous Lavender in Mounds

Lavender plants need full sun and good drainage to grow their best, so if your garden has less-than-perfect drainage, try planting lavender in mounds. You'll be rewarded for your effort with plants that look spectacular and have a longer life span.

The ideal time to prepare a planting mound for lavender is in fall before spring planting time to allow the mound to settle. To create the mound, start by marking the edges of the bed. Work in an area about 1½ to 2 feet wide and allow 2 feet between plants. Loosen the existing soil with a spading fork.

In a wheelbarrow, make a soil mix consisting of 1 part native soil, 1 part sand, and 1 part compost. Combine 2 parts of this mixture with 1 part either pea gravel or ½-inch-diameter mixed rock, and about 1 cup of lime. You may use more or less, depending upon how big your mounds will be and whether your soil is acidic or alkaline.

Pour this mix onto the site and shape it into a mound from 8 to 18 inches high, using higher mounds in wetter areas. Taper the edges of the mound to meet the soil level. (Within a year, the mound will settle to about half its original height.)

To plant the lavender in the prepared mounds the following spring, make a cone from the soil mix (try to use mostly soil around the roots, brushing any gravel away), and spread the roots of the plant over the cone. Cover the roots with mix, and water thoroughly.

Learn to Grow Lively Lemongrass

Gardeners who like cooking dishes with an Asian theme will want to grow lemongrass, which is used to season Vietnamese, Thai, and other Asian cuisine. The plant is easy to grow if you know how to help it survive winter—it's hardy only to Zone 10.

Lemongrass will grow well outdoors in summer in full sun and average soil. In fall, dig up your lemongrass plant and use pruning scissors to cut the crown into good-size chunks—about 4 to 6 inches in diameter. Disturb the roots as little as possible. Put each portion of crown that you want to keep into its own 8- to 10-inch container filled with potting mix. (Give the other portions to friends.) Keep the pots indoors in a sunny window or under light until all danger of frost has passed, at which time you can transplant the crowns back to your garden.

In the Deep South, you can overwinter lemongrass in place in the garden. Cut back the plant heavily in fall and mulch it deeply to help ensure its survival.

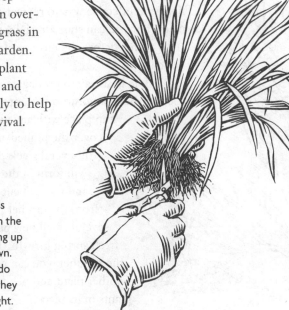

Keep lemongrass growing through the winter by potting up sections of crown. The plants will do well as long as they get plenty of light.

GARDENER TO GARDENER

Making More Lavender

I propagate lavender by taking cuttings in summer of half-ripe shoots with a sliver of the main stem. I plant them in a container of soilless mix or sand, water them, wrap the container in plastic, and provide bottom heat (you can do this by setting the containers on a heat mat or on top of a water heater).

In the garden, I make new lavender plants by hilling up soil around the crown of the plant and staking branches to the ground with wire. This can be done at any time of year here in western Washington. In spring, the staked branches will have rooted, and can be snipped off the main plant.

*David H.
Snohomish, Washington*

Help Rosemary Handle Winter

In Zone 8 or warmer, rosemary will grow into a good-size woody shrub. But in colder climes, you'll have to bring your rosemary indoors during winter if you want it to last. Be sure the pot and soil have good drainage—and water carefully because rosemary is very temperamental about water; it's easy to overwater or underwater it.

You may want to leave your rosemary in the pot year-round. In spring, after the last frost, sink the pot into a garden bed. At the end of the season, before the first frost, dig up the potted plant, repot it if necessary, and bring it inside. Your greenhouse or sunroom is the perfect winter site for your rosemary because it needs *lots* of light. If you don't have a greenhouse, give your potted rosemary your coldest, brightest indoor spot. Rosemary doesn't like hot conditions indoors, and it does like to be misted.

If the plant survives the winter, it will put on a big spurt of growth in late winter as the days get brighter—so don't forget to water your rosemary well at this crucial time, or it could die very suddenly.

Make Sage Last

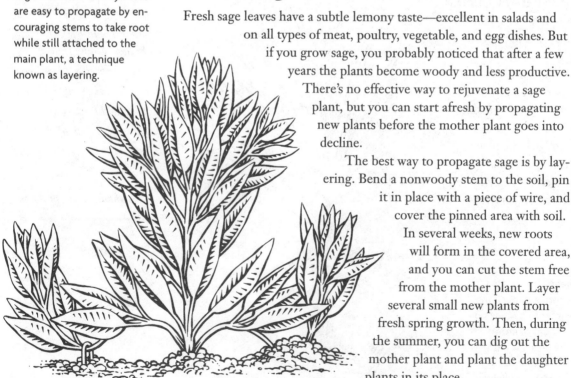

Sage and other woody herbs are easy to propagate by encouraging stems to take root while still attached to the main plant, a technique known as layering.

Fresh sage leaves have a subtle lemony taste—excellent in salads and on all types of meat, poultry, vegetable, and egg dishes. But if you grow sage, you probably noticed that after a few years the plants become woody and less productive. There's no effective way to rejuvenate a sage plant, but you can start afresh by propagating new plants before the mother plant goes into decline.

The best way to propagate sage is by layering. Bend a nonwoody stem to the soil, pin it in place with a piece of wire, and cover the pinned area with soil. In several weeks, new roots will form in the covered area, and you can cut the stem free from the mother plant. Layer several small new plants from fresh spring growth. Then, during the summer, you can dig out the mother plant and plant the daughter plants in its place.

Chapter 7

Tending a Bounty of Fruits and Berries

Pulses quicken when the backyard fruit or berry crop is ready to pick. Anticipation of the juicy sweetness of ripe peaches and strawberries and the tartness of a fall apple inspire us to put in the time and effort required to grow fruit crops.

Choosing the right varieties and the right planting location are extra important when planting perennial fruit crops, whether they're fruit trees or bushes. It's a multiyear investment that requires good seasonal care, such as pruning and protecting the fruit from animal and insect pests. With fruit crops, it's also important to understand the special requirements for pollination. Some crops can pollinate themselves, so it's sufficient to plant a single tree or bush. However, others need cross-pollination by another plant of a different variety, so you'll need to select and plant two compatible varieties that bloom at the same time.

Because growing fruit takes a little extra savvy, you'll surely appreciate the tips you'll find here, including a gardener-tested plan for preventing pests on apple trees, advice on growing grapes the easy way, and pruning and care pointers for peach trees. There are also tips that can double your raspberry yields and save your strawberries from a late frost.

No Need to Wait

For most gardeners, growing fruit means alternating dearth with glut. If you spend almost as much time waiting for your fruit as you do enjoying it, it's time to consider a new strategy. Grow more kinds of fruit, and plant an early, middle, and late-ripening cultivar of each fruit you grow. At the least, you'll double the producing season from a single fruit—and for some fruits, you'll do even better. For example, while many blueberry cultivars have month-long harvests, the blueberry season actually runs for up to 9 weeks, so plant early-, mid-, and late-producing varieties for continuous harvest. If your yard is small, stick with growing berry bushes, brambles, and vines, which require less space and are usually far less troubled by insects than are the tree fruits.

Berry-Freezing Facts

Freezing berries takes no time at all and keeps their natural sweetness and bright colors intact. Review these pointers before freezing berries.

Keep it simple. The simplest way to freeze berries is to pour them directly from the basket onto baking trays and then arrange them in a single layer. (With strawberries, remove the stems first and cut large ones in half; then put them on the baking trays.) Set the trays in the freezer. In a few hours, pour the frozen berries—now as hard as marbles—into freezer bags or containers, label them with the date, and store them in the freezer.

Don't wash. Don't wash berries before tray-freezing them. The drier the berries are when frozen, the better their color, taste, and texture will be when you use them. But before freezing the berries, sift through them to remove debris. Then, just before use, pour the frozen berries into a colander and rinse them under cold running water. This both washes the berries and partially thaws them.

Improve flavor with sugar. For even better flavor and color than from tray-frozen berries, toss rinsed and well-dried berries with sugar (½ to 1 cup for every 4 cups of berries) before freezing them. The sugar is incorporated into the cell walls, which become stiffer. (This isn't true for blueberries, though.) When defrosted, sugar-packed berries will be in a syrup.

Use them soon. Use tray-frozen berries within 6 months. After that, you can still eat the berries, but the color and flavor will deteriorate and the skins and seeds will toughen.

Respect tough skins. The skins of tray-frozen blueberries become tough in the freezer, so use them only in baked dishes and cooked sauces.

Plain Planting for Fruit Trees

The best nourishment you can give young fruit trees and vines at planting time is your native soil. Despite the advice you'll read in many books and articles, enriching the soil in planting holes with peat, sand, pine bark, or other amendments doesn't help fruit trees. Trees planted in unamended soil do just as well—in some cases better—than trees planted into amended soil. The best thing you can do is to plant trees that will do well in your conditions. In general, pears, apples, and grapes will do well in a wide range of soils. Cherry trees don't seem to thrive in clay soil, and neither do peaches.

Hang Up the Harvest

A coat hanger helps make fast work of harvesting small tree fruits such as apricots, cherries, and plums. When you want to pick, suspend your harvest bucket from a sturdy wooden coat hanger and position the hanger on a nearby limb.

Hang a harvest bucket from an ordinary coat hanger to save yourself unnecessary bending when harvesting tree fruit.

String Pruning

The best method I have found for keeping track of what to prune off my grapevine is my father's method: Tie colored yarn on the canes that have borne fruit in the current year. Then, between late November and early March, after the vines have gone dormant, prune the marked canes to the second bud from the main branch or trunk, 1 inch above the bud, with a downward slant.

Joan W.
Troy, Michigan

Frozen Berry Feasts

You may not need any encouragement to eat your bounty of berries, but just in case, here are five fine ways to feast on frozen berries.

Toss a few into fruit salad. You can add a handful of still-frozen berries to a fruit salad. If the berries have been frozen with sugar, they will create a sweet sauce when they defrost. Unsweetened berries will be mushy compared with the fresh fruit in the salad, but they'll provide color.

Make berry shakes. To prepare a nourishing, refreshing drink, combine about 1 cup of berries with one banana and about ¼ cup of orange, pineapple, or white grape juice in a blender; blend until smooth. Add sweetener if you wish, as well as yogurt or ice cream.

Perk them up with flavorings. If you find that the taste of your frozen berries has faded when you're ready to use them, add a few squirts of fresh lemon juice, a little extra sugar, or a splash or two of berry liqueur.

Bake with them. But before you toss them into your batter, take the time to defrost them. Frozen berries can chill the batter, which will then increase your baking time. And the result is often an overbrowned top and a gooey center.

Pep up your pancakes. Again, thaw your berries first. If you skip this step, you will end up with pockets of uncooked batter around the berries. Note that thawed berries may tint the pancake batter lavender or pink. Another option is to serve the thawed berries as a topping for your pancakes or waffles.

Drain Away Pests

Protect the tender bark of your newly planted fruit trees from gnawing rodents with inexpensive plastic drainpipe collars. These homemade tree guards will keep mice, voles, and rabbits at bay.

To make these collars, buy 10-foot lengths of 4-inch-diameter plastic drainpipe. Cut the pipe in 1- to 1½-foot sections. Slit each section so you can slip it around the tree base, taking care not to damage the delicate new bark. (The guards protect tree trunks from sunscald damage, too.)

Get Apples Up and Growing

Conscientious care of young apple trees after planting leads to best fruit production and tree health for years to come. Here are some tips for helping your trees get off to the best possible start.

- Spread a layer of mulch made of shredded newspaper after planting, and top it with straw to create a barrier that weeds and grass won't grow through easily. Use one bale of straw for four or five trees.

- Pull the mulch back about 3 weeks after planting and spread a balanced organic fertilizer in a 2-foot radius around the base of the trees, then replace the mulch.

- Pull the mulch back about 2 feet away from the trunk before the first frost so that rodents are less tempted to take up winter residence there.

A Dwarf for Your Garden

If you're stuck with a small yard but you really want to grow apples, then dwarf apple trees are what you need. Some dwarf apple trees grow no taller than 4 or 5 feet.

Dwarf apple trees are the result of grafting standard apple cultivars onto dwarfing rootstocks, and it is important to choose the right rootstock for your conditions. If you'll be growing apples in an exceptionally cold climate, look for rootstocks in the "Polish" series (referred to as P.2, P.22, etc.) or the "Bud" series. Most Polish rootstocks are hardy to Zone 3; Bud series rootstocks are hardy to Zone 4.

It also helps to choose rootstocks that are resistant to disease. The "Geneva" dwarf rootstock series is probably the most disease-resistant stock available.

The English rootstock MM.111 can survive in hot, dry, sandy soils and can also hold its own in heavy clay soil as well; it is probably the best rootstock for southeastern gardeners.

When you buy a dwarf apple tree, be aware that the final height of the tree when mature will depend on both the rootstock and the normal size of the grafted apple variety. For example, the semi-dwarfing rootstock M.7 will take a tree down to about 55 to 65 percent of its full size. So if the original tree would reach 35 feet (like 'Golden Delicious'), the "dwarf" would be around 18 feet high.

old-time wisdom

BE SURE APPLES ARE RIPE

Cut up an apple of the average ripeness of the crop, and examine if its seeds have become brown or blackish; if they remain uncolored, the fruit is not ready for pulling.

J. C. Loudon
An Encyclopedia of Gardening, 1850

Beautiful Blueberries

My blueberry bushes have been growing for 5 years now and are doing great. I used to feed them with compost and foliar sprays when the leaves were out, and I mulched with pine needles (to give the plants a little acid). Last fall I tried Gardens Alive "Shrubs Alive" plant food (it's organic). I gently worked $1/3$ to $1/2$ cup into the soil around the base of each plant. This year we had blueberries coming out of our ears and TONS of new shoots sprang up! I'm sold.

Under the blueberry bushes, I planted everbearing strawberries as a living mulch. They can tolerate the lower pH of the area and help to keep the weeds down and moisture in the soil. Plus, the flowers help bring in the bees for pollination. We like having fresh strawberries all summer long, too! Greens such as lettuce and spinach could be used as a living mulch instead.

Jamie H.
Waverly, Nebraska

Blueberries Love Sawdust

Sawdust can save the day for blueberries in the home garden. Blueberries like acid soil (pH 4.0 to 5.0), while most other garden plants like soil that's much closer to neutral (pH 6.5 to 7). You'll probably need to adjust the pH of your soil when you plant blueberries, which you can do by adding powdered elemental sulfur. To keep the soil acidity in your blueberry bed welcoming to the shrubs, try mulching with sawdust. The sawdust will decay slowly, acidifying the soil as it does so. A 1-inch mulch of sawdust worked lightly into the soil around your bushes annually should ensure an excellent harvest. Just be sure you aren't using sawdust from pressure-treated lumber, which contains chemicals you won't want to add to your organic garden.

Easy-Prune Blueberries

Blueberries are a great choice if you're a pruning-phobic gardener. Unlike fruit trees and grapevines, blueberries have very simple pruning requirements. All you'll need to do is to cut out weak or dead branches and remove thick, twiggy clusters to let in light. Once every few years, an old branch should be cut back to the ground to induce new growth. That's it!

Grape Growing Is a Snap

Plant grapevines and you'll have grapes—that's all there is to it. Here are some simple tips for growing bumper crops of homegrown grapes.

Choose disease-resistant cultivars. Check nursery and seed catalogs and your local Cooperative Extension office for grapes that resist anthracnose, black rot, botrytis, and mildew.

Don't sweat the pruning. One rule of thumb is to cut the vines back by one-third of their length in late winter. Pruning is really necessary only to confine the grapes to the structure you want them to grow on and to let light into the vines to stimulate fruiting.

Leave the extras for the birds. When you've had your fill of grapes, just leave the rest on the vine. Grapes ripen right around the time of fall bird migration. Depending on where you live, the grapes you don't want will attract migrating birds such as brown thrashers, cedar waxwings, grosbeaks, and mockingbirds.

Peach-Planting Pointers

No matter what type of peach tree you're planting, plant it during the dormant season. In areas where winter isn't bitter cold and the ground doesn't freeze, plant in winter or very early spring (before the trees leaf out). In areas where the ground does freeze, plant as early as possible in spring.

It's best to start with 1-year-old trees that are about 3 feet tall. Some gardeners think they are getting more for their money with a 2-year-old tree because it's bigger, but 2-year-olds have a higher percentage of failure and are more likely to go into transplant shock than a younger tree.

In a typical small orchard, full-size peach trees are set 15 to 20 feet apart. Dwarf varieties are spaced at about half that distance. Try not to cut it too close—trees spaced closely together need more water during periods of drought and may end up competing fiercely for available moisture and nutrients. The fruit on crowded-together trees is often smaller as well.

When *Is* a Peach Ripe?

Don't be fooled into thinking that a peach is ripe just because it's beginning to blush. You should always judge ripeness by the color of the nonblushed side of the fruit (sometimes you'll hear this called the "background color"). When that background starts to yellow, your fruit is beginning to ripen. Although you *can* harvest it at this time (and let it continue to ripen indoors), most gardeners agree that the fruit will be sweetest if left on the tree until fully colored—another week or two, depending on the variety.

Peachy Pruning and Thinning

Peach tree pruning is pretty basic—just keep the center of the tree open (free of overgrowth and dead wood) to allow air and sunlight in. That sunlight is *particularly* important in the cool, moist areas of the West Coast. Gardeners in this area may also want to prune out some of the foliage around the fruit in summer to make sure enough sunlight gets in; this really sweetens up some varieties. And yes, you should thin the fruits themselves as well. A peach tree will produce a lot more fruit than it should, and left alone the result will be a many small, ho-hum–tasting peaches. For the biggest and best-flavored peaches, thin young fruit to about 6 inches apart.

Saving Fruit from Pests

In my experience, it's essential to thin, thin, thin apples and pears to reduce pest problems. Nobody hates to pull baby fruit off the branches more than I do, but if you don't, fruit that touches other fruit forms moist feeding areas for nasty little bugs. Here are the steps I take to protect my fruit.

1. *Between Thanksgiving and Christmas, spray the branches and trunk with a fine horticultural oil.*

2. *In winter (after January 1), prune the trees to allow good air circulation between all the branches.*

3. *Just before the flowers bloom, spray again with the horticultural oil; after the flowers bloom, spray about every 30 days with insecticidal soap. Direct your spray to the branches, not the fruit.*

4. *Thin your fruit to one per cluster.*

Donna R.
Colchester, Connecticut

Meet Peach Water Needs

When it comes to water, peach trees can be fussy. They have very shallow roots that demand constant moisture, but they don't tolerate waterlogged soil. Choose a site for your peach trees that is well drained but tends to stay moist. If you live in an area that tends to have dry spells, your best bet is to set up a drip irrigation line around your trees to deliver a steady source of water.

Preventing weed competition for water is important, too. The best practice is to mulch newly planted trees with 1½ to 2 inches of weed-free organic matter.

Even if you have slow-draining or rocky soil, you can still grow great peaches. Build raised beds or terraces that are 18 inches higher than the surrounding ground. Backfill the planting area with loamy sand and plenty of compost, and plant your trees.

Conquer Peach Leaf Curl

Peach trees infected with peach leaf curl are truly ugly: The leaves become severely puckered, distorted, and curled and will drop prematurely. The tree will produce new leaves to compensate, which can reduce the tree's vigor and increase danger of winter injury. The good news is that you can easily prevent this disease organically. Buy a lime-sulfur spray, and apply it either in late fall after all leaves have dropped or in early spring before the buds begin to swell. Once the buds have begun to open, it's too late to spray. In addition to spraying, always remove and destroy any diseased leaves.

Try Pest-Free Asian Pears

If you're looking for fruit trees that produce sweet fruit and have virtually no pest woes, try an Asian pear tree. Asian pears aren't bothered by 90 percent of the pests that commonly bother other fruits. And compared with other fruits, they're easy to grow.

Prune Asian pear trees as you would an apple to keep the tree's branches open and to keep the fruit in easy reach. Asian pears are so productive that the fruits must be severely thinned to just one per cluster as soon as you see them developing. The heavy, yellow fruits are crisp and sweet, but flavor quality varies among the varieties. Before you buy an Asian pear tree, ask your supplier for recommendations, or try to taste some varieties that other gardeners in your area are growing.

Double Your Raspberry Yields!

Here are two great tips that can nearly double your raspberry yields.

Mulch with straw. A Cornell University study showed that 'Heritage' raspberries mulched with straw produced nearly twice as many primocanes (fruit-bearing stems) as berries grown using other weed-control methods such as plastic mulch, herbicides, and hand weeding.

Trellis against wind. If you garden where it's windy, tying your raspberry canes to a simple wire trellis can double your yields. A study at the University of Guelph in Ontario, Canada, compared the yield of unsupported plants with the yield of plants tied onto wires supported by steel T-shaped fence posts. The variety 'Boyne' yielded 68 percent more berries when trellised, and 'Regency' produced a remarkable 189 percent more. Researchers believe the yield increases in supported or sheltered plants are due to the greater leaf area they develop, resulting in increased photosynthesis, combined with better light penetration provided by tying the canes evenly along the trellis wires.

old-time wisdom

OATS AS RASPBERRY MULCH

A subscriber speaks highly of the practice of sowing oats in the fall among raspberries. Of course the winter kills the oats, but they afford a mulch for the soil.

Farm Journal, *1885*

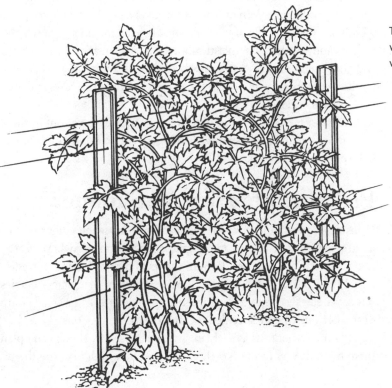

Trellising raspberries is well worth the effort for easier harvesting and much higher yields.

Freezing Strawberry Plants

Where I live in Florida, it's best to plant strawberries early—by early March at the latest. However, plants often aren't available from suppliers that early. So I ordered plants this spring and I'm keeping them frozen until fall. I placed the plants in a gallon-size re-sealable bag, covered them with Spanish moss, and put them in the freezer. Once a month, I take them out, thaw them, and open the bag so they can get some indirect sunlight and oxygen. Then they go back in the freezer for another month. I'll repeat this until planting time, which for me will be in October.

I have planted strawberry plants that were frozen before; a local berry farmer gave them to me. I swear, within 3 days the green leaves were popping out of those gnarly dead-looking things I had "just planted." Amazing!

*Lisa A.
Homestead, Florida*

Raspberries for Fall

Fall-bearing raspberries may be the ultimate low-maintenance bramble for gardeners in the northern two-thirds of the United States. You can plant fall-bearing raspberries in fall and harvest your first crop the following fall. A good straw mulch is the key to successful fall planting in the North. Prepare the planting site in advance so you can set out plants as soon as they arrive from the nursery. Don't thin the stand during the growing season; after your fall harvest, cut or mow all the canes off at ground level. New canes will sprout in the spring to bear fruit in fall.

To ensure that crops will bear fruit before fall frost in the North, cover the plants in early spring with row covers until the plants are 18 inches tall. This speeds growth so that flowering and fruit set happen earlier in fall. The plants have few pest and disease problems because you cut off all growth each fall, so pests and diseases have nowhere to overwinter. To prevent virus problems, avoid susceptible varieties and start with virus-free planting stock.

Save Strawberries from Frost

Black plastic can save tender strawberry foliage and flowers from spring frost damage. When frost seems likely, cover your berry patch with black plastic (rolls of black plastic are available in a variety of lengths and widths). The plastic absorbs heat rising from the ground and keeps temperatures underneath a full 10°F higher than the outside air. Between frosts, roll or fold the plastic between the rows and anchor it with rocks or bricks.

Another tactic for warding off frost damage is to get out in the early morning after a frosty night and wash the frost off your plants before it can damage the buds or berries.

Pick Strawberries All Summer

Nonstop crops of juicy strawberries can be yours when you grow day-neutral varieties. As their name implies, day-neutral strawberries are not as sensitive to summer daylight that cuts off production of traditional June-bearing strawberries. June-bearers produce bigger berries, but day-neutrals eclipse their June-bearing cousins with a steady output of smaller but equally succulent berries over three seasons.

Plant day-neutrals as early in spring as possible. If you can't plant them by mid-May in the North, it may not be worth planting them.

Set the plants about 4 to 5 inches apart in staggered rows. To prevent stunted growth, it's a good idea to pinch off their flowers for 6 weeks after planting to allow them to grow to sufficient size before bearing fruit. Thirty days after that, you should be picking berries.

Mulching the plants with a ½-inch layer of straw mulch immediately after planting helps because the plants have a shallow root system. The mulch also helps cool the soil, which increases yield in summer. In the hot days of August, try evaporative cooling. Rig a mist-type sprinkler that will release a low amount of moisture into the air to keep them cool in the heat of the day. Put the sprinkler in the middle of the bed, and make sure you don't flood the bed.

Day-neutrals need slow, steady feeding. Add compost or fish emulsion every 2 weeks or so throughout the growing season. Work a moderate amount into the top layer of soil. Pinch off runners throughout the season as well so that the plants will concentrate on berry production, not on the production of daughter plants. Try covering your berries with row covers in spring and fall to extend harvest. You may be able to pick strawberries right up to Thanksgiving.

You may want to treat the plants as annuals and replant them each year. To overwinter them, begin mulching in late fall with 1½ to 2 inches of loosely applied straw. Remove the straw when growth begins in spring. If the plants are becoming too dense in the second year of growth, thin the runners enough to be able to spot your closed fist in the growth before it touches the crowns of the plants. In their second year, day-neutrals have a flush of berries in June, then rest in early July, coming back with more berries in early August. Yields will not equal those of the first year of growth.

Bees Make Bigger Strawberries

Want bigger strawberries? Then encourage bees in your garden. A Cornell University study has shown that when bees are active in strawberry patches, the berries grow up to 40 percent bigger. Strawberry flowers are pollinated primarily by wind and gravity, but as with many other crops, they benefit greatly when bees are present to improve the pollination. The bees distribute more grains of pollen onto each flower, and this causes each "bee-blessed" berry to grow plumper.

To attract a variety of beneficial bees, grow lots of flowers (especially blue and yellow ones) near your berries. But avoid planting flowers that the bees prefer over your crop if the two are in bloom at the same time. You can determine this simply by watching which flowers the bees are choosing.

Transplanting Strawberries

A bulb-planting tool is a handy device for transplanting small strawberry runners into a new bed. And this technique should also work well to relocate seedlings of other crops and cause a minimum of root disturbance. Start by tucking the plant's leaves up into the bulb planter. Then press down to cut a circle of soil. Lift the planter, and slide out the plant and rootball. Use the bulb planter to cut a new hole where you want to place the plant. Set the transplant into the hole, and firm the soil around it.

*Mitchell B.
Greensburg, Kentucky*

Seek Apricots That Tolerate Frost

Apricots bloom in early spring, 2 weeks or more before peach trees. So if you live in an area where spring frosts are unpredictable, you may have assumed that you can't grow apricots. Not so! The critical factor is choosing a variety that can take moderate frost. Be sure to plant the tree on the highest ground possible, but in a protected spot near your home.

Make Pawpaws Feel at Home

Pawpaws are cold-hardy fruits with a flavor that's a mix of banana, pineapple, and mango. They are sometimes called "poor man's banana."

Large, lush leaves and rich, tropical-tasting fruit have made the native American pawpaw tree a cause célèbre as pawpaw fans extol the plant's virtues to an ever-growing audience. But a gardener's burst of enthusiasm is often tempered by the cautions about pawpaws being difficult to transplant and slow to establish.

One secret to growing pawpaws is to add a handful of soil from an established pawpaw patch to the planting hole when you plant a pawpaw tree. This soil may contain beneficial mycorrhizal fungi that help generate better root growth (each type of plant responds best to particular fungi).

Pawpaws require well-drained, fertile, loamy soil, but otherwise you'll need to do very little maintenance in the proper conditions.

Bareroot trees will establish themselves as well as container-grown specimens do. The trees grow slowly, so don't be discouraged. During the first few years, most of a pawpaw's growth takes place underground because it's developing a long taproot.

Chapter 8

Cultivating a Low-Care Lawn

The beauty of organic lawn care is that you spend less time tending your grass. Once you've established a healthy lawn using organic techniques, it will need little attention beyond mowing and trimming. Healthy organic lawns are deep-rooted, so they usually don't need watering, and they're sustained by the natural fertilizing that results when you use a mulching mower to return the clippings to the soil.

Switching from chemical to organic lawn care requires some time and patience, but the results are well worth it. This chapter will help you in making the switch to organic lawn care with gardener-recommended, nonchemical strategies for beating lawn weeds and instructions for fixing bare spots. Follow our mowing tips to help your lawn thrive, and investigate the secrets for helping a lawn green up fast with organic fertilizing methods. Learn about some simple fall lawn chores that will help your lawn look its best.

Also, consider converting some or all of your lawn to nonturf alternatives. It's easy when you follow the instructions for starting a moss lawn or establishing a mix of natural grasses and wildflowers.

Eating Oxalis

Oxalis grows as a weed in my lawn, but I don't mind it too much because it's pretty—and tasty too. (I just had some in my salad for lunch.) I've got several established plants now that I let grow, both the yellow- and violet-flowered varieties. And I've also planted a purple-leafed cultivar. I've been warned not to eat too much at once since this plant's high Vitamin C content is due to oxalic acid, which can cause convulsions in high dosages.

Otherwise, I hand-pull them. Semiannual applications of corn gluten meal seem to keep oxalis and other unwanted weeds down in the lawn.

*Jerry F.
Howard Lake,
Minnesota*

Mulch Makes Grass Seed Stay Put

End the frustration of watching your newly seeded lawn wash away in a sudden rain. You can save yourself from losing seed (and from the hassle of reseeding) by shaking a very thin layer of pine needles, straw, or hay over freshly sown seeds. Use just enough mulch to catch seed before it washes away, but not enough to shade seedlings. Individual pieces of straw or hay may seem too small to have any beneficial effects, but even the thinnest layer shields the soil and prevents it from forming a hard crust.

If you don't have pine needles or straw, you may want to try a commercial product called Pennmulch, made of pelleted recycled paper, developed at Pennsylvania State University.

Stop Weeds in New Lawns

When you start a new lawn from seed, weeds can be a big problem. To reduce the stores of weed seeds waiting to germinate in your new lawn, try this technique: Till the area, rake it smooth, and water. Wait a week or two for weeds to sprout, and then use a hoe to cultivate shallowly and kill the weeds. Wait another couple of weeks and go over the area again with your hoe. This process will eliminate most weed seeds near the soil surface, and you can then sow your grass seed.

Don't Mow Too Low

Set your mower blade so you remove no more than one-third of the grass blade at one time. This encourages deeper roots that give your lawn better access to soil moisture and nutrients. The resulting thicker, healthier turf will also do a better job of crowding out any weeds that try to move in. The recommended height for a healthy lawn is 2½ to 3 inches.

Sharpen Up before You Cut

Do your grass a favor and keep your mower blades sharp. Sharp mower blades give a lawn a neat, clean cut, while dull blades tear at grass, leaving it looking frayed and making it more prone to disease. Spring is the season to sharpen mower blades. If you're handy, use a file or grinder to restore the cutting edge on your blades; otherwise, take the mower to the repair shop. The cost is usually less than $5 a blade.

Mulch Your Clippings

Leaving properly chopped grass clippings on the lawn instead of bagging them adds valuable nitrogen to the soil, provides drought protection, and eliminates disposal problems. And, by using a mulching mower, you can reduce your average mowing time by as much as 30 percent because you don't spend time collecting clippings or emptying the mower's collection bag.

When you buy a mulching mower, look for a model with a doughnut-shaped deck, which channels air currents to lift the clippings so that they can be cut more than once before they are forced down onto the surface of the soil. The best mulchers also offer double rather than single blades.

Be Smart, Buy Nonspill

Did you know that an estimated 17 million gallons of fuel is spilled each year just from the refueling of small engines? That's more than the amount of crude oil that leaked from the Exxon Valdez in 1989. Do your part to reduce fuel waste: Be sure you use a "nonspill" gas container or a nozzle every time you fill your lawn mower.

Fork Fix for Lawn Problems

Shortcuts across your lawn to the driveway, swing set, and shed endure heavy foot traffic, which can cause the grass in those areas to suffer. If the informal paths in your yard are suffering from "brown-out," restore them to health with a simple hand-aerating technique. Simply thrust the tines of a garden fork 4 to 5 inches into the soil and then move the fork handle back and forth like a pump or jack handle. This action opens channels in the soil that will allow air and water to penetrate below the packed surface layer—without uprooting your lawn. Repeat this procedure at 6-inch intervals throughout the browned area.

Drop That Hose

Resist the urge to sprinkle your lawn each evening. Frequent watering promotes shallow roots. Deep watering encourages your lawn to send roots farther into the soil so your lawn can last longer between rains or watering without becoming stressed. Give the lawn one good soaking per week—and take rainfall into consideration.

GARDENER TO GARDENER

Dig Lawn Weeds When It's Wet

I've had luck pulling dandelions out right after it rains, when it's very wet. I stick my finger down next to the root as far as it will go, hold, and PULL! I've gotten 80 percent of the root this way. Using an asparagus cutter, sticking it down next to the root, also can help to supply the leverage needed to pull up most of the root.

Sara B.
Tipp City, Ohio

Get Greener Grass Fast

Give your lawn a green-up with these quick and easy fertilizing secrets.

Soothe sunburned grass with seaweed. To green up a lawn that's suffering from heat stress, spray liquid seaweed on the grass. A hose-end sprayer works well for applying the seaweed. Use a double dose along the edges of the lawn that border sidewalks and driveways (those areas suffer more heat stress). You may need to make several applications; keep the lawn watered once it greens up again.

Give hungry lawns a special mix. Use fertilizers that include mineral ingredients such as granite meal, greensand, seaweed, natural rock phosphate, and trace minerals. These tend to last longer than fertilizers that are high in compost, so you may need to fertilize your lawn only twice per year instead of three or four times.

Wait for the rainy season. If your region has predictable rainy and dry seasons, make the spring fertilizer application after the rainy season, not before. A newly fertilized, lush lawn is more susceptible to disease problems, especially when conditions are wet.

To Tackle Thatch, or Not?

To determine whether thatch (an accumulation of dead, partially decomposed roots and stems) is a problem in your yard, poke your finger into the grass. If it feels soft and springy and your finger doesn't reach soil, you need to get to work. The thatch layer is thick enough that it can prevent water from reaching the soil and may hold moisture near the plants, encouraging disease and pest problems.

The best time to dethatch is in early spring just after the first growth. If the thatch layer isn't too thick, a stiff rake will do. Thicker layers may require a vertical power mower or a regular mower fitted with a dethatching blade. An easier approach is to let compost do the work for you. Spread a light layer (about ⅜ inch) over your lawn, and the compost releases millions of active microbes that break down the thatch. It also suppresses many diseases. Field studies have shown that compost can be as effective as chemical fungicides in suppressing blight and root-rot diseases.

A Pretty Sod Patch

Restore a small section of weedy or bare lawn quickly by applying a sod patch. You can buy sod, or perhaps you have some healthy sod available from an area of your yard that you're converting to garden.

First, dig out weeds in the area you want to repair. Loosen the soil with a long-tined fork, spread a 1-inch layer of compost on the surface, and rake it smooth. Water the soil lightly before laying the sod. Place the strips tightly together without stretching them, staggering the ends. After you've laid the sod, fill in all cracks with screened topsoil. Soak the sod thoroughly, and water every 2 or 3 days for 2 weeks or until the grass has rooted securely. If the sod shrinks at the edges, top-dress with screened soil and seed with the same grass variety. You can walk on the newly planted sod, but don't mow until the grass is at least 2 inches high.

Switch Spreaders to Save Time

To spend less time fertilizing your lawn, try a cyclone spreader instead of a drop spreader. The faster application time is due to the design of the cyclone spreader, which makes a broader sweep than a drop spreader.

Cyclone spreaders are easy to find in hardware stores and garden centers. Be sure to choose an organic fertilizer mix, or make your own by mixing 3 parts blood meal, 3 parts bonemeal, and 1 part kelp meal. (Keep in mind, though, that you should always test your soil before applying any type of fertilizer. Contact your local County Extension agent for information on obtaining a soil-testing kit.)

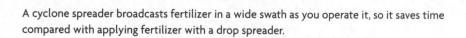

A cyclone spreader broadcasts fertilizer in a wide swath as you operate it, so it saves time compared with applying fertilizer with a drop spreader.

Vinegar Weed Spray

I use 20 percent vinegar ($12 per gallon at the feed store) to kill weeds in St. Augustine grass. I am having particularly excellent results against oxalis. Two hours after spraying, the oxalis is fried.

I mix 1 tablespoon of molasses and 1 tablespoon of dish soap into the vinegar to reduce the surface tension and allow it to stick to the weeds. I spray it full strength from a hand-held spray bottle. When I finish, I rinse the bottle thoroughly so the acid in the vinegar won't corrode the metal spring and balls inside the spray head. I use a piece of cardboard to mask off the grass when I spray so that I don't kill the grass along with the weeds.

I'm having good luck with other broadleaved weeds, too—except ivy, which is not affected by the vinegar.

David H.
San Antonio, Texas

Lawn Vac to the Rescue!

Your yard's a mess and company's coming. Don't panic—get out the shop vacuum! You can use the vacuum to extract crabapple and other fruit tree droppings from your lawn, as well as seeds from Norway maples and goldenrain trees that work their way into your grass. It's also handy for a final cleanup of leaves and small twigs that can get left behind after you haul away prunings from trees or shrubs.

Empty the vacuum into the compost pile, or pick through the crabapples for the good ones and make them into jam or preserves—just be sure to wash them first in case the inside of the vacuum is less than spotless.

Flood Relief for Your Lawn

Heavy rains can lead to temporary flooding around your yard from surface runoff. When the water subsides, don't be too concerned if there's a layer of flood-deposited soil on the grass: It may actually do your lawn some good. If the soil layer is an inch or so deep, don't walk on it or do anything at all until the soil dries. Walking on the wet lawn and compacting the soil even more is the worst thing you can do to the already-stressed turf.

In most cases the silt and muck will gradually filter down through the grass and can actually improve your lawn by acting as a mild fertilizer.

After the muck settles, test your soil's pH, just in case the runoff included some highly alkaline or acidic substance. Give your lawn plenty of time to recover, and don't let it suffer from drought later in the growing season.

If flooding deposits a layer that's more than 2 inches thick, you may want to lift or slice off some of the excess. Try using a broad, flat snow shovel to scoop off the soil. Stand on a board while you do this to distribute your weight more evenly and prevent yourself from sinking.

Fall Compost Boosts Lawns

The secret to beating weeds in lawns is to apply compost in the fall. Grind or sieve the compost first and spread a ½-inch layer over the surface of your lawn. Rake it into the soil; reseed bare spots. This treatment will make the lawn grow so vigorously that weeds, including quackgrass, will be crowded out. Your grass will get an early start in spring and cover the ground so thickly that the quackgrass, which spends the winter in the seed stage, won't get started.

Mow No More

Moss patches in your lawn may be a sign that your lawn could easily be completely converted from grass to moss. There are advantages to a moss lawn, not the least of which is no more mowing! Moss is lovely— and definitely low maintenance. It needs no cutting, liming, or aerating, and it thrives in precisely the situations—around knobby-rooted trees, beneath deep shade, and in moist, acidic, compacted soils—that thwart grass.

Here's what you need to know if you're considering making the switch from grass to moss.

- Make sure moss is already growing in your yard or in nearby areas. Moss grows best where it grows naturally in the wild. If you live in a dry climate, you'll have difficulty establishing it around your home.

- Start small because it's much easier to keep a small area free of weeds, leaves, and twigs, all of which deter moss growth.

- Begin by transplanting moss found around your property or your neighbor's yard. Moss native to your area works best, but don't pick wild moss from the forest. You can usually find what you need close by, perhaps in the sidewalk or even from potted perennials purchased at a nursery.

- Establish moss in a shady place first, preferably where it is already growing. Transplant small sheets of moss to bare spots after watering the area thoroughly. Moss doesn't have roots, so you can lift whole sheets, place them into position, and press them down firmly.

- Blend moss with yogurt and pour the slurry onto the ground. Some folks swear by this, and although this technique may sound odd, yogurt can help create the right growing conditions for moss.

- Water your moss lawn at least once a week. Moss tolerates some sunshine but favors consistent moisture.

- Walk on your moss (you won't hurt it), but keep your dogs and cats away from it. They will tear it up, and their urine will leave black rings that take time to fade.

old-time wisdom

FRAGRANT GRASS MIX

In our lawn grass we always put a little sweet vernal grass (*Anthoxanthum odoratum*) on account of its delightful fragrance.

Vick's Illustrated Catalogue and Floral Guide, *1872*

A Lawn without Turf

Converting lawn to garden is an exciting project that will open up new areas for experimenting. Perhaps you'll want to plant berry bushes, a mixed groundcover bed, or sow a natural lawn of native nonturf grasses. (For a comprehensive listing of meadow plants for your region and sources for them, go to www.organicgardening.com.) Remember to start small: Replace just a patch of the lawn with new plants. You'll learn from experience how much is involved in getting rid of the lawn sod and preparing the site. And you'll be able to observe the planting throughout the season before you commit to a complete makeover.

Here's how to remove an existing turf lawn and prepare the soil for a new natural lawn.

Strip the sod. Rent a sod-cutting machine to accomplish this task quickly and neatly. Or you can use a sharp spade or even a linoleum knife to separate the sod from the soil beneath it. Whatever tool you use, roll up the sod like a carpet, leaving bare soil behind. Compost the sod, give it away, or use it in another part of the yard.

Amend the soil. Established native grasses and wildflowers grow well without regular feeding, but seeds or transplants may need a nutrient boost to get off to a strong start. Before you plant, have the soil tested and add the recommended nutrients. Spread the amendments and mix them thoroughly into the soil.

Plant and mulch. Broadcast flower seeds evenly throughout the bed, and add any transplants. Spread a ¼- to ½-inch layer of straw or hay mulch over the bed to keep the soil moist and to deter weeds from sprouting while the new plants grow. Replenish the straw or hay as it deteriorates.

Water. Gently sprinkle the seeds and transplants to get them growing; however, avoid watering too hard or too much before the seeds germinate, or they could wash away. Keep the soil moist while the seeds germinate and the transplants' roots start growing.

Keep the birds away (for now). Ultimately, you'll love watching the birds flock to your new lawn, but until it's established, you want to keep them away from the seeds. To do this, attach flash tape to wooden posts around the newly planted area. When the tape whips around in the wind, the flashing reflections scare off birds.

Chapter 9

Starting Seeds Indoors and Out

The allure of starting your own plants from seed is less about saving money and more about creating a garden that's uniquely your own. Most garden centers sell the same old selection of annuals, perennials, and vegetables—or they all have the "hot" new choices of the season—but they can't begin to offer the full range of cultivars and species that are available from seed. Growing plants from seed opens doors to a smorgasbord of interesting and unusual plants that would be hard to find from a local source.

For those gardeners who enjoy the money-saving aspect of seed starting, there are plenty of tips for fashioning seed-starting containers and planting labels from household recyclables. And all gardeners can benefit from the recipes for an organic seed-starting mix.

The chapter also covers custom care for seedlings, in-cluding watering and heating tips, as well as an herb tea that will help keep your seedlings healthy. There are plenty of tips for starting specific types of plants from seeds, including secrets for starting seven of the most popular types of annuals. The chapter rounds out with new ideas for storing seeds for longest viability.

Baby-Wipe Seed Safe

*I used to keep my seeds in
the refrigerator in quart-size
yogurt containers, labeled
"summer" and "winter." That
way, I was able to organize
my seeds by the time of year I
planted them. This worked
until I moved and no longer
had room in the fridge. I
wanted one container that
would hold all my seeds but
still let me group them by
season. So I took a baby-wipe
container and made file labels
out of cardboard, marking
them "summer vegetables,"
"summer flowers," "winter
greens," and "fall flowers" to
reflect our planting seasons.
Because it's not airtight, I put
in a silica gel packet from a
shoebox to absorb moisture.*

*Karen S.
Austin, Texas*

Vermiculite-Free Mix

Most seed-starting soil mixes include vermiculite, a natural mineral
that helps improve aeration and water retention. However, vermiculite
contains small amounts of asbestos and has been linked to asbestos-
related illnesses. Gardeners using vermiculite are probably not in any
danger, according to the EPA. Nevertheless, if you'd prefer to avoid
asbestos altogether, try this simple, vermiculite-free mix.

> $3\frac{1}{2}$ gallons of peat moss
> $\frac{3}{4}$ cup of limestone (to adjust the pH of the acidic peat)
> $1\frac{1}{2}$ gallons of screened, aged compost (at least 8 months old)
> 1 to 2 quarts of perlite (optional)

You can boost this mix with 3 tablespoons of bloodmeal (for
quick-release nitrogen), 1 tablespoon of rock phosphate (for phosphorus), and 1 tablespoon of kelp or seaweed meal (for potassium). If
you don't have these materials on hand, then simply fertilize seedlings
with a liquid fish-and-seaweed fertilizer, but wait until their true
leaves appear.

The Big Chill

Some seeds, including those of many common landscape trees and
some perennials, are programmed to sit dormant until environmental
conditions are just right for germination. If you want to start seeds of
these plants indoors, you'll need to trick the seeds into breaking their
dormancy, a technique known as stratification. Here's one way to do it.

1. Soak the seeds in warm water for 24 hours to soften their coat-
   ings. Drain the seeds, but don't let them dry out.

2. Punch holes in the lid of a glass jar. The size of the jar doesn't
   matter because once the seeds sprout, you'll plant them into
   containers that can accommodate their subsequent growth.

3. Label the container with the seed type and date.

4. Mix the seeds with sand, peat moss, or sphagnum moss at a
   ratio of 1 part seed to 3 parts medium. This medium doesn't
   need to be sterile, but it must be clean—not previously used for
   planting or seed starting. It should be moist but not soggy.

5. Put the seed mixture in the jar, tighten the lid, and refrigerate the jar. Temperature requirements will vary by species, but they should not go below 32°F or above 50°F. Most seeds require 1 to 4 months at a consistent temperature to germinate. Check weekly to make sure the medium hasn't dried out. Once the chilling period has elapsed or the seeds germinate, pot them up.

Presprout in Paper

Sprouting seeds before you plant them can boost germination rates and give you more control when working with expensive or scarce seeds. Here's how to do it.

1. Spread a double layer of damp paper towels on a flat surface. Evenly space seeds about 1 inch apart on the moist towels.

2. Roll up the towels, taking care to keep the seeds from bunching up. Use rubber bands to keep each towel in the shape of a tube.

3. Label the seed roll and place it in a plastic bag. Close the bag loosely—germinating seeds need some air. You can put several rolls in one bag.

4. Put the seeds in a warm place—near a water heater or on top of the refrigerator. Note on your calendar to check them in 2 days. After that first inspection, check the seeds daily for signs of sprouting.

Plant sprouted seeds in individual containers using a fine, loose potting soil mix, or plant them directly into the garden. (Handle them gently—the fleshy roots and stems break easily.) Then treat them as you would any other newly germinated seedlings.

old-time wisdom

BE CRUEL TO BE KIND

The kindest gardener is the one who thins vegetable and flower seedlings most cruelly.

The Garden Magazine, 1908

Presprouting seeds saves time and money; otherwise, you waste time and space sowing seed that isn't viable.

Pinch-and-Drop Seeding

Rather than struggling to sow small seeds evenly along a furrow, use a pinch-and-drop technique. Take a small pinch of seeds between your finger and thumb, and drop it in the furrow as a cluster; repeat this at intervals down the row. In planting spinach, for example, drop three or four seeds every 3 inches. Later, all you need do is remove two or three excess seedlings in each group.

Cut a Yardstick Down to Size

When sowing vegetable or flower seeds into seed flats, lay out tidy rows for the seed using an old yardstick. Cut the yardstick into two pieces, one the length of the flat and the other the width of the flat, to mark rows in both directions. The yardstick lengths make uniform, evenly spaced rows, and the seeding goes quickly.

Spread moistened soil mix in a flat, and level it off. Take either of the yardstick lengths and use it to mark indentations about 1 inch apart, either across the width of the flat for short rows, or down the length of the flat for longer rows. You can adjust the depth according to the seeds you're using, indenting rows slightly deeper for normal-size seeds or barely denting the surface for small seeds, such as those for petunias, that won't be covered with soil mix after planting.

A Painter's Touch

To gently cover small seeds that you've carefully arranged in a flat or garden furrow, use an old paintbrush to sweep soil over the seeds. You'll have more control than you would with a trowel or your hands.

Shiny Shoe Box for Sturdy Seedlings

To start heat-loving tomato and pepper seedlings, all you need are a shoe box and some aluminum foil. For early seed starting, line the shoe box with foil placed shiny side up.

Poke drainage holes through the foil and cardboard, then fill the box with potting mix and plant your seeds. The top of the soil should be a few inches below the top of the box so the foil can magnify the heat and light of the sunshine onto the seedlings. You can set the box outside in the sun on nice days.

Test Your Broadcasting System

Broadcasting is a fast way to sow seeds, but if you don't do it carefully you'll lose the saved time in thinning. To get the knack of broadcasting, set up a practice area by spreading a white sheet on a floor. Use carrot seeds or other small seeds, and scatter them over the sheet at various rates. Your goal is to have a regular pattern of coverage with seeds falling 1 or 2 inches apart. Practicing and seeing the results really will improve your technique!

Burlap Shield for Seeds

Here's a trick to ensure success with direct-sown small seeds in the garden. After you sow seed, spread a single or double thickness of natural burlap over the seeded area and water it well. The burlap breaks the force of the water, preventing seeds from washing out before they germinate. Between waterings, the surface of the burlap will dry out but the underside will remain moist, providing the right environment for germination. Leave the burlap in place, and peek underneath daily to spot the first seed leaves.

TP Your Seed Rows

Do you have trouble seeing tiny seeds when sowing them in rows? You can make the seeds more visible by lining your rows with ribbons of toilet paper before you sow the seeds. The toilet paper quickly decomposes after being covered with moist soil.

Sow a Summer Seedbed

Starting seedlings in late winter and early spring is an indoor job, but in summer you can create a seedbed right in the garden for seedlings of cabbage, broccoli, and other fall crops. Work the soil finely or spread a layer of sifted compost over the soil surface before sowing seeds. After sowing, cover the seedbed with wet burlap or other light fabric. This covering prevents the soil surface from drying out in summer heat. Check the seedbed daily. Keep the covering and soil surface moist at all times, and remove the covering as soon as seedlings start to germinate. Protect the tender seedlings from hot sun by placing some brush loosely over the seedbed. Or place a piece of lattice over the bed; support it with rocks, cinder blocks, or boards so it doesn't crush the seedlings.

GARDENER TO GARDENER

Deluxe Row Markers

Many gardeners like to mark their plantings with empty seed packets stuck onto stakes. But it doesn't take long for sun and rain to take their toll on unprotected paper packets. To protect seed plackets, recycle clear plastic bottles into row markers that will keep the seed packets looking good all through the season.

1. *Cut a rectangle of plastic from the plastic bottle. Make it large enough to fold over and cover both the front and back of your seed packet.*
2. *Cut a triangular section about 3 inches long.*
3. *Fold the plastic rectangle over the seed packet and then staple the triangular section to the bottom of the packet.*
4. *Place your nifty new row marker into the garden and head for the nearest bench for a break.*

*Sondra F.
Independence, Kansas*

Go for the Big Roots

The trick to getting the best results from home-started seedlings is to choose the seedlings with the biggest root systems when you transplant. The length of the stem and size of the leaves isn't as important as hearty roots. Throw out weak plants with few roots because they won't do well anyway. Transplanting only those seedlings with strong root systems will be more time- and cost-efficient in the long run: The plants will establish themselves more quickly and need less coddling.

Seed Starting on Wheels

If you garden in Florida or another mild-winter area, you don't need an elaborate indoor setup for seed starting. You can start seeds outdoors for most of the year. To make a highly portable seedbed, fill an old metal wheelbarrow with seed-starting mix and plant into it. You can move the wheelbarrow around to give the seedlings sun or shade as desired, and even wheel them inside if a cold spell is predicted. When it's time to plant the seedlings into the garden, it's a cinch to transport the transplants right to the planting site.

For warm-climate gardeners, an old wheelbarrow is a handy place for a portable seed-starting area.

Help for Seed-Starter Hands

Save your skin from that red, raw, chapped look and the abrasions that can result when you spend lots of time with your hands in soil-based potting mixes. Before you dive into the seed-sowing season, buy yourself a box of thin surgical gloves.

Surgical gloves will protect your hands and wrists from the unpleasant aftereffects of otherwise enjoyable tasks like seed sowing and transplanting. And unlike heavy garden gloves, they're specially designed to give your fingers a no-slip grip—even when they're wet. They're also great for keeping your hands clean when you're doing other messy jobs like spreading fertilizer. When your work is done, rinse the gloves if you plan to use them again.

Scattered Seeds

Instead of planting in rows, broadcast radish seeds over a wide area. You will harvest about three times the radishes per square foot compared with row plantings, and as you thin the largest radishes, the smaller ones around them will then mature, giving you the effect of a long-season staggered yield without multiple seedings. This technique works for most root crops and greens.

Wonder Water

Studies by *OG* readers and staff show that degassed water (water that's been boiled to drive off dissolved gases) can benefit seedlings. Seedlings watered with this "wonder water" show earlier, stronger germination and better root branching. Houseplants benefit from it, too. Here's how to make "wonder water."

1. Gather some glass canning jars, rings, and lids.

2. Fill a pot with enough water to fill the jars. Bring the water to a rolling boil, and keep it boiling for 5 minutes.

3. Heat the jars under hot water so that they won't crack when you fill them. Fill each jar to the top with boiling water. Screw a lid tightly on each jar to prevent air from getting in.

4. Allow the jars to cool. The water will remain degassed until you open the jars.

Buffer the Heat

If you start seeds in flats on top of heat mats, you may need to raise the flat a bit to help diffuse the heat. You can put a screen, a brick, or a plastic tray across the rack that extends over the mat.

Heat mats made for home-scale use are usually set at 72°F, which is too hot for most transplants. You can stack the flats so the heat lovers get the most heat. Another tactic is to put the heat mat on a timer and set it so that it shuts off at night.

Or put it where it catches a draft—someplace where the air keeps moving so that it varies the heat level, like near a door that's opened frequently or near where you walk around and stir up air currents.

The key is to mimic nature as much as possible by creating "daytime" heat and "nighttime" cooling.

Tickle Your Tomatoes

To avoid that long, leggy look (good for fashion models; bad for tomato starts) in your seedlings, try tickling young tomato plants. Brush tomato seedlings with your fingertips for 90 seconds twice a day, and you'll get plants that are 25 to 35 percent shorter than unbrushed plants. According to studies at the University of Georgia, the resulting seedlings are sturdier and transplant better than spindly, leggy ones. Just don't brush your seedlings when they're wet because you can injure the leaves.

Snip to Thin

A cuticle scissor is the perfect tool for thinning seedlings. Instead of uprooting unwanted seedlings, snip them off at soil level. This technique lets you avoid disturbing the delicate roots of young seedlings, which often grow intertwined with their neighbors. No scissor on hand? Pinch the stems between your fingernails instead.

Treat Touchy Transplants Tenderly

Put an end to transplant shock by planting tough-to-transplant vegetables in the little plastic mesh baskets in which berries or cherry tomatoes are sold. The baskets are perfect for giving cucumber, melon, and squash seedlings an early start since they have plenty of room for their long roots. When the seedlings are grown, you can set the basket directly in the ground so these touchy plants won't even know they've been moved.

To get started, line each basket with two or three thicknesses of newspaper or paper towels and fill it with potting mix. Sow four or five seeds per basket and put them in a well-lit spot.

Once warm weather arrives, plant your seedlings, basket and all, making sure the basket and lining are buried. The roots will grow through the paper and basket into the surrounding soil. At the end of the season, you can lift the baskets, clean them, and store them for future use.

Ready, Set, Rotate

Standard cool-white fluorescent light tubes work well for lighting seedlings indoors. Light intensity is highest near the centers of the tubes, so to prevent any seedlings from getting "leggy" set up a rotation schedule for your flats or pots from end sites to center stage. This will ensure the most even growth.

Make a Simple Seedling Sprinkler

Remember the old sprinkler bottles that moms used to spritz clothes before ironing? Even though you can't buy them anymore, you can make a suitable substitute to water tender seedlings or seeds that haven't sprouted yet. All you need is a 1-quart plastic bottle with a lid about 3 inches across. Poke about five holes in the lid with an awl. Fill the bottle with water and compost tea or fish fertilizer, and sprinkle your seed flats.

Fluffy Soil Isn't Fine

In preparing a seedbed, don't overwork the soil until it's too fine or fluffy; you'll end up causing soil compaction and may wear a path to a poor or failed crop. The person who tills till the cows come home may end up with light soil that appears to be the perfect medium for seeds, but the compaction caused just a few inches below the surface may make it hard for roots to catch hold, absorb air, and penetrate deeply into the soil.

Herb Tea for Healthy Seedlings

To prevent damping-off from killing seedlings, try watering them with chamomile tea. Make a strong tea with 3 teaspoons of dried chamomile in 6 cups of boiling water. Let the tea steep and cool. Water the seedlings two or three times until all signs of damping-off vanish.

Seed-Starting Paper Pots

These newspaper pots for seed starting are easy to make in a variety of sizes by using empty cans for molds.

1. *Cut or tear a page of newspaper into strips, making the strips wide and long enough to provide the pot depth and diameter you want and allowing enough extra width to fold under to form the bottom of the pot.*

2. *Wrap a newspaper strip around a can of any diameter. Fold under the extra width to form the pot bottom.*

3. *Remove the can, and staple the seam to secure the paper. Place the pot into a container that will support it securely.*

4. *Fill each with potting soil, and water until the soil is evenly moist. Sow your seeds, and label the pot.*

When it's time to plant the seedlings out in the garden, you can just leave them in their pots.

Kathryn K.
Kutztown, Pennsylvania

Humidity Helper

A good way to increase humidity around potted seedlings is to set a couple of seedling pots in a larger container of pebbles. The pebbles should be about fingernail size, and there should be just a small amount of water in the pebble container—enough to create humid conditions, but not enough to touch the bottom of the pots. (If potted seedlings are left in standing water all the time, the roots will rot.)

Secrets for Starting 7 Annuals

Starting annual flowers from seed can save you plenty over the cost of bedding plants. Many popular bedding plants are fairly easy to grow from seed if you know their individual quirks. Here's some advice for success with seven types of popular annuals. (In all cases, cover seed flats with plastic and provide bottom heat if possible until the seeds germinate. Then remove the plastic and move the plants to a cooler spot.)

Impatiens. Don't cover impatiens seeds because they need light to germinate, and the pores in the planting mix are like the Grand Canyon to the miniscule seeds. Most of them fall well below the surface. Try adding a little sand to your seed-starting mix, and sift a thick layer of pure peat over the surface of the flat before scattering pinches of seed as you would sprinkle salt over food. Begin looking for the first flush of tiny green leaves about 10 days after sowing, and then move the seedlings to a cooler place that has plenty of light. Transplant them when young—about 1 inch tall. Older plants don't recover as easily from transplanting.

Marigolds. Marigold seedlings can take some abuse, but coddle them and you'll be happier with the results. Lay marigold seeds on the surface of soil in flats, then sprinkle on enough sphagnum peat to keep the soil moist. With bottom heat, seedlings will be up in 5 to 7 days. Move them to a cooler area immediately, and transplant them to larger containers when they're 1½ inches tall.

Petunias. The secret to starting petunia seedlings is to never let them become crowded and never let the roots dry out. Petunia seeds are very small; plant them as described for impatiens above. Petunia seedlings like even cooler temperatures than impatiens. If your petunia plants become woody before you can move them to the garden, cut them back drastically before transplanting, then keep them well watered and well fed.

Portulaca. Skip seedling flats with portulaca because seedlings come up so quickly. Fill cell packs with germinating mix and put three or four portulaca seeds in each cell. The seeds like darkness, so cover them with sifted sphagnum peat. After danger of frost, you can plant the cell packs outside without need for thinning or separating the seedlings.

Salvia. Salvia is a joy to transplant. Sprinkle the large seeds on top of the flat and cover them with a fine dusting of peat. Without the peat the seeds would dry out, but don't put on too much because salvia needs light to germinate. Seeds will sprout in 10 to 15 days. Move the young plants from the seedling flat to larger containers when the plants are about 1 inch tall.

Sweet alyssum. Start seeds directly in cell packs because sweet alyssum is hard to transplant. Your goal is to transplant young and disturb the roots very little. Sow the seeds as you would portulaca. After germination, the seedlings like 60°F at night and about 70°F during the day. Transplant the seedlings outside when they are about 1 inch tall.

Zinnias. You don't need to start zinnia seeds early. They'll sprout in 4 to 5 days and shouldn't grow in containers longer than 4 weeks. Sow the large seeds a bit sparsely on the soil surface in a flat and cover them with ⅛ inch of peat. Transplant them to individual pots or cell packs within 1 week.

Pepper Seeds Like It Hot

Starting your own pepper plants from seed increases your range of choices greatly, but be prepared to give pepper seeds what they need. Raising pepper seedlings requires 8 to 11 weeks, and it's easy to derail the schedule right from the start if you allow the seeds to languish in less-than-ideal temperatures. At 85°F, pepper seedlings will pop up in 1 week, but at 60°F or below, the seedlings can take up to 3 weeks to germinate. Keep seed flats of peppers on propagating mats or on a shelf near a furnace, water heater, or woodstove. If you need to water, be sure to use lukewarm water. Cold water will add to the plants' germination time.

Baby Corn Seedlings Are Best

Corn seed needs warm soil to germinate (it does best between 70° and 85°F), but when planting fever is on, it takes lots of self-control to wait for soil to reach that range. To assuage your urge to plant, start some sweet corn seed indoors about a week before the last expected frost. When the seedlings are about 2 weeks old, harden them off by setting the plants inside a coldframe or any sheltered outdoor location for about a week. Transplant them very carefully because the roots are easily damaged.

Resist the urge to let the plants grow much larger before transplanting them to the garden. A study at Iowa State University showed that growth of 4-week-old corn transplants was poor when compared with the growth rates of 2-week-old seedlings and direct-seeded corn.

Keep Basil in Clumps

When starting basil from seed, pot up seedlings in clumps rather than as individual plants. Basil seedlings are quite delicate, and transplanting clumps of seedlings from the seed flat to containers reduces the risk of transplant shock. Plus, when you eventually set out the clumps into your garden, you see that they develop into vigorous, multistemmed plants that provide more foliage per square inch of garden space than single-stemmed plants.

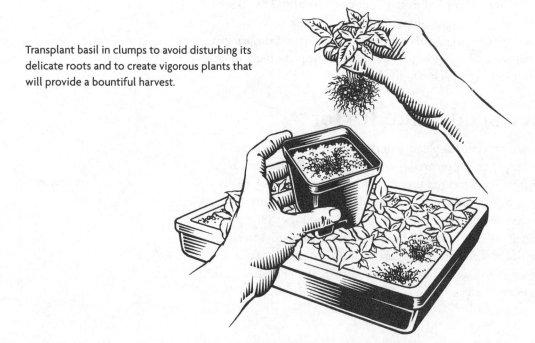

Transplant basil in clumps to avoid disturbing its delicate roots and to create vigorous plants that will provide a bountiful harvest.

Avoid Onion Seedling Stress

Starting onion seeds in flats can result in better germination and seedling growth than sowing the tiny seeds directly into the garden. But don't leave onion seedlings in their flats longer than 8 to 12 weeks from seeding, or they will bulb prematurely because of the stress.

Hostas from Seed

Starting hostas from seed is as easy as starting your own tomato or pepper plants indoors. Sow seeds in February in small seed flats filled with seed-starting mix. After moistening the mix, sow the seeds onto the surface and cover them very lightly with mix. Then cover the trays with plastic bags and set them in a warm spot to germinate. Check the flats frequently to make sure the mix stays moist. In about 2 to 4 weeks, the plants will have sprouted.

Remove the plastic bags and place the flats under lights. About 6 to 8 weeks after sowing, when the seedlings are starting to get crowded, transplant each plant into a 3-inch pot. As the weather warms, move your baby hostas to a coldframe in the garden and then to a temporary nursery bed for their first season outdoors.

Hostas stay fairly small in their first year of growth, usually reaching no more than 3 to 4 inches tall. Keep the plants in the nursery bed through their first winter, covered with a 2-inch layer of shredded leaves. Hostas are very winter-hardy, even when young, so the plants should be fine.

The following spring, transplant the 1-year-old hostas to their permanent homes. Some varieties will reach their mature size by the third season, while others need 5 years or more to reach their peak. Be aware that if you grow hostas from seed collected from plants in your garden, the offspring may not resemble the parent plants. Hosta plants cross-pollinate easily, so when you use seed from your garden, you usually get new plants that are different from the parents.

Seed Organizer

Keep leftover seeds handy for next season in a 3 × 5-inch card file. Make a card for each kind of seed you plant and organize the cards by planting date. Attach small seed packets to their cards with a paper clip; store larger seeds in a separate container and use cards to hold their place in your planting lineup. Add a picture of each variety, cut from a catalog, to make your favorites even easier to locate.

GARDENER TO GARDENER

Soda-Bottle Seed Starter

I start seeds in 2-liter plastic bottles. Excess water drains away from the roots into the bottom half of the container, where you can see it. I use colored plastic bottles so that the roots are not exposed to direct sunlight.

1. Measure up 6 inches from the bottom of a 2-liter bottle and make a mark. Place a rubber band around the bottle on your mark as a guide to ensure an even cut.
2. Using scissors or a knife, cut along the rubber band and detach the top of the bottle.
3. Make a 2½-inch cut in the top piece so it can be compressed and inserted into the bottom part of the bottle. Invert the top piece into the bottom piece so the spout becomes a drain.
4. Fill the part of the bottle that has the spout with potting mix, and plant your seeds.

Lamont L. E. Jr.
Lynchburg, Virginia

Bread-Bag Tags

When I need to mark a specific color of flower for seed gathering in the fall, I attach a plastic bread-bag tab to the stem while the flower is in bloom. To save seeds from more than one color of the flower type, I use tabs with different colors or write on the tabs with a fine-point permanent marker. The tabs are also handy as plant markers, price tags at a plant sale, or a place to record pertinent information, such as height, color, and variety.

Ruth M.
Truro, Nova Scotia

Timing Transplants for Hot Climates

Most gardeners need to time their seed starting to make sure transplants aren't ready too early, or they'll become pot-bound before the weather is warm enough for planting. But gardeners in areas with blistering summer heat, such as Southern California and some parts of the Southwest, should start tomato and pepper seeds by mid-February at the latest so that the plants can get established in the garden before the hottest part of the summer.

Tips for Seed-Saving Success

Saving your own seed is a rewarding way to complete the cycle of life in your garden, and it's not difficult to do. Here are some things to keep in mind if you decide to try a seed-saving project.

■ Avoid saving seeds from hybrid plants, which usually do not produce true offspring from seed.

■ Save seeds only from strong, healthy specimens that display desired traits. Observation is key to successful seed saving. Pull up, or *rogue*, any plants that are not true to the plant characteristics.

■ Label your plants at every stage from seedling through drying to finished seed.

■ Save seeds from as many plants as possible. With self-pollinating plants, a minimum of 6 to 10 plants is necessary to maintain a wide genetic representation; 25 is even better. Seeds saved from just one self-pollinating plant will grow well, but you may be losing some background genetic material.

■ Cross-pollinating plants rely on larger populations to sustain their integrity. A minimum of 16 plants is adequate for some, although many need at least 64. Fewer numbers of cross-pollinating plants compound the presence of unexpectedly harmful genes. This can result in weak, stunted, low-vigor plants.

Chapter 10

Extending the Harvest

Eating fresh, organic produce for a lot longer than you might imagine—that's the appeal of using season extension techniques. You can't change the weather, but you can use old-fashioned and newfangled methods to encourage plants to grow earlier in spring and later in fall.

Using a coldframe is one time-tested method for extending the harvest, but today, fewer gardeners use traditional wooden coldframes and more use some type of plastic-covered plant shelter. In this chapter, you'll find plenty of great ideas for improvising cloches from a hodgepodge of household items. Other tips offer ideas for using row covers to protect plants, and one old-time method to tell you how to create an earth-sided coldframe.

Ready for something more sophisticated? You'll like the hints for setting up a hoop house over a framed raised bed and the tips from home greenhouse owners about how to use pipes, bricks, and barrels to help store heat.

Another theme of the chapter is planning and planting in summer for harvest into fall—and even winter—including strategies for starting cool-loving crops in the heat of summer.

GARDENER TO GARDENER

Slow Cook for Heat
    I heat my 4 × 6-foot mini-greenhouse with a slow-cooker filled with water. I top off the water regularly and it works fine. Because I garden in Zone 5, I use my greenhouse only to start seedlings; I don't try to use it year-round. I'm delighted to be able to start the season a little early.

    Mavis B.
    Blacksburg, Virginia

Let Your Garden Rock

If you have poor soil and a short growing season, improve your harvest by using rock in your vegetable gardens. Fashion 6-inch-high, compost-enriched beds bordered by 2-foot-wide sections of flat stones, and you'll be rewarded with earlier and better crops. Your vegetables will grow faster from the compost and increased soil temperatures. (Heat absorbed by the rocks during the day is sustained in the soil at night.) The rocks also help conserve soil moisture.

Fall-Built Bed for Early Spring Start

Raised beds warm up and dry out fast, just what you need for an early start on your spring planting. And late summer or early fall is the perfect time to build a raised bed. In late August or September, pile compost and other materials 12 to 15 inches high to form a bed of the desired size. Top the bed with some soil or fine compost. The bed will settle over winter, and it will be warm and dry weeks before your regular garden soil is ready to plant. Plant onions, lettuce, and other cool-season crops as early as March, and you'll be harvesting by June.

Search for Winter Cheaters

Wherever you live, if you want to stretch the season, seek out the little islands of warmth in your yard. Look for the places where the ground freezes last in fall and thaws first in spring. Masonry walls are excellent winter cheaters. They act as heat sinks, storing warmth during the day and slowly releasing it at night.

Mulch in Fall, Plastic in Spring

To get the earliest possible start on planting, prevent the soil from freezing over winter by piling a 1-foot-deep blanket of organic mulch—such as leaves or grass clippings—on beds in fall. In late March, rake away the mulch (and sometimes snow) to expose the soil to sun.

    Lay a clear plastic sheet over the cleared bed, and seal the edges with soil or rocks. The plastic layer traps the sun's heat and quickly warms the beds. Lay the plastic over rough ground rather than on smoothly raked soil because air pockets enhance the warming effect. (Place a few fist-size rocks beneath the plastic to create such pockets if there aren't many.)

After 2 weeks, uncover the bed, cultivate, and replace the plastic sheet until the soil temperature reaches 45°F or warmer. Then it's time to plant peas, lettuce, beans, potatoes, and possibly sweet corn. Replace the clear plastic to keep the beds warm. Check them daily. Seeds usually will sprout in 7 to 10 days.

Frost-Defeating Fencerow

Gardens located at the bottom of a slope are prone to frost damage. If you can't change the location of your garden, try planting a dense fencerow along the slope uphill from the garden. This fencerow will break the downhill rush of cold air that can nip your garden on chilly nights in spring and fall (or even summer in some high-elevation areas). The fencerow will also benefit your garden by providing food and shelter for birds.

Slope Soil for Solar Surge

Subtle changes in your garden layout can pay off in faster soil warming in spring. Lay out your raised beds to face south and slope the soil 5 to 10 degrees toward the south to capture even more of the sun's heat. Because of its low angle, the spring sun strikes the earth obliquely. A sloped bed is more perpendicular to the sun and therefore receives the rays more directly. Framing your sloped beds with rocks, bricks, or cinder blocks will also help with warming because they act as heat sinks.

Because of settling, the beds may lose their tilt by summer, but by then, the sun will be high overhead and your soil will be plenty warm.

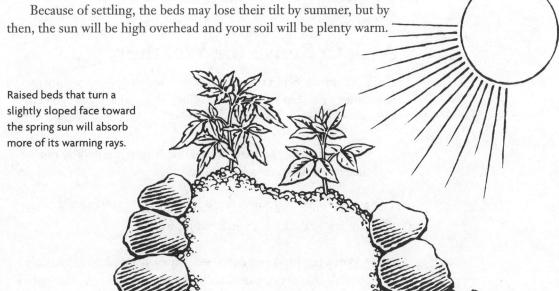

Raised beds that turn a slightly sloped face toward the spring sun will absorb more of its warming rays.

Electrify Your Soil

Get a jump-start on spring by heating your soil with electric heating cables. Use a self-regulating type of cable, such as the kind used to keep exposed water pipes from freezing.

These cables are available at hardware stores and home centers. You will need to buy and install a fused plug and an end seal for the end of the cable that will be buried in the soil. Instructions for doing this will come with the components. (Make sure to follow the instructions carefully.)

Before laying the cable in spring, prepare your soil. Then, snake the cable throughout your planting area, spacing the links about a foot apart. The cable is flexible, but you may need to pin it down with tent stakes or wire pins if you make sharp curves.

Push the cable a few inches into the soil, then plant in the foot-wide area between the cable lines. You can turn on the cable only at night, or let it run during the day, too. Once cold weather is over, pull up the cable gently to avoid damaging nearby roots, clean it, and store it until next year.

Early Bucket Tomatoes

Eager to have some tomatoes ready to pick by July 4th? Start a few plants early in 5-gallon buckets. Set the plants outdoors during the day, but bring them indoors overnight whenever temperatures below 40°F are predicted.

A Sixth Sense for Weather

Can you "smell frost in the air?" It takes time to develop sensitivity to weather signs, but it's worth the effort. Here are some weather signs worth noting.

- Some gardeners have observed that frost is often likely during the last week before a full moon.

- If the sky is clear, the air is calm and still, and there is no breeze blowing as dusk falls, watch out for frost!

- When temperatures dip to 40°F by early evening, it's entirely possible that they'll plummet to the freezing point by the early hours of morning.

Down in the Trenches

To hasten your sweet corn harvest, plant your sweet corn seeds in trenches about 4 inches deep. Dig the trenches a week or so before you plan to plant and cover them with clear plastic. This helps warm the soil, which is essential for faster corn seed germination. When the soil is warm, uncover the trenches, plant your seeds, water them well, and then put the plastic back in place. Leave it there until the tips of the corn seedlings just touch the plastic. By then, the weather should be warm enough for the corn to survive without cover.

Kelp Spray for Frostproof Plants

Believe it or not, many growers report that spraying plants with kelp solution can help the plants tolerate frost better. The secret may be that seaweed helps the plant compensate for the growth-inhibiting effects of low temperatures by supplying vital elements for growth that the plant would otherwise be unable to make for itself.

If you live near the coast, you can collect seaweed for your garden and even make your own spray solution. Most gardeners, though, will find it more convenient to purchase a kelp concentrate to make the solution. Granular kelp may also be applied to the soil, but the foliar spray is more rapidly absorbed. Frequent, light applications of the kelp are more effective than occasional heavy treatments.

The Great Melon Cover-Up

Melon production can be disappointing in short-season areas. To maximize your melon harvest, warm things up by covering beds with plastic (black, clear, or IRT—infrared transmitting film) and your plants with spun-bonded polyester (floating row cover) or slitted clear plastic.

Sheer Substitute for Row Covers

Sheer curtains can go from window covers to row covers to extend your growing season. It's easy to buy gauzy sheer curtains secondhand at garage sales for pocket change. They make a reasonable substitute for row covers for short durations. To make a simple protective cover for fall crops, fasten the curtains to sections of 4-foot welded wire fence about 3 feet wide. You can clip the curtains to the wire fence using clothespins. Arc the fencing over the plants you want to protect, and anchor the sections in place with stakes made by bending cut sections of clothes hangers.

Weighted Row Cover

Draping floating row cover over a bed of plants is a fast, easy way to provide a few degrees of frost protection. However, the cover won't do any good if it blows off during the night. To keep the cover in place, fill some plastic gallon jugs nearly full with water. Put the caps back on and set the jugs at intervals along the edges of the row cover.

Easy Cloche Keeps Out Cold

If you have $5 and a screwdriver, you can build a simple A-frame cloche that will protect low-growing plants from spring or fall cold. All you need is some inexpensive 1 × 3 furring strips of whatever length will work best for your garden and a few pieces of hardware. To make the frame: Simply butt the ends of two long furring strips against two 2-foot sections. To make sure the boards are perpendicular, measure diagonally from corner to corner—when the distances are the same, the corners are square.

Join the boards with bent framing plates, which you can buy—unbent—from building supply centers for less than 25 cents. Screw the plates into place on both sides of the board, using ⅝-inch Phillips-head screws. Make two rectangular frames.

Cover the top side of each frame with inexpensive 6-mil plastic sheeting, stapling it in place. Attach hinges to a long edge of each frame, and your frame will fold flat for easy storage.

Put Row Covers in Their Place

The perfect tool for firmly anchoring both plastic mulch and floating row cover is a wheel hoe equipped with a furrower, or moldboard. Start by running the wheel hoe down each side of a bed, keeping the vertical edge next to the bed and throwing soil away from the bed. Unroll the row cover over the plants and anchor the edge into the furrow you opened by backfilling with the soil you just turned over.

Umbrella Cloche

Broken umbrella? Remove the fabric from the umbrella frame and recover the frame with floating row cover to make a cloche. And when you don't need it for covering plants, you can call it into duty as a handy gadget for keeping flies off food at a picnic.

Avoid the Crunch

Clear plastic 2-liter soda bottles with the bottoms cut off serve to protect seedlings from the cold early in the season. But the bottles can also serve another purpose. On very cold nights when the bottles alone won't do the job, bury the bottled-covered plants under a thick layer of loose straw—up to 1 foot deep. The bottles will protect the seedlings from being crushed by the straw. If you don't have straw on hand, try covering the plants with a blanket for insulation.

A Sackful of Frost Protection

Hang an old burlap sack or large plastic garbage bag in your garage or shed, and stash it full of berry baskets, coffee cans, plastic flowerpots, and bottomless gallon milk jugs. If frost threatens in spring, toss the sack in your garden cart and head out to the garden in the evening to cover seedlings that might be damaged by frost. For very tender crops like cucumbers, melons, and tomatoes, try draping a clear plastic dropcloth over plants in late afternoon. It will trap heat and thus defeat the frost.

Anchored Milk Jugs

Covering cold-sensitive transplants with plastic milk jugs is a popular way of encouraging growth and preventing frost damage early in the season. To keep these jugs in place, cut around the bottom of the jugs on three sides, leaving a hinged flap. After you put the minigreenhouse over a young plant, hold it in place by weighing down the flap with a mound of soil or a rock. These jugs should last for 2 years before the plastic breaks down.

Jug Insulators for Plants

Opaque plastic jugs filled with water can help protect your plants from an ill-timed hard freeze. Use dark-colored jugs, such as those for laundry detergent or antifreeze. They will absorb heat better than clear jugs. Set three filled jugs around a seedling or small transplant and four around a larger plant. Throw a blanket over the top, and you can bring plants safely through a night when the temperature drops as low as 24°F. That can give you as much as a full month's head start on planting warm-season crops.

Jug Protection

I like using jugs in the garden—big jugs, small jugs. My husband gave me the idea; he suggested filling up containers with water, and he was certain this would keep the plants from freezing. Here in California, using water-filled jugs protects my plants down to about 25°F, depending on whether the previous day was sunny. If so, these jugs can absorb a lot of heat, and thus keep the plants a tad warmer during the night.

In a greenhouse, one way to generate heat is to make a nice, fresh compost pile under your beds. As the compost cooks, it releases heat into the greenhouse. Last winter, I kept a tomato alive with just the greenhouse compost (coldest nights got to about 25°F, and I used no jugs).

Jacki W.
Kernville, California

Balancing Heat

I've had good results this past year with my 300-square-foot Quonset-style greenhouse. One electric radiator heater kept it frost-free through a mild winter at 5,400 feet in suburban Denver. The house has double plastic walls. I've corrected one original flaw—30 water-filled barrels were sitting directly on the ground, but now I've raised them on frames of 2 × 4s. (Ever sleep out on the cold ground without a foam pad? Chilly, isn't it?) I grew lettuce all winter and started seedlings on heat mats. I estimate I spent about $20 a month heating it during December and January. My main problem is avoiding overheating on sunny days. When it's 60°F outside, it can be 100°F in the greenhouse.

*John M.
Naperville, Illinois*

Bag Some Heat

Keep early transplants warm by lining plant rows with dark plastic bags filled with leaves. Cover the rows at night, bags and all, with cloth or plastic sheeting. The dark bags absorb heat during the day and release it under the sheeting at night.

Sleepover in the Garden

When an Arctic blast threatens to bring a surge of superchilled air to your garden, a sheet of plastic just won't cut it. For these times, it's a good idea to have some old sleeping bags on hand (you can buy them cheaply at garage and yard sales). Keep them stashed in your garden shed, and throw them across coldframes or sturdy wire supports over a garden bed. Then put your plastic over the sleeping bags to prevent them from soaking up moisture from heavy frost.

Bare-Bones Protection for Fall Crops

One simple way to protect leafy greens and other fall crops from frost is to assemble a simple cover from scrap wire and clear plastic. Bend the ends of long pieces of stiff wire down at 90-degree angles to form flat-topped hoops. Push the ends of the wires into the ground along the edges of a bed until the flat tops of the hoop are just above the plant's tops, then cover the hoops with plastic. Weight the plastic with rocks or plastic jugs filled with water.

Split-Season Planning

The heat of July too often brings the activities in the vegetable garden to a close. July is the dividing line between two parts of an active gardening season, each consisting of about 90 days: April–May–June and July–August–September.

Some time in late March, gardeners set aside time to prepare for early spring crops. In July, or a little before, it's time to make preparations for a fall garden. The wise gardener keeps both of these time periods in mind and uses them to advantage. The unwise gardener, on the other hand, takes it easy during midsummer, harvests what there is, and reaps only half of what might have been harvested.

Think Deeply about Fall Crops

When it's planting time for seeds and transplants for fall gardens, the weather is often hot and dry. Help crops handle drought conditions by planting a little deeper than in the spring. If rain is lacking, be sure to soak seedbeds and young plants.

Allow much more space between plants than you would in a spring garden. With moisture at a premium in late summer, crowded conditions lead to water stress and slowed growth.

Find New Favorites for Fall

Once you get the hang of fall gardening, you may want to expand your palate of crops. Here are some out-of-the-ordinary crops that will thrive in cold weather.

Overwintering cauliflower. Gardeners in mild winter areas can grow cauliflowers such as the heirloom variety 'Purple Cape' over the winter. These cold-loving cauliflowers don't even begin to form heads until they've been exposed to frost, so in mild winter areas, start plants indoors in July and transplant them out early in September. They'll be ready for harvest by late February.

Celeriac. This crop is a close relative of celery that forms a large, turniplike root that you can eat raw or cooked. Plant it outdoors in June to harvest in late fall (it takes as long as 200 days to mature).

Corn salad. Also called mâche, this nutty-flavored salad rosette is sown in fall and overwinters with minimal protection even in sub-freezing temperatures. Mild winter days perk up its leaves for fresh salad fixings. Even as far north as Zone 4, you can sow this crop in late August for a fall harvest.

Radicchio. Radicchio is a red-headed chicory; it's a salad green that you don't want to eat until it has weathered a frost—or at least until low temperatures bring out its best flavor. In areas with cold winters (Zone 6 and colder), plant radicchio in early summer, then cut back the plants around Labor Day. They'll resprout and be ready for harvest a month or so later. In warmer areas, plant radicchio in fall for spring harvest.

*Hoophouse
Testimonial*

*In spring, we get an
8-week jump on tomatoes in
an unheated hoop house. We
put down black plastic mulch,
then put on clear plastic and
let that sit for about 10 days
(more if not sunny; less if
sunny) until the soil warms to
60°F. Then we put in the
plants and put Wallo'Waters
around them. We also have
many 5-gallon buckets of
water in the hoophouse (at
least eight) plus a 50-gallon
tank from a defunct water
softener. We keep the plastic on
until a few weeks after the last
frost date then take it off and
let the tomatoes live outdoors
for the rest of their lives.*

*In fall, we can extend the
tomato season by 4 to 6 weeks,
but not longer because of the
cold and also because there
is not enough light after
mid-November to stimulate
tomatoes to flower and set
fruit (same with peppers and
eggplant).*

*Lucy G.
New Paris, Ohio*

Is There Still Time to Plant _____?

How can you tell exactly which varieties you still have time to plant and mature in your fall garden? It's easy! Just calculate how many frost-free days you have left, then subtract 14 days from that number to compensate for the shorter, cooler days at the end of the season. If the days-to-maturity of the variety in question is less than the number you calculated, then it's fine to plant. Follow this formula and your crops should be 90 percent grown by the first frost, and they should be able to handle "cold storage" in your garden well.

For example, let's say it's July 15 and the first frost date in your zone is September 15. You have 60 frost-free days left; subtract 14 for that end-of-the-season allowance and you'll see that you still have 46 days—enough time to plant, for example, 'Kentucky Wonder' bush beans (45 days) or 'Goldrush' zucchini (45 days), but not 'Derby' bush beans (57 days).

Planting Tips for Hot Soil

Spinach and lettuce are great crops for fall gardens, but it can be a challenge to get them to germinate in hot, late-summer soil. For example, spinach won't germinate when soil temperature is over 85°F. Try these techniques for coaxing the seeds to grow.

- Soak spinach seed for a few hours, then place the seeds between damp paper towels and refrigerate them for several days before planting.

- Store lettuce seed in the freezer for a day or two, then presoak it before planting.

- Carrots can take up to 3 weeks to germinate in hot soil (by then, weeds may have overtaken the seedbed). The solution is to pre-sprout carrot seeds before planting. Soak the seeds overnight, then place the seeds between damp paper towels and put them in a plastic bag. Check them daily. When the first three or four seeds sprout, carefully sow all the seeds into your garden and water well.

- Cool the soil before planting by setting scrap pieces of plywood on top of bricks over the garden bed where you plan to plant. Remove the plywood each night so the soil is exposed to the lower air temperatures.

A Simple Hoophouse

Unheated tunnels of plastic, whether knee-high or large enough for a person to work inside, make year-round harvesting possible. You can assemble a low hoophouse in just a couple of hours, at a cost of $1 or less per square foot. Here's how.

1. Prepare a south-facing garden bed, 2 feet wide × 12 feet long.

2. On each long side of the bed, drive four 18-inch-long rebar stakes 12 inches into the ground, leaving 6 inches exposed. The stakes should be spaced 4 feet apart.

3. Fit 10-foot lengths of ¾-inch PVC pipe over the rebar stakes to form arches 3 feet high across the bed.

4. For added stability, stretch nylon cord or baling wire from hoop to hoop, wrapping it around the top of each one, and stake the wire at both ends.

5. Cover the framework with a 12 × 20-foot sheet of heavy clear plastic, anchoring it along the soil line with bricks, rocks, or soil. Leave enough plastic at each end to fold together and clip shut.

To access the bed, simply pull back one side of the plastic covering. This hoophouse is easy to take apart for storage during the regular growing season.

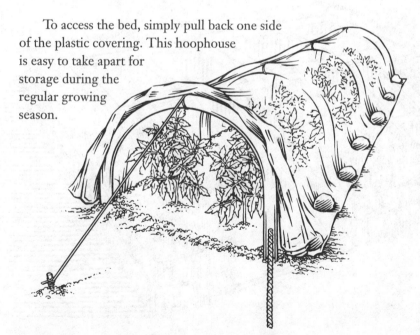

A simple low hoophouse extends the season in spring and fall, adding several weeks of extra harvest enjoyment to your gardening year.

Raised Bed Hoophouse

I have twelve 4 × 8 wood-framed raised beds and they are all made so hoops can be put up over them. My husband attached ¾-inch pipe clamps every 1½ feet on the inside of each 8-foot-board. Then I bend ½-inch-diameter black plumbing plastic (cut in different lengths depending how much height I want) into the hoops (five per bed). I drape floating row cover or plastic over the hoops. This year I ordered some plastic clips from Charley's Greenhouse Supply to help hold things in place. I sometimes attach an 8-foot furring strip to the tops of the hoops to give them more stability in the wind. I use my hoophouse to get a jump on planting. I have started tomatoes as early as March.

I sometimes put 2-gallon jugs of water under the covers to help keep things warm at night or if we get snow.

Karen B.
Glens Falls, New York

Hay-Powered Hotbed

If you live in an area with cool summers where growing cantaloupes and watermelons is an exercise in frustration, try raising your success rate with a hay-powered hotbed. All you need is some bales of rotting hay and old window frames. Procure some old hay bales from a local farmer—ones that have gotten wet and are rotting and warm. Put three or four bales end-to-end in a line, and then set other bales at right angles to the line, forming three attached U-shaped frames. Mulch the ground in the openings with about 6 inches of compost. Set one window on top of each opening and tilt down another on the open south side. In effect, you've created three miniature heated greenhouses, in which the temperatures in the protected spaces can be as much as 20°F higher than the outside air temperatures.

You can use these spaces for starting a range of warm-weather crops from seed early in the season, including tomatoes, eggplant, peppers, and sunflowers. Start your cantaloupe and melon seedlings in the frame, too. In late May, add sand and more soil, and the vines will thrive. In June, when the weather is warm enough to suit the plants, dismantle the coldframes and use the rotting bales to mulch your garden.

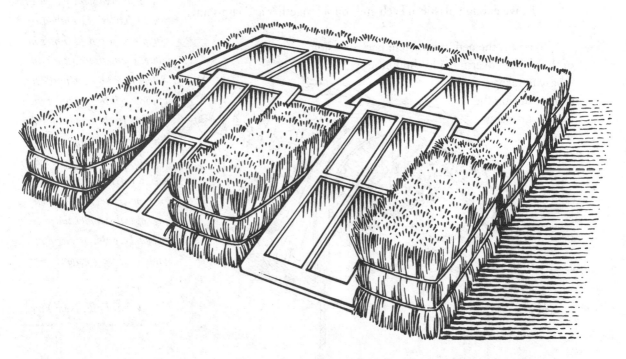

Heat from rotting hay supercharges the atmosphere in this improvised hotbed, so you can grow even the tenderest long-season crops in cool-summer areas like the Pacific Northwest.

Hay Frame

Improvise a coldframe with bales of hay, old bricks, and clear plastic sheeting. Build a three-sided frame out of the hay bales, using two layers of bales for the back wall and one layer on the sides. Lay bricks on the floor of the frame and stack them against the back wall (they'll retain heat). Drape plastic over the top, using bricks to weigh it down. In the spring, when you don't need the coldframe anymore, you can use the hay for mulch. Remember to place the bales so the binding twine is on the sides, not the ground, or the twine will rot, making it difficult to move the bales.

Once-Living Mulch Covers Crops

Another way to shelter hardy greens like spinach over the winter is to use cuttings from a cover crop as mulch. Plant your greens and a crop of oats together in late summer. After broadcasting the oats and raking them in, overseed spinach in rows. By the time the spinach greens have four or five leaves, the oats will be about 5 to 8 inches tall. When the oats winter-kill, they will cover the greens.

For a thicker, denser mat, try using a mixture of ryegrass with clover instead of oats.

A variation of this method for fast-growing spinach is to start the spinach in mid-August, so you can make one or two cuttings in fall. Then, about mid-September, rake in spring oats between the spinach rows. The oats will grow 6 to 8 inches tall before they're killed by cold temperatures and become a protective mulch for the spinach.

Winterkilled oats provide an insulating cover for spinach or other hardy greens through winter.

Winter Beet Boost

If you love beet greens as much as the beets, you can have them at home all winter, as we do in cold and snowy New Jersey. At the end of last year, I gently pulled some beets from the garden, potted them up individually, and put them in my "cold room." This is a southwest-facing, unheated room with windows.

Throughout winter, I watered them sparingly and picked the outer leaves off as they got big enough to eat. I steamed the leaves for about 5 minutes right after picking. The leaves kept coming up from the roots for months. Although you'd need a lot of pots for any great quantity, the occasional beet-green boost I got was a real winter blessing.

*Sally A. W.
High Bridge, New Jersey*

Winter Crops in a Coldframe

Few gardeners make full use of a coldframe. We pop seedlings into the little shelter to harden them off before the big shift to the garden, and that's about it. Yet in the deep of winter and earliest spring when the grocery store offers only pale, plastic-wrapped produce, the coldframe is truly at its best. For gardeners daring enough to use one at that time, it becomes the source of crackling-fresh, delicious gourmet greens, the basis for vitamin-rich salads. Many varieties of lettuce, kale, oriental greens, chicory, endive, spinach, cress, and mâche are good candidates for winter coldframe gardening.

To keep these crops growing even longer, try lining the walls of your coldframe with black-painted milk jugs filled with water. The jugs will store heat during the day and release it at night. Sometime in December, your plants may just stop growing. When you notice this, gradually mulch around and over the plants inside the frame and cover the outside with an insulating blanket topped with straw or snow. Re-open the frame in late February or early March and your plants will resume growth.

Nature's Own Root Cellar

Want to enjoy garden-fresh carrots, beets, and other root crops all winter? No need for a special root cellar—you can store these crops right in your garden. Just before the ground freezes in late fall, mulch your root crops with a heavy layer of leaves or straw (pile it on about 1 foot thick). The mulch cover prevents the ground from freezing, especially when snow provides an extra insulating layer on top. When you need some veggies, just push aside snow and mulch and dig out as much as you need. Replace the mulch to protect the remaining roots. Other crops that store well this way include parsnips, turnips, celery, rutabagas, cabbages, leeks, kale, and spinach.

Chapter 11

Creating Great Container Gardens

Have you ever grown a tomato plant upside down? Or tended a banana tree in your living room? You can try either or both of these creative gardening projects, plus many more, when you garden in containers.

Growing plants in containers may be the only option for gardeners with limited space, but whether you try container gardening out of necessity or just for fun, you're sure to enjoy the results. With the wide range of small-size cultivars available and numerous low-cost containers, you can express nearly every gardening urge through a container garden.

This chapter focuses on some of the basics of container gardening, and it presents some unusual container garden projects. Tips include how to find inexpensive sources of containers, how to use lightweight fillers to make large containers less weighty, and some great ideas for keeping containers watered while you're away.

As for projects, beyond the upside-down tomato and the banana tree, look for ideas on forcing layers of bulbs in containers, fashioning a mini tree centerpiece from a fragrant herb plant, and harvesting coffee beans from your own potted coffee plant.

Pot Parameters

Matching plants to the correct-size pot is a crucial part of success with container gardens. Small plants, like lettuce and chives, can get by in a 6-inch-diameter (1½-quart) pot, but they'll probably do much better in a container that's 8 inches across (3 quarts). They'll surely thrive in a 10-inch (6-quart) pot.

For large plants, like peppers and tomatoes, think big. Peppers require a pot that holds 2 to 3 gallons of soil (about 12 inches across). Most tomatoes need at least a 5-gallon pot; commercial ones this size usually run 15 inches in diameter.

You can create containers from recyclable items. Plastic 5-gallon food buckets often discarded by delis, supermarkets, and bakeries are great pots. Just be sure to punch drainage holes in the bottom. You can cut 55-gallon plastic barrels in half to make 25-gallon plant containers. You can also plant a whole garden in an inexpensive plastic wading pool or a cement-mixing tray.

Bottom or Sides?

Drainage holes are a must for a plant container, but should the holes be in the bottom of the container or on the sides? In some cases, holes punched about 2 inches up from the bottom rim of the container may be just right. Positioning drainage holes this way creates a reservoir that holds extra moisture in the bottom of the container. In a hot climate, vegetables will thrive on the extra moisture, and you won't have to water as often. If you try this technique, be sure to use a very loose growing mix.

Build a Wooden Window Box

Although you'll find plastic window boxes galore at garden centers, it's still a fun and relatively simple project to build your own wooden version. Good-quality pine boards are fine for building a window box. (Avoid spruce; it is much less durable.) Although somewhat more expensive, both cedar and California redwood are excellent choices, as they have far greater moisture resistance and will give more lasting service. Use boards at least 1 inch thick; thinner wood is likely to warp when it gets wet.

Window boxes can vary in size. Minimum inner width should be 7 inches to allow enough space for at least two rows of plants (generally an upright kind in the back, and a hanging type to spill over the outer edge). Best inside depth is also 7 to 8 inches. A shallower box will not provide sufficient room for roots, and the soil mix will dry out too quickly.

Use screws rather than nails to fasten the box together—preferably brass screws because they won't rust. For drainage, drill a series of ½-inch holes in the bottom of the box, spaced 6 to 9 inches apart and alternating in two long rows.

Containers on the Cheap

You don't need to spend hundreds of dollars on pots for the garden and patio. Instead, use your imagination and you'll keep those dollars in your wallet. An old watering can or a galvanized tub can add a dash of creativity to an otherwise boring deck. A salvaged animal trough can take on new life when planted with annuals such as impatiens. And a terra-cotta chimney flue has a pleasing rectangular shape and can raise an arrangement of succulents such as hens-and-chicks to new heights.

Location Is Everything

Think carefully about the location of container gardens. It they're out of sight, will they also be out of mind? It's easy to kill potted plants with neglect if they're set in spots that you don't see very often. Try creating a large container garden along the path leading to your front door. You'll pass those plants every day, so you'll be likely to water and care for them right when they need it.

The Plastic Bag Garden

Fill heavy-duty (4-mil-thick) trash bags with potting mix to create contained growing beds on a patio—or in a garden with truly terrible soil. Good ingredients for the mix include compost, peat moss, coarse sand, and perlite. Be sure to poke drainage holes in the bottoms of the "bag beds" before filling the bags. You can grow all kinds of crops and plants in these growing bags, including pumpkins.

Best for Hanging Baskets

Try these beauties for attractive indoor hanging baskets.

Lipstick plants (*Aeschynanthus* spp.)
Angelwing begonia cultivars (*Begonia* 'Tom Ment 1',
    'Orange Rubra', and 'Elaine')
Columneas (*Columnea* spp.)
Kalanchoes (*Kalanchoe pumila, K. uniflora*)
Ivy geranium (*Pelargonium peltatum*)

"Peanut" Planters

Instead of throwing away the Styrofoam "peanuts" that come in packages, I recycle them to provide drainage in the bottom of plant containers. Whether I am repotting houseplants or making containers for the outside deck, I first put a 1- to 3-inch layer of the peanuts in the bottom of the container. They weigh almost nothing, so it's easier to lift and move large planters.

Rosalie S.
Shelburne, Vermont

Container Soil Specifics

Commercial soilless potting mixes generally contain mostly peat moss or shredded wood, with some vermiculite and/or perlite (natural mineral substances) added to help hold moisture and for better aeration. But since these mixes contain few plant nutrients, mix it half-and-half with equal parts mature compost and your absolute best garden soil when you fill pots. The compost will provide slow-release nutrients and introduce its innate disease-fighting microorganisms to the mix. And your own soil particles will help hold those nutrients in place until the plant roots take them up.

If you need lots of mix for big containers, find a nursery willing to sell you some in bulk. Or make your own by mixing 1 part loamy soil (not too much sand or too much clay) with 1 part mature compost. If you can't get that much compost, substitute aged shredded leaves.

Some other materials can make useful additions to homemade potting mixes. Coarse (not fine) sand can improve drainage and/or anchor tall plants so they don't blow over in strong winds. Perlite makes a mix lighter, and composted manure provides much-needed nutrients.

If you're growing nitrogen-hungry crops like corn, lettuce, and potatoes in containers, add 1 to 2 tablespoons of bloodmeal to 5 gallons of soil-compost mix. Eastern gardeners should add about ⅓ tablespoon of sul-po-mag (an organic fertilizer) to 5 gallons of soil-compost mix because eastern soils tend to lack magnesium. Container mixes made with western soil should be fortified with ⅙ tablespoon of sulfate of potash to 5 gallons of mix to supply potassium. To add calcium to a mix, include ¾ tablespoon of gypsum per 5 gallons of mix.

6-Pack Planting

Save potting mix—and your back muscles—by using aluminum cans to take up some of the space in supersize planters. Shallow-rooted annuals—and even some perennials—are unlikely to root deeply enough to reach the bottom of a very large container, so filling the entire pot with potting soil is a waste of time and money. But by filling the bottom of a large container with empty cans you'll reduce the amount of soil mix you need. Plus, the planters will be much easier to move. Other lightweight fillers that work well (and that you may have lying around your yard) include pinecones and sweet-gum balls.

A Fishy Solution

A fish tank makes an excellent companion for houseplants. The water that evaporates from it provides humidity for nearby plants. And when you clean the tank, water your plants with the dirty water from the tank. The fish waste in it is an excellent natural plant food.

Tub-Watering Wisdom

Watering patterns for large patio containers, such as half-barrels, change as the plants grow. Early in the season, the soil in these large containers tends to hold more water than the small young plants in them can use, and so the soil may not dry out enough—especially during cool, cloudy periods. To prevent this, always water sparingly at this time, or grow your container plants in small to medium-size containers for a few weeks; you can transplant them to big tubs when they have developed a large root system.

The larger your container plants grow, the more water they will need. Try to keep your soil mix evenly moist, and avoid running excess water through the pot because this will wash out nutrients your plants need to thrive.

By the end of the summer you'll probably have to water at least once and maybe even twice a day, depending on how large your containers are and how many plants you put in them. If you're the forgetful type, consider using an automatic timer and a drip irrigation setup to be safe.

Lighten Up

To increase the chances that your tropical houseplants will produce flowers or fruit, consider giving them supplemental light. For flowering and fruiting tropicals, wide-spectrum lights work best. By supplying both blue ("cool") and red ("warm") light, they simulate natural ultraviolet light.

A less expensive way to combine red and blue light is simply to buy both cool and warm white fluorescent tubes. Try using four fluorescent tubes positioned no closer than 6 inches above the plants. As the plants grow, raise the lights to maintain the minimum distance.

Another option is a high-intensity sodium or halogen light, the kind used by many commercial growers. These are more expensive than fluorescent tubes but will probably give you even better results.

GARDENER TO GARDENER

Fighting Fungus Gnats

I have over 20 houseplants and more fungus gnats than you can imagine! I tried soapy water, which didn't seem to faze them. I also tried Bt (Bacillus thuringiensis) and definitely saw signs of improvement for a few weeks, but they soon rebuilt their population. I e-mailed our state Extension office and was told that fungus gnats are a sign of overwatering. The agent recommended that I allow my pots to dry out completely between waterings—to the point of leaf wilting—as fungus gnat larvae cannot survive in a dry climate. Now I only water when the soil's completely dry. This has really reduced the fungus gnat population. I also use window flycatchers to catch the adult fungus gnats. These clear traps are coated with an adhesive that insects stick to. They cost $2 for four traps—pretty inexpensive for the work they do.

Vicki N.
Gaffney, South Carolina

Pill Bug Cleanup Crew

I raise pill bugs in my indoor container plants to help get rid of the plants' dead matter. I also like to see pill bugs in my garden because they eat decaying material, turning it into a fine, finished compost. Gardeners occasionally have trouble with pill bugs attacking living plants, but in most normal garden conditions, pill bugs leave fresh plants alone.

Richard N.
Carmel, California

Pots That Self-Water When You're Away

The biggest problem with a container garden is that it often requires daily watering. So, does that mean you can't take a summer vacation without risking a total loss? No! Try one of these self-watering techniques to keep your container plantings thriving when you have to be away for a few days.

■ Slip a plastic saucer or shallow pan under each pot; water the plants well and fill the saucers just before you leave.

■ Build a watering reservoir into your containers. Start with a 5-gallon bucket or other container that doesn't have holes in the bottom. Drill drainage holes 2 or 3 inches up on the sides of the bucket. When you water deeply, you'll create a self-contained reservoir of moisture at the very base of the container.

■ Make a self-watering system out of an old T-shirt. Tear the shirt (or other rag) into long strips. Bury one end of a strip several inches deep in the soil of a pot, and hang the other end into a pan or bucket of water set beside the pot. The cloth will act as a wick and draw moisture into the soil in the plant pot. Set a rock on the strips to keep the wind from blowing them out of the pan of water.

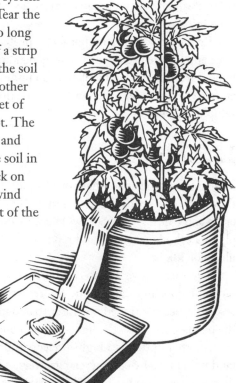

A strip of cloth buried in the soil of a pot acts as a wick to draw water from a reservoir, supplying steady moisture for several days.

Shield Container Gardens from the Cold

When you have a small city of containers on your apartment porch, it may not be possible to bring all of them inside if frost threatens. Instead, create a protected space by suspending sheets of clear plastic from the porch ceiling in front of your plants.

A Tree from the Supermarket

You can turn an avocado from the grocery store into a beautiful houseplant by following this simple procedure.

1. Select a fully ripened avocado. Summer varieties are dark brown when ripe; winter strains will be bright green. The fruit should yield slightly when touched.

2. Slit the avocado and carefully remove the pit.

3. Wash the pit free of flesh. Insert four sturdy toothpicks into the flat, fat side of the pit.

4. Place the pit into a container of water with the flat side down; the toothpicks will support the pit.

5. Put the container in warm, filtered light. Monitor the water level; the bottom ¼ inch of the pit should be in water at all times.

6. In 2 to 6 weeks, the avocado will develop a main root. When you see small hair roots developing, it's time to pot the pit.

7. Fill a clean 6- to 10-inch clay pot with a standard potting mix that contains a small amount of sand. Remove the toothpicks from the pit, position the pit in the pot, allowing the top third of the pit to show above the potting mix.

Your tree may grow about 1 foot each year if you keep it in bright light (full sunlight isn't needed), water it with tepid water, feed it with liquid fish emulsion solution every 2 to 3 months, transplant it as needed, and never allow it to get too cold.

An Herbal Centerpiece

A myrtle or rosemary topiary "tree" is a great centerpiece and conversation starter. Start by creating a "standard" as described here, and if you enjoy it, move on to trying more intricate shapes.

1. Choose a plant with one straight stem at least 4 inches long. Pot in a 4-inch-diameter container with a drainage hole, using a potting mix that drains well. Push a 16-inch support stake into the soil next to the plant.

2. Use a small shears to remove side branches from the main stem to form a "trunk." Secure the trunk to the stake with twist ties, using one tie for about every 2 inches of stem. The ties should be secure but allow room for the trunk to grow.

3. As the plant grows, continue to prune the lowest-growing branches and secure the stem. Allow the top to grow.

4. About 6 months later, when the stem has reached the top of the stake, use scissors to snip off the growing tip. Allow four to six sets of leaves (and any developing shoots) at the top of the stem to remain intact, and remove any branches below. This encourages the development of side branches.

5. To create the "head" of the standard, trim the side branches as they grow, allowing four or more sets of leaves to remain. Shape the crown into a sphere of foliage. Maintain the shape of the standard by periodically trimming the crown as needed.

Repeatedly trimming and shaping a potted woody herb such as rosemary leads to a topiary "tree" with an exquisite form and fragrance.

An Italian Deck Garden

Dream up a theme for a garden of containers on a deck, such as an Italian garden. It could feature tomatoes, sweet pimiento peppers, and classic Italian herbs like oregano, rosemary, marjoram, and flat-leaf parsley. Plant the tomatoes and peppers in the center of large (about 12 × 24-inch) containers supported by wire cages. Plant 'Miniature Globe' basil in each corner and other herbs along the edges. For a colorful flourish, tuck in a couple of nasturtiums or fragrant 'Lemon Gem' marigolds, both of which have edible flowers that add a nice touch to salads. Be sure to include some leaf lettuce, and you can make a fresh salad any time.

Be creative when it comes to themes: You could also grow a pesto garden, salsa garden, mixed greens garden, or medicinal herb garden. The possibilities are almost endless.

Yummy Tree Tomatoes

For a truly novel fruit that tastes something like strawberry-raspberry custard, try the tree tomato or tamarillo (*Cyphomandra betacea*). It bears egg-shaped red fruit the first year if grown from cuttings. Like our common garden tomato, tree tomatoes are nutritious, supplying vitamins A and C. Eat the 2-inch fruits plain, or use them to perk up salads or to make jams.

The tree tomato will grow well in a bright, south-facing window. Although you can grow your own plant from seed, it may take several years to fruit. For faster fruit, buy a plant that has already started from a cutting.

A vigorous grower, the plant can shoot up 1½ feet high the first year, and up to 5 feet when mature. It's sturdy, though, so you won't have to stake it. To help keep it compact, cut it back as often as necessary. Fruit forms on new growth, so occasional pruning won't hurt fruit production.

The plant doesn't need pollination to set fruit, but moving it outdoors for the summer where it will be pollinated by bees will lead to more abundant fruiting. While it's outdoors, be sure to water regularly during prolonged dry spells to prevent the fruit from dropping. (The trees are shallow-rooted and sensitive to drought.)

A word of caution: Although the small flowers are fragrant, the large leaves have the musky odor characteristic of this family. So if the smell of tomato leaves bothers you, you may not want a tamarillo in your house.

GARDENER TO GARDENER

Topsy-Turvy Tomatoes

Have you ever grown tomatoes upside down in a bucket? I did it 2 years ago and it worked great! I used empty cat litter buckets (5-gallon size) with handles and lids. I cut a hole in the bottom of the bucket about 3 inches across, shook most of the dirt off the roots of the tomato plant, and worked the roots through the hole so that they were inside the bucket and the plant was hanging out of the bottom. (I laid the bucket on a table while doing this.) Then I added potting mix until the bucket was about half full and hung it from a STRONG hook anchored into a heavy wooden beam on the south side of my front porch.

I wired the handle of the bucket to the hook to secure it against strong wind. I added more soil mix as the plants grew. The lids helped prevent moisture loss and kept the soil warm.

Dee M.
Springdale, Arkansas

African Violet Pots

I love African violets! Unfortunately, I don't have enough room to grow many of them. My family already barely has room to eat at the kitchen table due to the houseplants that nearly cover it. Last year I received an "African violet pot" as a gift. This is essentially a porous pot that sits inside another glazed pot. They look really cool and water the violets from the bottom up, which is what these plants like best. My violet hasn't stopped blooming since! I put in some diluted kelp/fish fertilizer every third or fourth watering.

Keli W.
Lake Oswego, Oregon

Dig That Dwarf Banana

Banana trees can grow as tall as 30 feet, so choose a dwarf variety such as 'Dwarf Cavendish', 'Dwarf Red Jamaican', or 'Zanmoreno' for a unique houseplant.

Like other tropical plants, bananas need evenly moist—but not saturated—soil. Plant the corm in a 5-gallon (or larger) container, and be sure that there is at least 3 inches between the corm and the sides of the container. Allow the very top of the corm to remain above the surrounding soil. To keep the corm from rotting, let the top 2 inches of the soil dry out between waterings.

When the plant that sprouts out has four to six leaves, repot it in a larger container that is 18 to 24 inches in diameter. Eventually, you'll need a container at least 3 feet deep and as wide. (Set it on a dolly so that you can move it easily.) Give the plant as much light as possible—move it outdoors to a bright porch or patio for the summer. Be careful about temperature, though. When nighttime temps drop to 50°F, bananas will stop growing. For fruiting, bananas really need at least a year of consistently warm (70° to 80°F) weather.

Bananas are *heavy* feeders. Mix an organic fertilizer blend into the soil before planting and again at regular intervals so the plants receive a total of 10 pounds per year. (Allow the plants to rest in December, January, and February.) When they are flowering, provide a boost of phosphorus and potassium as well.

You can expect to get some bananas 18 months or so after planting. When you do, you'll taste nature's ultimate convenience food at its best—fresh off the tree. Cut back the fruiting stem after harvest.

Homegrown Coffee

A coffee tree makes a great houseplant and, if you're patient, you can eventually harvest beans from the plant for a homegrown cup of java. Coffee plants have glossy foliage, tiny white fragrant flowers, and green berries ("cherries") that ripen very gradually. Inside the berries are the "green" beans that are roasted, ground, and then brewed to make coffee.

To keep your java plant happy, place it in bright but indirect light in winter. In their native habitats, coffee plants grow as "understory"—surrounded by towering trees—so an east or west window will work fine. If you move your coffee plant outdoors in summer, be sure *not* to set it in direct sunlight.

Pot your coffee tree in a standard organic soil blend, but mix in about one-quarter peat since the plant likes a slightly acid pH. If your tap water is alkaline, water the plant with distilled water. While the plant is actively growing, feed it with half-strength odorless fish emulsion every 2 weeks.

For most of the year, try to keep the soil moist without allowing it to become waterlogged. Then pick an appropriate time when, by temporarily reducing water, you can induce flowering.

Once the plant flowers, you'll need to encourage pollination by tickling the blossoms with a feather or small paintbrush. Check the plant often while it is blooming—coffee flowers are open and ready for pollination only for a very short time.

You may have to wait as long as a year after flowering, but eventually the "cherries" will turn dark red, signifying that they are ripe. Pick the cherries and remove their seeds. Soak the seeds in water overnight to remove the slippery covering, then rinse them. Let the seeds dry for 5 to 6 days, then squeeze the seeds with your fingers to remove the beans inside. Also remove the skin around the bean.

To roast the beans, put them in a single layer in a shallow pan with a lid over medium heat. Use no oil; just shake the pan constantly to avoid scorching. The beans will darken and pop. First pop indicates light to medium roast; second pop is a dark, espresso roast.

Double Your Bulbs, Double Your Bloom

For pots of blooming bulbs that burst with color on a gray winter day, you need to jam-pack your containers with bulbs, one on top of the other. Here's how to do it.

1. Fill the bottom one-third of a pot with soil mix, then put in a layer of bulbs pointed side up.

2. Add mix until the tops of the bulbs just poke through the surface, then position a second layer of bulbs in between the tops of the first layer.

3. Add another layer of mix until you can barely see the tops of the bulbs poking through.

This method works best with tulips and daffodils. Be sure your bulbs have had the cold treatment needed for forcing blooms out of season.

GARDENER TO GARDENER

Forcing Hyacinths

To force hyacinths, all you need is a 4-inch pot for each bulb or a shallow "azalea pot" for multiple bulbs. I use regular packaged potting mix, fill the pot about halfway, set the bulb in place, and then add more soil. The tops of the bulb can peek out of the mix. In the azalea pot, you can cram the bulbs in so they are nearly touching each other.

Water your containers well and keep them someplace cold (like your refrigerator) for 10 to 14 weeks. Different bulbs have different chilling requirements, but you're usually safe potting them up in October or November and chilling them until February. Check them occasionally to see whether they need water.

When you can't stand winter any more, take a pot out and put it in a bright, warm location. Within a couple of weeks, you'll have flowers!

Kathy T.
Northfield, Minnesota

Porch Orchard

The art of growing fruit trees in containers is an easy one to master due to the development of improved dwarf cultivars. Many fruit trees—especially peaches, nectarines, sour cherries, and plums—are self-fruitful and require no cross-pollination, so you can enjoy fruit from even a single planting. Some miniature cultivars grow only about 6 feet tall.

A pot 2 to 2½ feet in diameter and 2 to 2½ feet deep is the ideal size for planting dwarf or miniature trees. Drainage holes on the side, near the bottom, are necessary. Avoid planting in polypropylene tubs; though they retain moisture and seem easier to move around, they're usually not sturdy enough for the weightiness of soil. If you'll need to move the plant or take it inside for the winter, choose a container with sturdy handles or gripping areas, or place it on a dolly.

To plant a bareroot fruit tree in a container, follow this procedure.

1. Fill the container about one-third full with a porous, well-drained soil mixture.

2. Loosen roots for planting, mound the soil up in the center of the container, and spread the roots over it.

3. Add soil mixture to fill the tub two-thirds full.

4. Use a tree wrap to cover and protect the tree trunk from sunburn during the first growing season.

5. Soak the mixture to settle the soil and roots, then add more soil to within 3 inches of the top of the container. Firm and water thoroughly again. Mulch with 2 to 3 inches of compost.

Give your tree a site in full sun in your yard or on your terrace, porch, or balcony. Most trees won't bear fruit until their second or third years. Once they do, it's important to thin the fruits to ensure larger, finer quality. Thin most varieties when the young fruits are about 1 inch in diameter. (Peaches, plums, and cherries generally don't need thinning.)

Your tree can stay outdoors year-round unless you live in an area with extremely cold winters. In this case, place the pots in an unheated garage during the heart of winter, or use snow as an insulator around the container.

Plant a dwarf fruit tree in an oversize pot that's supported by a dolly. You can move the tree as needed to maximize light exposure during the growing season and provide some shelter from wind and winter weather.

Impatiens in a Pot?

Impatiens are hard to beat for nonstop color in sun (New Guinea varieties) or shade (traditional varieties), which is one reason why they've become such popular bedding plants. Now there's an impatiens that's perfect for containers: 'Fanfare' trailing impatiens. 'Fanfare' has a mounded, trailing habit, which makes it a better choice for growing in hanging baskets and window boxes than more upright varieties. It will thrive in full to part shade.

All Peas on Deck

While air temperatures may be warm enough to plant peas on Easter in your area, the soil is often too cold and wet for good germination. As a result, early pea plantings tend to germinate poorly.

To get an early crop and avoid the hazards of overly cold and wet soil, plant a first crop of peas in containers. Sow your peas in a round container such as a half-barrel and install a tube of chicken wire in the center of the pot for the peas to climb. This will allow you to plant as early as 2 weeks before Easter. The container can do double duty as the growing season progresses, too. After the pea harvest is finished, use the tub for annual flowers.

Tomatoes on the Wagon

An old-fashioned wagon makes an easy-to-move base for off-season tomatoes. Pot up two tomato plants into two 10-gallon containers in August and put them in the wagon. Let the plants grow outdoors as long as warm weather lasts; as temperatures begin to fall, wheel the plants indoors overnight. It doesn't take long, and if you have a protected, south-facing spot for the plants outdoors during the day, you could harvest fresh tomatoes all the way until Christmas.

Potted Roses Outside and In

If you grow your roses in pots, you'll get two benefits—convenience and low maintenance. Plant miniature and small shrub roses in pots, and set those pots into other pots sunk into the ground in your garden. When you want roses indoors simply lift the potted roses from their in-ground container, wash the pots, and bring them inside.

Double-potting also helps to keep roots cool and protected from hot summer sun and drying winds, so you won't have to water as often.

Double-Duty Poinsettia

Poinsettias bring holiday cheer, but they inevitably seem to decline after a few weeks. To help your poinsettia stay healthy and happy to bloom another year, try the following.

1. At Christmastime, keep the plant in a sunny, draft-free location for as long as it blooms.

2. In late spring, cut stems back to 6 inches and sink the plant, pot and all, into a sunny garden bed outdoors.

3. During the summer, water as needed and trim to maintain an attractive plant shape.

4. When fall arrives, but before frost, lift the pot and bring the poinsettia indoors. Set it in a bright window, either in a room where the lights are never on after dark or where you will re-member to cover the plant every night. (Poinsettias won't bloom unless they have a sufficiently long daily period of darkness).

5. Next December, watch it bloom!

Top 5 for Hot Pots

If you need perennials that can stand hot, dry conditions in containers, try these five.

Willow blue star (*Amsonia tabernaemontana*)

Butterfly weed (*Asclepias tuberosa*)

Blanket flowers (*Gaillardia* spp., especially *G.* × *grandiflora* 'Baby Cole')

Prickly pear (*Opuntia humifusa*)

Yuccas (*Yucca* spp., especially *Y. filamentosa* 'Golden Sword')

Chapter 12

Protecting Your Garden from Insect Pests

Insect pests may be part of the natural world, but they're a part that we'd rather do without. When pests chomp our perennials or tunnel into our apples, we're ready to do battle.

Organic gardeners approach insect pest problems with passion, but it's also important to keep in perspective the bigger issues of what's safe for people, garden plants, soil, and the environment. A very effective array of organic pest-fighting tactics are available that don't require the use of synthetic chemical poisons.

You'll find some of the best strategies for fighting pests in this chapter, as gardeners share a recipe for a spicy spray that will banish pests, ideas for making insect traps, suggestions for pest-repelling companion plants, and their favorite ways (sometimes gory) to attack slugs. You'll also learn how decisions as simple as when you plant and whether you cover a crop with floating row covers can make a big difference in preventing pest damage. There are tips to encourage birds and beneficial insects to do pest-control duty for you, as well as effective ideas for controlling specific pests, from aphids to yellow jackets.

GARDENER TO
GARDENER

*Homemade
Sticky Traps*

*Here's a new twist on
sticky traps that will eliminate
having to mount them on
stakes or hang them from
branches. You'll need to buy
yellow, blue, or white posterboard from your local drug-
store or art supply store, and
Tangle-Trap from the garden
center or hardware store.
Cut the posterboard into 3- to
6-inch-wide strips. Apply the
Tangle-Trap to one side of
each strip. Bend the strips into
circles (sticky side facing out)
and staple.*

*Remove any severely dam-
aged leaves from the infested
plants and place the free-
standing sticky cylinders
around the plants. This works
very well in my garden, and
you can make about six traps
for less than a dollar.*

*Kristen L.
Naples, Florida*

Kill When Cold

One basic rule of organic pest control is that the early hand-picker gets
the pests. Most flying insects are very sensitive to temperature
changes. When they're cold, insects move slowly and will not or
cannot fly. It's no trick at all to catch and kill them in the coolness of
early morning. A few hours later, when the midday sun has warmed
them up, pests are much better escape artists.

Trap Nests Net Many Pests

Earwigs, pill bugs, sow bugs, slugs, and snails like to hide out in damp,
shady places during the heat of the day. To take advantage of this habit,
lure them with attractive "trap nests" (damp boards, pieces of paper,
crab claws, or broken crockery). Then get out every afternoon, check
every single trap, and dispatch the pests into a container of soapy water.

Color-Coordinated Traps

Many flying insects are attracted to certain colors, which has given rise
to the use of colored sticky traps. Be sure you're using the right color
trap for the pest you want to catch. Yellow is most attractive to aphids
and whiteflies, blue is best for thrips, and white is recommended for
flea beetles. These traps can also attract beneficial insects, so don't put
out traps unless you know the pest is present.

Growing-Degree Days
Help Bypass Pests

The time that certain insects or plants emerge differs from region to
region. Nature doesn't use a calendar. Instead, insect and plant development are governed by signals from nature—especially the light and
heat that have accumulated during the season.

So how can you plan for the onset of particular garden pests, such
as Japanese beetles, forest tent caterpillars, and gypsy moth larvae?
There is a formula, used to measure accumulated heat, called growing-
degree days (GDDs). This formula is the key to intelligent pest management. For instance, there is no point in taking any steps toward
pest control if the pests aren't there yet.

Your local Cooperative Extension office or other educational
sources can supply charts of GDDs for insect and plant behaviors, and

they're useful tools. Ask your local Cooperative Extension or weather station for the current GDDs, and then check the chart to anticipate when insect pests will emerge in your area.

Here are some smart garden timing tips for better pest management.

Cabbage loopers. Plant cabbage early (about 4 to 5 weeks before the last frost), and harvest by late spring—before the cabbage loopers emerge and begin chewing.

Carrot maggots. These pests are the worst when you plant early to get those first sweet carrots. Instead, wait until after June 1 in the North (or until early summer) to plant your carrots.

Corn borers. If you plant corn 2 weeks after the last frost date, you may just be able to avoid these pests.

Potato leafhoppers. These insects come on strong in July, so plant your potatoes as soon as possible in spring and try to harvest them all by late July.

Break the Pest Cycle

For fruit trees, one of the most important steps in reducing pest problems is to clean up *all* fallen fruit. Many fruit tree pests, such as codling moths, overwinter in fallen fruit. Removing all fallen fruit doesn't guarantee that you won't have insect damage the following year, but at least you'll know you didn't raise the pests on your own property.

This strategy can also help with ornamentals. If you have perennials that were infested with pests during the growing season, remove all the spent plant parts from your garden in the fall so the pests can't overwinter as eggs, larvae, or adults in the foliage or flower pods. Burn the infested material or seal it in plastic bags and put it out with your trash.

Make a Contract with the Birds

Inviting birds to your yard can be the best pest control deal you'll make. If you have fruit trees, stack a rough brush pile near the trees in winter to provide shelter for birds. Supply water, too. Birds will take up residence and comb your trees for overwintering insect eggs and larvae. In early spring, build and set out nesting boxes and nesting shelves. Help birds furnish their nests by putting yarn, string, feathers, and old socks cut into strips near your feeding stations.

Use a Good-Neighbor Policy

One of the most interesting tactics for foiling insect pests is companion planting. Pair plants that repel a particular pest with the plant that pest attacks. Here are some combinations to try.

Basil and tomatoes: The basil is reputed to help tomatoes overcome both insects and disease.

Beans and cilantro: The cilantro attracts a species of parasitic wasp that attacks the Mexican bean beetle.

Beans and potatoes: The beans dispel Colorado potato beetles, while the potatoes repel Mexican bean beetles.

Lettuce and sweet alyssum: The alyssum attracts predatory insects that feed on aphids.

Tomatoes and asparagus: Asparagus beetles don't like tomatoes.

10 Plants That Bring In the Birds

Plant these now; be pest-free later!

Serviceberries (*Amelanchier* spp.)

Native ornamental grasses, such as bluestems (*Andropogon* spp.) and Indian grass (*Sorghastrum nutans*)

Cotoneasters (*Cotoneaster* spp.)

Hollies (*Ilex* spp.)

Junipers (*Juniperus* spp.)

Mulberries (*Morus* spp.)

Virginia creeper (*Parthenocissus quinquefolia*)

Pines (*Pinus* spp.)

Cherries (*Prunus* spp.)

And don't forget annual and perennial flowers, such as cosmos, amaranth, bachelor's button, marigold, zinnia, coreopsis, purple coneflower, and goldenrod.

Weed Strips Shelter Good Bugs

Raise a crop that will encourage beneficial insects to call your garden home: weeds. Allow weed strips to grow every 10 rows or so in your garden, or let a weedy border grow up around your garden. Flowering weeds such as dandelion, wild carrot, lamb's-quarters, goldenrod, and evening primrose seem to be particularly effective for sheltering beneficials. When the weeds begin to shade your vegetables, cut them back to about 1 foot high.

Post a Perch for the Birds

Welcome insect-eating birds to your garden with an 8- to 10-foot-tall perch made from a pole topped by a wooden crosspiece of any length. You can use a ½-inch wooden strip, a piece of molding, or any small scrap of lumber for the crosspiece. However, a bird's little feet may feel best perching on a round piece of dowel.

    If you have tall tomato cages or melon trellises in your garden, birds may like perching on them as well. Try using one stake that is a foot taller than the top of the cages, and add a short crosspiece to it as well.

A garden stake with a perch that projects above your tomato cages and other garden structures provides a vantage point for visiting pest-hungry birds.

old-time wisdom

INVITE TOADS IN TO KEEP INSECTS OUT

There is no better insect destroyer than the toad. He will eat 100 rose bugs or slugs in one night. If you haven't plenty of these sturdy little hoppers in your garden, go on a hunt to collect some and bring them home in a bag.

Loring Underwood
A Garden Diary and Country Home Guide, 1908

Clover Oases for Beneficials

Red and white clover are excellent plants for attracting beneficial insects. Provide "island refuges" for good bugs by planting two or three clumps of clover near the garden. Mow them one at a time over the season to force the insects from the clover into your garden plants.

Save Beneficials—Mow Just Half

You may have cover crops like clover or buckwheat planted for soil improvement or to control erosion, but they're undoubtedly sheltering beneficials, too. When you mow or turn under the crop, you will kill or disrupt these beneficials. You can use a strategy similar to the one described above to avoid decimating populations.

No matter what your "cover and mow" or "cover and turn" routine, do it in halves. Till or mow down the *right* side of every row the first time, then do the *left* side 2 weeks later. Although you can't save every beneficial insect, this method helps you maintain a permanent habitat and some good places for the population to hide in and grow at every stage of the insects' development.

Row Covers Add a Few Ounces of Prevention

The old "ounce of prevention" adage is surely correct when it comes to using floating row covers (polyethylene fabric) to prevent many insect pests from getting to crops. However, it's important to have a good seal around the edges of the covers to prevent pests from sneaking through gaps to get at your plants.

If you haven't been successful weighting down row covers with boards, rocks, or pins, try stapling ½ × ½-inch wooden strips on the long edges of the covers. (Strips used for interior trim or moldings work great.) These prevent the row covers from blowing loose in the wind. When it's time to remove the row covers, just wrap the fabric around the wood strips and store the whole thing.

Panty Hose Keep Bugs off Produce

Pest-free produce is a cinch with this easy trick. It works the same way as floating row covers without the cost. Just use old panty hose to cover individual fruits and vegetables when they first start forming. Slip a length of panty hose over corn, cucumbers, grapes, melons, peaches, small pumpkins, and squash to protect them from birds, ear-wigs, slugs, snails, and other munchers. Tie knots at the top and bottom of the hose to prevent openings. The nylon panty hose work great because they dry quickly after a rain and don't hold heat.

Turn Torn Row Covers into Plant Hoods

If your floating row covers are torn from heavy use, cut the salvageable sections into squares, which you can fashion into little bags for individual plant covers. If you're handy with a sewing machine, fold the squares in half and sew down each side; or, you can use clothespins. Place the individual bags or hoods over vulnerable plants in any part of the garden.

Top 10 Ornamentals for Friendly Bugs

It's the best possible news any gardener could ask for: You can prevent many pest problems simply by growing the right flowers. What gardener wouldn't rather grow beautiful blooms than spray dangerous poisons? Research studies have shown that the following ornamental plants are highly effective at drawing and sheltering bugs that help keep our gardens healthy.

Bachelor's button (*Centaurea cyanus*)

Borage (*Borago officinalis*)

Corn

Cup plant (*Silphium perfoliatum*)

Fennel (*Foeniculum vulgare*)

Golden marguerite (*Anthemis tinctoria*)

Mountain mints (*Pycnanthemum virginianum* and *P. muticum*)

Ornamental grasses

Pussy willows (*Salix* spp.)

Sweet alyssum (*Lobularia maritima*)

To learn more about these plants and other bug-beating blooms, go to www.organicgardening.com/library/beneficialborder.html.

Aphid Magnet

I grow an abundance of greens (spinach, chard, kale, collards, beet greens, and romaine) in a small salad garden. For two consecutive years, I have allowed a 'Red Russian' kale plant to mature and produce seedpods. By doing so, I seem to have solved the aphid problem in my garden. As the kale pods form, small clusters of aphids attach themselves to both the pods and plant stem. By the time the pods mature, the aphid clusters are dense to the point of saturation. The bugs remain on the kale throughout their life cycle, leaving the other greens untouched.

Duane S.
Tacoma, Washington

Turnoff Tea

Brewing teas that are a turnoff for insect pests is a smart way to protect your plants from harm. Teas made of wormwood or horseradish are very effective. To prepare wormwood tea, gather early-summer leaves in the morning, dry them in shade (or start with dried leaves), then cover with water and bring to a boil. Remove and dilute with 4 parts water, stirring for 10 minutes to mix thoroughly. For horseradish tea, pour boiling water over the leaves, then dilute with 4 parts water.

A word of caution: Be sure to test any homemade spray on just one plant before you spray your entire crop!

Bugs Don't Like a Hot Shower

A few seconds and a spray of hot water are all it takes to wash small pests such as aphids, mites, scales, thrips, and whiteflies out of your garden. Water heated to about 160°F gets rid of insects without hurting a wide variety of woody and herbaceous plants. Here's how to set up a simple system for delivering a hot-water spray.

1. Set your water heater so the water is a little too hot for home use, about 160°F. (Remember to turn down the hot-water thermostat when you finish treating your plants.)

2. Attach a fitting to the hot water spigot for your washing machine or laundry sink so you can hook up a ¾-inch insulated automotive heater hose to it.

3. Attach the insulated hose to the fitting. The length of the hose depends on how far you have to go to reach insect-infested plants—it comes in 50-foot rolls.

4. Feed the hose out a window or your dryer vent. (If you're dealing with a lot of hose, feed it in from outside.)

5. On the "plant end" of the hose, attach a nozzle that can apply the water in a soft spray of large drops.

6. Spray the stems and trunks as well as the tops and undersides of the leaves of your plants with hot water for 1 to 3 seconds. Also spray the surrounding ground to kill insects that might have been knocked off the plants.

Weed Juice for (Parasitic) Wasps

Spraying a fresh mixture of "weed juice" on plants can attract *Trichogramma* wasps to your garden. These wasps parasitize the eggs of many species of leaf-chewing pests. To make weed juice, blend 1 ounce of leaves or stems of weeds with 1 quart of warm water. Apply the spray to your crops; repeat every 2 weeks.

Soap Spray for Stubborn Pests

When a pest problem gets out of control, you may need to take more serious action than hand-picking or companion planting will solve. A homemade insecticidal soap spray will help control a variety of caterpillars and other soft-bodied pests. To make a spray, mix 1 tablespoon of liquid soap into 1 cup of canola oil; measure out 1 tablespoon of this mixture per quart of water.

Nasturtium Decoy for Aphids

Because aphids are attracted to the color yellow, they're also attracted to yellow-flowered nasturtiums. Try planting yellow-flowered nasturtiums at the base of tomato plants or other plants in your garden that are bothered by aphids. Monitor the nasturtiums closely, and once they've drawn in the aphids—but before the aphids produce any young—pull the decoy plants and destroy its load of insects.

Aphids Arrive after You Prune!

You can avoid a lot of aphids by pruning most of your trees and shrubs while the plants are dormant. Aphids are attracted to new leaves and shoot tips because nitrogen is concentrated in areas of new growth. Pruning your trees and shrubs, including roses, signals the plants to produce new, nitrogen-rich growth. So by trimming your plants while they're dormant, you'll ensure there is no nitrogen signal to attract aphids, and few—if any—aphids to attract.

Note that some shrubs, such as lilacs, should be pruned during the growing season, after they finish flowering. But these shrubs seem to be less prone to aphid problems and have already produced their new leaves and flowers.

To keep aphid problems in check in your perennial beds, go light on nitrogen when you fertilize because it also triggers nitrogen-rich, aphid-attracting growth.

Spicy Spray Banishes Bugs

After pests devoured most of my tomato garden last year, I changed my tactics. I made a spray consisting of a handful of chili peppers, a couple of tomatoes, a few cloves of garlic, some cinnamon, ½ cup of vinegar, a shot of olive oil, and a small squirt of dish soap. To this I added 2 cups of water. Then I mixed it in the blender and strained out the solids. I put the liquid into a plastic spray bottle and applied it to the plants about once a week after the fruit started to appear. Then when I watered the plants, I soaked them at their bases, near the roots, so I wouldn't spray off the solution. After a rain, I reapplied my concoction. Also, I picked off the flower tops from my basil plants as needed and spread them among the tomatoes. The results this year were no more bugs—and beautiful, healthy tomatoes!

Kathy D.
Sarasota, Florida

Cover Crops Aid Apples

Plant a cover crop to put a cap on apple pest problems. Studies show that apple orchards cover-cropped with rye, vetch, and clover have fewer codling moths, aphids, and leafhoppers than orchards with no plant cover between the trees. The cover crop shelters natural pest predators. Damage from codling moths in cultivated orchards was nearly 8 times greater than that in the cover-cropped orchards.

Trapping Apple Pests

Apple maggots and codling moths are two major pests of apples, but easy-to-make traps can save your crops from damage. For apple maggots, paint apple-size wooden balls red. Let them dry, slip a plastic sandwich bag over each ball, and coat the plastic with Tanglefoot. Hang the balls in your fruit trees (two traps per dwarf fruit tree), and the apple maggot flies will be attracted to them and get stuck. Remove the bags every 2 weeks and replace them with new ones.

For codling moths, cut a hole in the side of a plastic milk jug and add a vinegar-molasses mixture (2 parts vinegar to 1 part molasses). Hang the jug from an apple limb and you'll catch dozens of moths. Clean out the jug and replenish the liquid periodically to maintain its attractiveness.

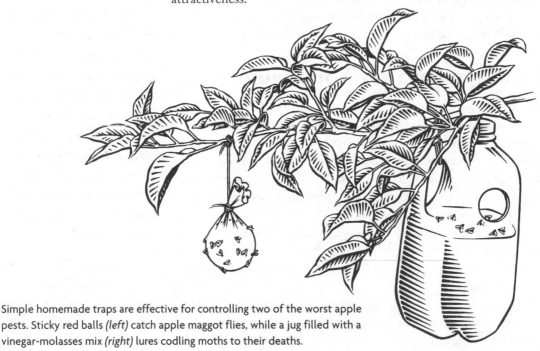

Simple homemade traps are effective for controlling two of the worst apple pests. Sticky red balls *(left)* catch apple maggot flies, while a jug filled with a vinegar-molasses mix *(right)* lures codling moths to their deaths.

Clay Spray for Codling Moth

If you have so many apples that bagging fruit isn't an option, try spraying fruits with kaolin clay to defend against codling moths. The clay forms a powdery film on fruit that acts as a barrier to feeding and egg laying. Beginning at petal fall, spray young fruit once a week for 6 to 8 weeks.

Asparagus under Attack

Two kinds of beetles dine on asparagus spears: the asparagus beetle (blue-black with white spots), and the spotted asparagus beetle (shiny orange with black spots). If you've noticed either of these small beetles in your asparagus patch in the past, take two steps to prevent future problems. First, clean up the patch well in fall, removing all dead fronds, and wait until late fall to mulch—otherwise the beetles will hide in the mulch. Then, in the spring, cover emerging asparagus shoots with floating row covers to prevent reinfestation, and handpick any beetles you see. In most cases, these steps will go a long way to reducing beetle damage.

Garlic Offends Cabbage Loopers

Southern gardeners can foil cabbage loopers by companion planting. Plan the layout of your cabbage bed in July, using small stakes to mark the locations where you'll set your cabbage transplants. At the same time, plant two garlic cloves between each stake. When the garlic sprouts are about 2 inches tall, set out the cabbage plants. The garlic immediately works to repel the cabbage loopers through the late summer and fall growing season, so your cabbages will be free of holes and unsightly frass.

Garlic planted ahead of cabbage creates a repellent atmosphere that prevents cabbage looper moths from laying eggs on the cabbages.

Cabbageworms Don't Like Red

Are cabbageworms ruthlessly butchering your cabbage? To save some for yourself, try planting red-leaved cabbage. Studies indicate that cabbageworms don't like them as well as they like green-leaved varieties. (And maybe the gardener can see the pest better and will hand-pick it more often!) It is also true that cabbages that have smoother leaves are attacked less frequently than crinkly leaved varieties.

To protect green cabbage varieties, try turning the leaves of broccoli, cauliflower, cabbage, and brussels sprouts white by dusting them with all-purpose flour. (It sticks best after a rain or on the morning dew.) Caterpillars eat the flour, bloat, and die.

Block Out Carpenter Bees

To repel carpenter bees, which tunnel into weathered or unpainted wood (such as the eaves of a shed), paint or varnish exposed wood surfaces. Keep in mind that these bees will chew through uncoated rot-resistant woods such as redwood, cedar, and cypress, too. Fill entrance holes with steel wool and cover with mesh screening. Remember that carpenter bees are valuable pollinators, so aim for an exclusion strategy, rather than eradication.

Spread the Sheets under the Pines

Conifer sawflies are a serious problem for pine and spruce trees in many parts of the country. To catch a lot of the pests in late spring, spread old bedsheets around the base of your evergreen trees. The conifer sawfly larvae will drop to the ground to pupate. A brisk whack or shake of the tree a few times will encourage the sawfly larvae to drop. You can gather them up and carry them to the trash or the bonfire before they have a chance to develop.

Worms in Your Ears?

The most common pest of corn is the corn earworm. Some gardeners control these tip-nibblers by squirting a medicine dropper half-filled with mineral or vegetable oil into the tip of the husk 4 days after silks appear (when they've just started browning at the tip). Or try a strong garlic water spray (a couple of mashed cloves per quart of water, left to steep overnight) or a shot of *Bacillus thuringiensis*, a natural caterpillar killer.

Catch Cucumber Beetles with Old Squash

Spotted cucumber beetles chew holes in all sorts of vine crops as well as in corn, potatoes, and some fruit crops. Even worse, they can spread serious diseases to your garden. But smart gardeners can put a stop to these troublesome pests early in the season. If you have winter squash in storage, keep some until spring—even if they are getting soft. Scoop out a hole in each squash, and place it by the vulnerable crops soon after planting. Once these traps hold lots of cucumber beetles, toss squash and pests in the trash.

Commodious Cutworm Collars

Use toilet-paper cylinders to protect young garden plants from cutworms. Cut the paper cylinder so that it can be wrapped around the plant stem. Push the cylinder into the soil so half is below ground. Cutworms can't get through the collars, so plant stems stay safe. The collars will deteriorate naturally during the growing season.

Nail Those Cutworms

Stick a nail into the soil next to each seedling—any size nail will do. Simply place it about ¼ inch away from the stem. The nail keeps cutworms from wrapping around a plant's stem, which is how they feed on—and sever—young plants.

Stuck in the Bucket

If fire ants have built a mound in your yard or garden, here's a safe, organic way to get rid of them. In the late morning on a sunny day when the ants have moved up inside their mound, assemble your garden hose, a 5-gallon bucket, a shovel, dish detergent, and baby powder or cornstarch. Spread the baby powder or cornstarch around the inside of the rim of the bucket and on your shovel handle (to make the surfaces slick so the ants can't crawl on them), tuck your pants inside your socks, and proceed with your equipment to the ant mound. Quickly shovel the mound and a foot or so of soil from under the mound—ants and all—into the bucket, add a generous squirt of dish detergent, fill the bucket with water, and stir well. Let it sit at least overnight to drown the ants. (Don't omit the soap. Without it, the submerged ants can live for several days.)

*Pine Needles
Annoy Slugs*

Our large hosta garden is
heavily shaded by pine and
spruce trees. Each year there
were tons of pine and spruce
needles to clean up. Slugs devoured the hostas, and mosquitoes ate us whenever we tried
to use the seating area in the
center of the hosta beds. Then
one year I didn't bother
cleaning up the needles, and I
noticed there was less slug
damage. Now I leave this fragrant carpet of needles, and
the slugs have all disap-
peared—I assume they don't
like to crawl over the needles.
The fragrance is wonderful,
and for some reason the mosquitoes have also gone away
(even though they are still
plentiful in our other gardens).

Claire W.
Crete, Illinois

Fancy Greens for Flea Beetles

Even if you don't like to eat arugula, consider sowing some in your
garden as a trap crop for flea beetles. They will flock to arugula, where
you can suck them off with a handheld vacuum.

Gummy Grasshopper Flour Formula

Stop grasshoppers from eating your plants by making them eat flour.
When you use this simple flour dust, grasshoppers, blister beetles, and
other chewing insects will end up with their mouthparts so gummed
up that they can't eat another thing.

Put 3 cups of all-purpose flour in a garden duster or, if you're
treating only a small area, put a small amount of flour in a saltshaker.
Go out in your garden and jiggle the plants that the grasshoppers or
other chewing pests are feeding on (this gets the insects moving). Dust
the insects and the leaves with flour.

After 2 days, rinse the flour off the plants using a fine spray from a
hose. On plants with hairy leaves, such as tomatoes, you may need to
rinse twice to clean off the flour.

When the grasshoppers eat dusted leaves, they ingest so much
flour that they become sick and stop eating. Since the success of the
method hinges on getting plenty of flour on the leaves that the bugs
are eating, it's best to apply the dust in the morning, while the plants
are damp with dew.

As long as you rinse off the flour after 2 days, you won't harm your
plants. But don't use self-rising flour—the salts in that type of flour
may injure plant leaves and aren't good for your soil.

Rub Out Pests with Rubbing Alcohol

Houseplants bothered by pests? Rub them out with rubbing alcohol.
An alcohol spray is effective against mealybugs, whiteflies, red spider
mites, aphids, fungus gnats, and scale. To make the spray, mix ½ to 1
cup of alcohol with 1 quart of water in a pump-spray bottle. Test-spray
one leaf of an infested plant and wait 1 day to check for damage. If the
plant is unaffected, spray the whole plant. Treat at 3-day intervals for
10 days or as needed.

Japanese Beetles Like It Wet

Female Japanese beetles feed only for about 2 days before laying their eggs in the soil. Many of the eggs dry out and cannot mature, so let your lawns and gardens dry out well between waterings. The adult females may seek other, damper places to lay their eggs, which means they may be drawn away from your yard to feed elsewhere as they get ready to start the new generation.

Japanese Beetles Drop and Disappear

Every Japanese beetle you catch early is one that won't be laying eggs. So at the start of the season, set your alarm clock before 7 A.M. to get up and out there to catch those beetles.

Spread an old sheet under the plants the beetles prefer. Some say roses suffer the most, but there are hundreds of target plants—everything from grapevines to fruit trees. Gently shake the plant or whack it with a broom and watch the beetles fall and "play dead." Toss them into a bucket filled with soapy water and put them in the trash.

Plant Rotten Onions for Maggots

Stunted, yellowed onion plants that wilt on hot afternoons are probably the victims of onion maggots, which tunnel into the roots. The maggots may also attack garlic and leeks. If you've had problems with onion maggots in your garden in the past, set out a "trap" for them by "planting" a few rotting or sprouting onions from the kitchen in your garden. Onion maggot flies will be more attracted to the odor from these onions than to your seedlings, and that's where they'll lay their eggs. Always remove and destroy the trap crops, including roots and surrounding soil, to reduce problems next season.

Drown, You Drunken Slugs!

Trap plant-munching slugs by setting out shallow pans of beer in your garden. (Any type of beer will work—slugs don't seem to have a favorite label.) The following morning, the containers will be full of the slimy creatures, either dead or dead drunk. Either way, you can dispose of the slugs and replenish the traps for another round.

Slug Behavior

I recently did some experimenting with copper strips for slug control and discovered that the instructions I received with the strips were grossly inadequate. To figure out how to do it right, I captured three large, juicy slugs. They did not hesitate to slither across the strip of copper I put in their pen. I then stood the strip up at a 90-degree angle to the ground to see what would happen if the slugs' antennae came in contact with the copper. When the slugs' antennae touched the copper, the slugs reacted as if they had been given an electric shock. But if the slugs could cross the copper without touching it with their antennae, they were off to the salad patch! I watched these slugs for a long time, and they never changed this pattern of behavior.

L. E. S.
Diamond Springs,
California

A Slug Solution

Here in Oregon, slugs are a huge *problem. The first seedlings of spring veggies are consumed in days. One year I planted Chinese cabbage seedlings and discovered that the slugs preferred Chinese cabbage to the lettuce, spinach, and other veggies that I planted. They chewed on the Chinese cabbage and let the other plants alone. Chinese cabbage grows so fast that it's able to keep up with the damage. I've been using this trick for 3 years now.*

Roberta P.
Beaverton, Oregon

DE Is Death to Slugs

Another slug-fighting tactic is to sprinkle diatomaceous earth (DE) around susceptible plants. DE contains the skeletal remains of tiny sea creatures, and the sharp crystals in the remains pierce the slugs' skin. Wear a mask when you apply DE, and reapply it after every rainstorm. Be sure to buy natural-grade diatomaceous earth and not pool-grade diatomaceous earth, which is used in swimming-pool filters.

Blast Those Spittlebugs

White foam on the leaves of vegetable plants, strawberries, and even some lawn grasses is a sign of a spittlebug infestation. The distinctive little clumps of white foamy stuff hide young spittlebug nymphs while they suck plant juices. If you are seeing lots of spittle spots in your garden, try spraying them away with a strong blast of water. If they reappear, repeat the water spray and follow it up with insecticidal soap to kill the nymphs before they can re-create their protective spittle.

Spider Mites and the Wet Blanket

If spider mites are a problem on some of your landscape plantings (they especially like junipers), use the wet blanket trick. Spider mites dislike cold, wet conditions, so when you have a cold rain, make the most of the situation. Put a blanket over the shrub, and keep the blanket wet for a few days. (Don't deny your plant light for too long, of course.)

If blankets are too much trouble with a larger planting, just keep hosing the shrubs every day to simulate a cold, wet spring. Besides discouraging the problem mites, you will be helping beneficial predatory mites, which eat the "bad" ones. Unlike problem mites, the beneficial mites happen to thrive in moisture.

Wash Away the Telltale Web

Fine webbing on the leaves of your houseplants is often a sign of spider mites. Infested leaves have yellow speckles and will eventually drop off the plant. The first line of defense against spider mites is a lukewarm shower with plain water. Wash the plant's leaves, especially the undersides, with running water. Then mist the plant every day for a week. Keep the humidity high around your plants by placing the pots on gravel in water-filled trays. If you have a major infestation, you may have to resort to spraying insecticidal soap.

Undercover Squash Beats Bugs

To foil squash bugs, vine borers, and cucumber beetles, cover your squash and cucumber vines with floating row covers right after planting. Weight the edges of the covers with boards or soil so there are no openings. Squash flowers must be pollinated by insects (or hand-pollinated) in order to set fruit, so check under the row cover daily once plants reach flowering size. When you find female flowers, lift off the covers for 2 hours twice a week. This is sufficient for pollination, but usually isn't enough time for pests to find your crop.

Multistemmed Defense

Squash vine borer larvae burrow into the stems of squash plants and destroy the vines from the inside. To prevent these pests from ruining your entire crop, force your vines to develop multiple stems. Pinch off the growing point while the plant is young—before borers attack (the adults lay eggs in July). With luck, the adult borer moths won't lay eggs on all stems, allowing you to salvage some of your crop.

Beetles Prefer Pigweed

Striped blister beetles seem to love redroot pigweed. Allow some pigweed to grow among your tomatoes, and the beetles will congregate on the pigweed. In the early morning, when the beetles are moving slow, shake them off the pigweed plants, gather them in a gloved hand, and dump them into a bucket of water.

Dust Mop to the Rescue

Eastern tent caterpillars and fall webworms are destructive caterpillars that make white or gray webs, or "tents," in trees. To rid your trees of the caterpillars, try drenching a dust mop in *Bacillus thuringiensis* (BT) and shaking it over the nest to try to saturate the nest with the caterpillar poison. The long-handled dust mop makes it easier to get the BT through the webs and onto the pest caterpillars inside.

Straw Mulch Stifles Slugs

If slugs are a problem in your garden, try using straw as your mulch instead of a fine mulch. Even in cool and rainy weather, slugs don't seem to frequent straw-mulched beds.

Trip Up the Thrips

Many summer-flowering bulbs, such as freesia and gladiolas, are very susceptible to flower thrips, tiny insects that deform buds and ruin blooms. Here's an easy way to protect these bulbs: Soak them in a mixture of 1 gallon of warm water and 2½ tablespoons of Lysol. Allow the bulbs to sit in the solution at least 12 hours, then plant them immediately. At bloom time, you shouldn't have any problems with thrips.

Quick Ways to Handle Yellow Jackets

Leave yellow jackets alone when you can—they're good for your garden because they prey on insect pests. But if they're nesting too close for comfort, try these quick ways to get rid of them.

- Spray yellow jackets with cold water from a hose. It won't kill the bugs, but it will knock them out for a couple of hours, so it's easy for you to get them while they're down.

- In the evening, when the wasps are calm, pour honey next to their in-ground nests. Raccoons, skunks, and other nocturnal animals may dig up and destroy yellow jacket nests while trying to find more honey.

- Lace canned dog food with parasitic nematodes—sold as entomogenous nematodes by companies that sell beneficial insects—and place the food where foraging wasps can find it. They'll take the food back to the nest and feed it to their larvae, which will die. To prevent your pets from eating the food, place it in a margarine tub with quarter-size holes cut in the lid. The food wouldn't harm your pets, but if they eat it, it won't be available for the yellow jackets to snatch up.

- Trap yellow jackets in a commercially available bag that contains an attractant.

Chapter 13

Intercepting Animal Pests

When it comes to animal pests, the underlying theme is to stop them along the way *before* they find your garden. Unlike our fight against insect pests, where killing off the offenders is an acceptable strategy, most of us aren't willing to fight animal pests to the death. The troublesome task is to find a way to live and let live.

Gardeners seek to outwit those hungry rabbits, raccoons, deer, birds, and other animals with an appetite for garden goodies. Tips in this chapter for outsmarting animal pests include an herbal repellent and a special homemade rhubarb concoction that's strong enough to scare off a moose! There are also suggestions for using decoy crops to lure animals away from your garden.

Check the techniques for protecting crops against specific animals, including fencing out armadillos, using CDs to scare birds, fooling crows intent on raiding your corn patch, combining peanut butter and electricity to shock deer, employing subtle tactics in the war against woodchucks, and kenneling corn to keep raccoons from stealing the ripe ears. You'll even find some helpful ideas for preventing pet cats (yours or your neighbors') from becoming a garden annoyance.

Vole Defense

I've seen my plants "sucked" underground by voles, right before my eyes. To protect plants from voracious voles, I sprinkle crushed oyster shells around the plants, or into planting holes for bulbs. I buy a 40-pound bag of crushed oyster shells (commonly used as poultry feed additive) for $10 at a local feed store. (It works against slugs and cutworms, too—and it's cheaper than diatomaceous earth.) I've also taken to planting new specimens inside buried hardware cloth "cages" to prevent voles from nibbling roots. So far, that's been my only successful line of defense!

Linda F.
Jackson, New Jersey

Spicy Pest Deterrents

Keep rabbits and mice from raiding your garden by dusting your plants with ground cayenne pepper. There's no need to apply the hot pepper powder heavily. Simply walk down the rows and shake the pepper container lightly as you go. Or make a hot-pepper spray by combining 2 tablespoons of cayenne pepper with 6 drops of dish detergent and 1 gallon of water. (Keep in mind that you'll have to reapply the pepper after rain.)

Hot-pepper powder mixed into birdseed also deters marauding squirrels. The hot pepper burns squirrels when they eat it the same way it does humans, but birds are unaffected. Keep in mind that the hot pepper could get into the squirrels' eyes and be very painful. You'll have to weigh your need to deter squirrels against the possible pain the hot pepper could cause them.

Hot Pepper Product Breakthroughs

While hot-pepper sprays have been used as home remedies to solve many garden pest problems, they do present a problem of their own—they wash off easily during rainy weather. Try one of the new products that combines ground-up hot-pepper sauce with wax, and the essence of hot pepper will last longer. Studies have shown that red pepper often discourages rabbits, chipmunks, and squirrels, and it's an effective insect repellent and miticide, too. You can use the products on house plants, where studies have shown they are as effective as insecticidal soaps and better than traditional pesticides. Some of the products, such as Hot Pepper Wax, are labeled as safe for use on vegetable plants, too.

Stop 'Em with Southernwood

A hedge of southernwood (*Artemisia abrotanum*) around your vegetable garden may deter rabbits and other small animal pests. The camphor oils in southernwood are a repellent—both to animals and some insects. Trim the foliage of southernwood to make a dense, attractive edging. Get good use from the trimmings by boiling them in water, straining the liquid, and applying the liquid (using a plastic spray bottle) to the foliage of cole crops to repel cabbage moths.

In a Dither over Armadillos

You may think the armadillo, resembling an armored anteater the size of a terrier, is a comical creature—that is, until you wake up one morning and find your yard looks as if it has been under artillery fire all night. Armadillos can be garden pests in parts of the southern United States, ranging as far north as Arkansas, Oklahoma, Kansas, Louisiana, and Texas.

If it weren't for this critter's excavating habit, you'd probably call it a backyard friend. The armadillo feasts on the soil-dwelling larvae of June bugs and other beetles that are highly destructive to lawns and gardens. But when plants are uprooted and the lawn is riddled with ruts, it's hard to feel kindness toward armadillos.

You can keep armadillos out of a garden by surrounding it with chicken wire or other metal fencing. A fence 12 to 18 inches high will do; armadillos can't climb. Sink the fencing a foot deep into the ground so they can't tunnel under it. For beds you do not want to fence, lay chicken wire over the soil and pin it down with bent pieces of clothes hangers to deter the animals from digging. Cut holes into the wire to set plants, then mulch over the wire to hide it.

Unbearable Compost

Compost piles that include kitchen scraps can be very attractive to bears, whose diets include a variety of berries, roots, and seeds. While suburban gardeners probably don't have to worry about bears, gardeners who live in or near woods or mountains may find bears raiding the pile. There's no surefire way to bearproof a compost pile, but you can make the pile less appealing by using it for composting only grass clippings, leaves, and other nonedibles. Recycle your kitchen scraps indoors by setting up a worm bin like the one described on page 8. Use the worm compost outdoors in your garden only when you're sure it is fully composted.

Bar Birds from Your Berries

Strawberries tempt many a bird to investigate and eat, but you can bar their way with strips of hardware cloth. Use ½-inch mesh that is 2 feet wide, and cut it into 6-foot lengths for easy handling. Bend the wire lengthwise into a V-shaped trough and invert it over your rows of berries. You can use it year after year—and it completely foils the most persistent birds.

GARDENER TO GARDENER

Garden-Munching Moose

I'd like to share my experience of encountering moose in Fairbanks. For years, I gardened with only a 5-foot chicken-wire fence around my vegetables, which worked quite well until the moose discovered the garden. Now I have a 7-foot fence around the garden, and the moose respect it completely. As a good-behavior treat, I pull the old broccoli plants in fall and pile them up far away from the garden so the moose can munch on them during winter.

Ruth M.
Fairbanks, Alaska

Keep Cats at Bay

*The best solution I have
found to keep cats out of the
garden is orange peels. Just
grate your orange peels or
grind them up, and sprinkle
them in your garden. It
doesn't take much, and you
need to do it only a couple of
times a season. Works like a
charm! I grate or grind all of
my peels and store them in the
freezer until needed.*

*Betty H.
Presque Isle, Maine*

A slightly raised cover of
chicken wire will allow
young seedlings to estab-
lish themselves—free from
the unwanted attention of
neighborhood cats.

Spuds Keep Crows from Corn

Crows will yank up corn seedlings to get the sprouted kernel beneath.
A half-dozen of the raucous birds can wipe out a garden corn patch in
short order. An ingenious way to stop crows from pulling up young
corn plants is to plant potatoes in the corn patch. Plant the potato
rows about 3 feet apart. When the potatoes are about 1 foot tall, plant
corn seeds between the potato rows. Crows won't come calling, perhaps afraid that predators are lurking under the potato foliage.

A straw mulch can also hide a fledgling corn crop from crows.
Sprinkle straw on corn rows immediately after planting. Use just a thin
layer of straw so that you don't shade and cool the soil.

Creative Cat Barriers

All the lovely, soft soil of a garden makes it the litter box of your cat's
(and your neighbors' cat's) dreams. Once the garden fills in with plants
it will lose its appeal, but until that happens the simplest and best solution is to fill the space with some kind of physical barrier. You can use
odds and ends of scrap iron, cast-off children's toys, or anything you
have on hand. Many gardeners have extra flowerpots in the shed or
garage, and they'll work, too. Just set the items of your choice among
your seedlings, leaving no bit of ground big enough for a good dig.

A Catproof Bed Cover

Another tactic for deterring digging cats is to cover newly seeded beds
with galvanized chicken wire. Leave it in place until the seeds have
sprouted and are starting to grow through the wire mesh. Then place
bricks under the perimeter of the mesh to raise it a few inches, and
weight the edges with another layer of bricks to anchor it. Once the
plants are a few inches tall, you can remove the mesh. By then the bed
will be less attractive to cats.

Deer Won't Dine on These

Deer don't eat everything, though it often seems that way. If you choose your landscape plants carefully, you can reduce deer damage—and the time, effort, and money you spend protecting plants with sprays, soaps, and fencing. No one can predict which foods deer will eat when the pickings get slim, but there are some plants that are less likely to become lunch for Bambi.

Deer food preferences may vary depending on where you live, but here is a basic list of plants that deer generally don't like. When you're considering plants that aren't listed, remember these guidelines. Deer especially like young fruit trees and lush, well- to overfertilized plants with lots of new growth. They tend to avoid aromatic herbs like rosemary and leathery, fuzzy-leaved, or spiny plants.

Columbines (*Aquilegia* spp.)
Barberries (*Berberis* spp.)
Clematis (*Clematis* spp.)
Delphiniums (*Delphinium* spp.)
Foxgloves (*Digitalis* spp.)
American holly (*Ilex opaca*)
Irises (*Iris* spp.)
Common lilac (*Syringa vulgaris*)

Repel Deer with Runaway Mint

At last! There *is* a use for the excess of mint that almost inevitably follows the planting of this fragrant herb. Plant divisions or rooted stems that threaten to grow out of control into plastic pots, and sink them at intervals throughout your flowerbeds (leave a 2-inch lip above ground to stop runners from spreading into the beds). Plant these containers in areas of the garden where deer tend to browse, especially along the semishady edges of flowerbeds, and they will deter the nibbling deer.

Static-Free Deer Repellent

If deer are a problem in your landscape, tie antistatic strips or strips of dryer sheets to your shrubs every few feet. These strongly perfumed white strips that go in the clothes dryer to prevent static and scent the clothes work just as well to deter deer from browsing, even on favorites such as rhododendrons. An extra advantage with dryer sheets is that periodic rains revive their scent—at least a few times—so that they need replacing only every couple of months.

GARDENER TO GARDENER

Roses vs. Felines

Roses are my passion, and I also focus on making the garden an enticing habitat for birds and other wildlife. One day I noticed that our neighborhood cat never stalked the birds that were visiting the feeders I had hung over my roses, probably because of the thorny stems on the rosebushes. So I decided to plant a climbing rose at the base of an oak tree that had always attracted lots of birds, often with the cat lurking hungrily nearby. Now the rose keeps the cat at bay and is an awe-inspiring traffic stopper when in bloom.

Tina B.
Knoxville, Tennessee

*Herbal Bunny
Repellant*

 *Our neighborhood is
plagued by rabbits, which destroy tender annuals and other
emerging plants. I've even lost
marigolds to their voracious
appetites! We have no dogs or
cats to patrol and chase them
away. While trimming back
an overgrown rosemary bush, I
decided to toss the cut branches
around the new plantings. My
hope was that the strong odor
would ward off the bunnies.
Even as the rosemary branches
shriveled and turned brown,
they continued to give off their
pungent fragrance. The result
has been quite good; I have
lost no plants this season.*

 *Helen L. S.
Chapel Hill,
North Carolina*

Single-Strand Deer Deterrence

An electric fence is a reliable barrier for keeping deer out of the
garden, but a multistrand electric fence can be a big investment. You
can keep costs down by installing just a single-wire electric fence
around your garden. To increase its effectiveness, drape aluminum foil
spread with peanut butter over the wire at several spots. The deer will
be attracted to the peanut butter, and when they put their noses on the
highly conductive foil, they'll receive a shock.

If You Plant Lettuce, They Will Come

Outsmart garden-nibbling neighborhood rabbits by taking advantage
of their timid nature and their love of lettuce. Plant a lettuce border
around the vegetable garden on the side where rabbits most often approach. Then leave an open space of lawn or mulch between the
lettuce and the rest of your garden. Plant onions—not a rabbit favorite—on the edge of the main garden next to the open space. The
rabbits will content themselves with the lettuce and likely not venture
past the open space and onions.

The Hairy Wreath

Decorative grapevine wreaths eventually become too ragged to remain
hanging over the mantel or on the front door, but don't throw them
away. Recycle wreaths in the garden and decorate them with dog hair,
a deterrent to rabbits and other animals. The wreaths are perfect re-
ceptacles for holding the dog hair. Just brush your dog and poke the
tufts or clumps of hair into the spaces in the wreath. Hang the wreath
so its lowest point is about 9 inches above the ground. And don't worry
about the weather. When it rains, the wet-dog smell gets even
stronger. In this case, the doggier it smells, the better!

Raccoon Remedies

Try this grab bag of tips from *OG* readers to protect your sweet corn
from ravaging raccoons.

> ■ **Outfox them.** When your corn begins to form kernels, put a
> few drops of fox urine (a liquid scent sold in sporting goods
> stores) on the ground around the perimeter of your corn patch.

■ **Draw a line they won't cross.** Spread a wide border of lime around your patch. Make sure to reapply the barrier after heavy rain.

■ **Keep cool with cucumbers.** Interplant cucumbers or squash with your corn to confuse the critters.

■ **Use B.O.** Hang some dirty shirts—the more odoriferous, the better—from the fence around your garden, or from stakes around your corn patch. The scent of humanity may keep the raccoons away.

■ **Go for the net effect.** When corn ears start to form, cover the plants with bird netting, making sure that the net reaches the ground on all sides. Secure the net to the ground with metal garden pins or pieces of clothes hangers.

■ **Send 'em packing.** Protect your ears by taping them to their stalks with ¾-inch packing tape. Wind a strip of tape around an almost-mature ear about 1 inch above its attachment to the stalk and again about 1½ inches below the tip.

■ **Try shock therapy.** Surround your corn with two or three strands of electrified wire; the lowest strand should be about 6 inches above the ground. Put the fence up before the crop matures—once raccoons have tasted corn, a small shock won't keep them from it.

Win the Woodchuck War

Take advantage of the fact that woodchucks like to have a well-hidden entrance to their burrows, and "landscape" the entrances to make them woodchuck-unfriendly. Remove all brush, tall weeds, grasses, and other forms of protective cover near woodchuck burrows. Replace the plants with onions and garlic, which repel woodchucks.

Another defensive tactic is to put out an "unwelcome" mat. If you have a dog, give your pet a small scrap of carpet remnant or an old throw rug to sleep on for a week or two. Then place the canine-scented unwelcome mat among plants favored by woodchucks and give your pet a new carpet bed, also destined for the garden. Swap the beds every few weeks, keeping the rotation going for the whole growing season.

GARDENER TO GARDENER

Rhubarb Repellent

Here in Alaska, I grind up rhubarb leaves in a blender and spray or fling the mixture on my flowering plants. Moose avoid the treated plants completely, so it might work against deer, too.

Alison H.
Anchorage, Alaska

Bury Your Garden Fence

If rabbits are munching away at your lettuce and broccoli, a simple 3-foot-high fence made of chicken wire should take care of the problem. Not so with woodchucks and other burrowing critters, though. For these garden raiders, you'll need a fence that keeps critters from climbing over *and* from tunneling under. Here's how to install a woodchuck-resistant fence.

1. Dig a trench about 6 inches deep and 12 inches wide around the outside of your garden.

2. Set metal or fiberglass fence posts on the garden side of the trench. You'll need one post for each corner and additional posts for long stretches of fence.

3. Attach 4-foot welded-wire fencing to the posts—but before you clip or staple it in place, bend the lower 1 foot of the fence outward at a right angle so it lines the trench bottom.

4. Fill the trench with dirt and, using the safety procedures recommended by the manufacturer, add a single strand of electric-fence wire a few inches above the top of the welded-wire fence.

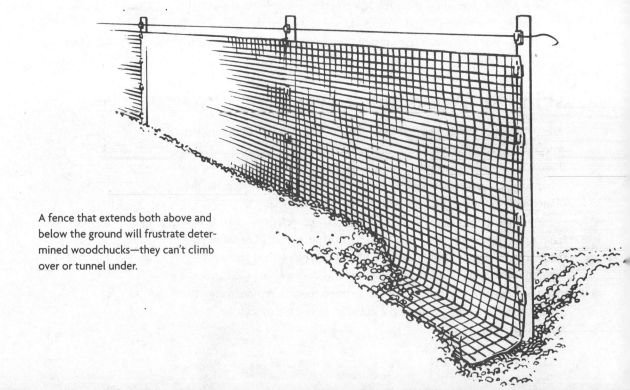

A fence that extends both above and below the ground will frustrate determined woodchucks—they can't climb over or tunnel under.

Chapter 14

Staying Ahead of Weeds

In an organic garden, there's no need to strive for total weed control. Weeds can serve a purpose in organic gardens, such as keeping the soil covered, sheltering beneficial insects, and even providing a tasty addition to salads.

The goal is keeping the balance in your favor—exploiting weeds for their benefits while preventing them from becoming a problem.

Thus, many of the tips in this chapter focus on secrets for stopping weeds early on. You can experiment with a technique for "cooking" weeds to death and with using a variety of interesting weeding tools. For patches of problem weeds, simple solutions for smothering them out may work just fine. And don't overlook the tips on that tried-and-true approach: hand weeding.

You'll find out how to prevent weed problems from springing up while you're away on vacation, how to suppress weeds with a living mulch, and the right way to use a string trimmer for fighting weeds. And for those times when weeds need to be stopped in their tracks quickly, there's advice on safe, organic sprays you can use to kill weeds.

Weeds in Your Wildflowers

In the first year after sowing wildflower seeds to start a prairie planting, it's inevitable that weeds will sprout along with the wildflowers. To prevent weeds from taking over the planting, *don't* hand-pull the weeds. If you do, you'll disturb the emerging wildflowers. Instead, three or four times during the growing season, mow the bed with a string trimmer or a hand scythe. Cut plants back to 6 inches tall—always before the weeds set seed. Leave the cuttings in the bed as mulch.

The following year, your prairie plants will be taller, so raise your mowing height to 12 inches. Mow once or twice this season, beginning in June when biennial weeds—Queen Anne's lace, bull thistle, and sweet clover—are flowering but not yet setting seed. If you notice perennial weeds such as Canada thistle, dandelion, and bindweed, pull them carefully by hand, but only after a soaking rain when the roots pull easily and you are less likely to disturb your prairie seedlings.

The third year, mow the entire planting to the ground early in the season—about the time maple trees begin to bud. Rake out the cut material. In subsequent years, your established prairie will fend well for itself. The spring mowing is usually all the maintenance that's needed.

Beat Weeds Early

You can reduce your weeding chores dramatically if you launch your control effort *before* you start planting seeds. Here are the basic steps.

1. Cultivate your beds or seed rows about 2 weeks before you begin planting the garden. Water them if the soil is dry. Cultivation kills weeds and loosens the soil so crops can grow well, but it also brings more weed seeds to the surface, where they sprout. (Many weed seeds are "smart" and go dormant when buried; they sprout when they are brought near enough to the surface to survive. Sometimes it takes several years of diligence to eliminate this "seed bank" from your garden.)

2. Hoe the bed shallowly just before planting seeds. Cultivate just deeply enough to kill the newly sprouted weed seedlings without stirring up any buried weed seeds. The best hoes for this and other weeding chores are diamond, stirrup, and collinear types with thin blades that are angled so you can slice just under the soil surface.

3. Plant your seeds, then spread a 1-inch layer of weed-smothering fresh grass clippings on all the bare soil in your garden—except that directly over your newly planted seeds. When all areas are covered, add a second layer. The more you mulch, the less you have to weed or water. Grass clippings are superb as mulch because they look great and are as rich in nutrients as most compost. Best of all, you can usually get as many as you need from your neighbors—for free. Shredded leaves also work well.

Hoe or pull any weeds that come up through your mulch during the growing season. By removing them before they set seed, you will reduce your weed problems for years to come. At the end of the growing season, add another couple of inches of grass or leaves to the entire garden, and you probably won't even need to cultivate next spring.

Prevent "Vacation Weeds" Now

If you're planning to be away from your garden for any length of time during the summer, you can prevent a weed crisis by mulching heavily before you go. Spread newspaper (at least six sheets thick) in the exposed areas between your garden plants, then cover the newspaper with a layer of organic matter such as pulled weeds, hay, leaves, or grass clippings. This mulch will also protect your garden from drying out if it doesn't rain while you're away.

Time Paper Placement to Win over Weeds

Newspaper mulch makes a great weed blocker around vegetable crops such as potatoes, but it's important to mulch at the right time to stop the weeds without slowing down your vegetables.

As potato plants grow, their size makes it hard to weed between the rows. Yet the weeds can still sneak in there with no trouble. To stop weed problems before they start, wait until your potatoes are growing and well established but not yet filling in the rows completely. Then hoe between the plants one last time and lay down a two-sheet-thick layer of newspaper. Toss soil on the edges of the paper to hold it down, or cover it with grass clippings or straw. The timing of this mulch gives the potatoes a boost and will save your back in weeks to come. This system works well for beans and other crops.

Grass Clippings Conquer Weeds

We have a large garden. Once our plants have gotten established, we pull out every weed we can spot. Then we place lots of grass clippings around the plants and between rows (anywhere there is soil visible). The grass clippings keep the moisture in the ground, so I don't have to water, and they don't allow the weeds to grow because they block out light. My plants really thrive.

Kristin B.
Covington, Ohio

Swipe Soil to Prevent Path Weeds

"Scalp" the topsoil from garden pathways to stop them from becoming weedways. After you dig your garden beds, remove the topsoil from the paths. Since you don't want plants to grow in pathways, you don't need "good" soil there. Pile the swiped topsoil on your beds, add some organic matter, and you'll have ready-to-plant raised beds.

Once you've stripped the good soil off your paths, top them with a thick layer of wood chips. You'll never have to worry about weeding again. To get chips for your paths, check with local arborists, who often give away the chipped prunings that result from their work. Local municipal recycling centers also often have wood chips available free or for a minimal charge.

Cook Out the Weeds

You can use heat to your advantage and the weeds' disadvantage: Use the summer sun to fry your weeds by covering them with a layer of heat-trapping clear plastic. This technique, known as solarization, destroys existing weeds and any weed seeds in your soil (plant diseases, too).

Solarizing is a great technique to try right before you go on vacation. You just roll the plastic out over vacant beds and relax, knowing that weeds are wilting while you're having fun in the sun.

To prepare a bed for solarizing, rake the soil smooth. If there's some weedy growth, don't worry about pulling it out—it will be torched by the solarization process. Use a sprinkler to wet the plot thoroughly. Roll clear plastic over the bed (UV-resistant greenhouse plastics hold up the best), stretch it tight, and then seal all the edges of the plastic with soil. Leave the plastic on for 2 to 3 weeks.

Weed-Whacking Wisdom

Terminating weeds in your vegetable garden with a string trimmer would seem to be a simple process, but here's how to do it right. First, use your mower to cut back overgrown weeds in the paths between your garden beds. (If your garden is in rows rather than beds, mow down weeds between rows if there is enough space between the rows for you to maneuver without cutting your crops.) Then, use a string trimmer to whack weeds between plants in the bed or in the row. The string trimmer works especially well between caged crops such as tomatoes and peppers; the cages protect the plants from an accidental slip of the trimmer. It is essential that you wear protective eye gear and gloves when you are using a mower or string trimmer! And don't forget to protect your garden plants from a slip of the wrist—cover smaller plants with buckets or boxes, and have a helper protect uncaged large plants with a large sheet of cardboard.

Use a Pitchfork Comb

When invasive grasses such as Johnsongrass occupy your vegetable garden, tackle them with a pitchfork. Work the soil until it is loose and open, and then go over it with a pitchfork. Stab the fork into the ground and lever it back so it combs upward through the soil. The tines will catch the grass roots, and you can handpick them off the fork.

Try a Berry Living Mulch

Believe it or not, strawberries can be used as a living mulch to suppress weeds. The strawberries spread by runners, and they're invasive enough to smother many competing weed crops. They won't produce too much of a crop unless they're planted in full sun, but you will get some berries as a bonus even when you plant them in light shade under other plants such as rose-bushes or blueberry bushes.

old-time wisdom

HOT WEEDING TIP

A hot, windy day is a good time to hoe between your plants because the wind and sun kill the uprooted weeds in a short time. They dry up, and there is but little to remove.

W. C. Egan
Making a Garden of
Perennials, 1912

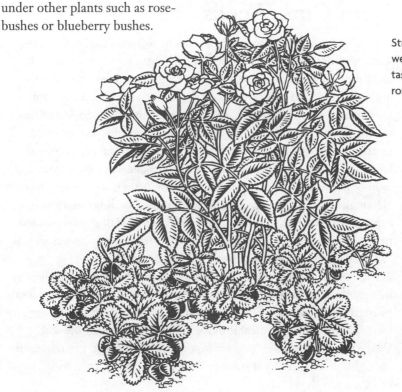

Strawberries serve as a weed-suppressing (and tasty) living mulch under roses or other shrubs.

GARDENER TO
GARDENER

Kudos for Corn Gluten

I have used corn gluten several times. It is an effective organic course to take for weed control, assuming the weeds you want to stop are growing from seed, although it is not 100 percent effective in preventing seed germination. It will not stop weeds that put out runners. In my experience, it will slow the spread of dandelions.

Ray W.
Bristol, Virginia

Smother Weeds with Buckwheat

Got a weed problem? Sow buckwheat thickly to create a dense "smother crop" that efficiently chokes out even the most aggressive invaders, including quackgrass. Buckwheat offers other benefits, as well. Its delightfully fragrant blooms will draw swarms of bees and other beneficial insects to the garden. And at the end of the season, you can turn it under to enrich the soil with nutrient-loaded organic matter.

A Suppressing Story

How can time spent planting a cover crop next fall save you hours of weeding the following summer? If the cover crop is annual rye and you turn the crop into the top few inches of soil in spring, it will suppress emergence of ragweed, pigweed, and purslane for more than a month. One caution: The toxins from the decaying rye will also inhibit germination of small-seeded vegetable crops such as lettuce and carrots. Reserve the rye-planted area for transplants and sowing corn, beans, peas, and other larger-seeded crops.

Corn Cuts Weeds

Corn gluten meal, a nontoxic by-product of corn processing, prevents seedlings from growing new roots and kills them within a few days. Because it's 10 percent nitrogen, it feeds your grass with an essential element. And kids and pets can play on the lawn right after you apply it. How effective is this natural herbicide? Researchers at Iowa State University found that applying corn gluten meal one time—before weeds emerged—reduced the survival rates of dandelions, crabgrass, annual bluegrass, buckhorn plantain, curly dock, purslane, lamb's-quarters, and redroot pigweed by an average of 60 percent. After several years, the corn gluten meal provides as much as 90 percent control. Remember to use corn gluten meal only on established lawns—it will kill newly sprouted turfgrass. Also keep in mind that it provides 10 percent nitrogen, so you can cut back on nitrogen fertilizer.

To use corn gluten meal in garden beds, first prepare your bed by tilling or raking the soil, then spread the meal over the surface at a rate of 20 to 40 pounds per 1,000 square feet (2 to 4 pounds per 100 square feet). Till (or rake) the meal into the top 2 to 3 inches of the soil. Water the bed thoroughly to prompt any weed seeds to germinate (the corn gluten kills any "just sprouted" seeds), then avoid watering the bed for a few days.

A Shot of Vinegar

If you're tired of hand-pulling broad-leaved weeds such as henbit and dandelion from your lawn, you can thwart them with a well-placed shot of vinegar. Fill a spray bottle with undiluted vinegar, or with 3 parts vinegar and 1 part dishwashing liquid. Spray weeds in a narrow stream, dousing the weed's leaves and crown.

Take care not to splash the spray on the turf or any plants you'd like to keep, though, because vinegar will kill grassy plants as well. Carry a section of newspaper or a piece of cardboard with you and use it to shield desirable plants. And don't get carried away with this weed treatment—repeated applications of vinegar will acidify the soil so that nothing will grow in it.

Weed Early, Weed Easy

Want to get a jump on weeds? Pick an unseasonably warm day in February—it's too early to plant, but it's a great time to pull perennial weeds. In fact, it's the best time. Taprooted perennials are much easier to uproot earlier in the season than later, and perennial grasses are especially vulnerable to pulling in early spring. By late spring, grasses have a robust, spreading root system that has to be dug out.

Machete Makes Mincemeat of Large Weeds

When weeds threaten to go to seed, it's important to get rid of them fast to head off an explosion of future weeds. For example, a single fleabane plant can produce over 200,000 weed seeds. A machete makes quick work of chopping down large weeds. Try to incorporate weeding into whatever other tasks you're doing, such as thinning, sowing, or transplanting, so that you won't ever have to deal with large weeds. But for the occasional weed that escapes your notice until it's a monster, the machete is a powerful and effective weed stopper.

Cut Annual Weeds to the Quick

Use utility scissors to clip off annual weeds like lamb's-quarters, pigweed, and purslane below the soil surface. The scissors hardly disturb the soil, and whatever bits of root remain just break down and add more organic matter to the soil.

GARDENER TO GARDENER

Corn Gluten on the Cheap

The cheapest source I've found for buying corn gluten is a feed store or grain elevator. It is sold in 50-pound bags as animal feed. I've never paid more than $17 a bag.

Kathy T.
Northfield, Minnesota

Match the Glove to the Weeds

Wearing gloves while weeding can save you from the annoyance of grubby fingernails and worse. Choose a glove that works the best for the type of weeding at hand.

For pulling small weeds, try a pair of disposable latex gloves. You'll have better dexterity than you would with fabric or leather gloves, and you won't end up with mud under your nails. The most economical place to find disposable latex gloves is in the paint section of home-improvement stores. As long as you don't puncture them while weeding, you can wash and reuse them many times.

Heavy-duty latex dishwashing gloves are the best choice when you need to pull poison ivy. Use an extra-large pair (the longer they are, the more protection for your arms). Pick a cool, cloudy day in early summer and patrol your whole yard, pulling every piece of poison ivy you see. Pull the poison ivy, roots and all, out of the ground. Place the plants in a plastic grocery bag, tie the handles closed, and toss the bag in the trash. Toss the gloves out, too, so that you don't get the oil on anything else. Avoiding a bad case of poison ivy is well worth the price of the disposable gloves.

Polish Up Those Handles

To keep from losing or misplacing your hand weeder, paint the handle bright orange or red. And rather than buy paint when you need only a small amount for this purpose, use some old red nail polish. This is a job children really love. Let them mix all your old bright colors together, do their nails—however messily—and color the tool handles at the same time. Materials needed: one or more children, red nail polish, and nail polish remover for their hands and your yard furniture and deck.

Hand-Pulling Hints

For those times when pulling by hand is the weeding method of choice, such as when perennial weeds have already started to set seed—be sure you're working efficiently to avoid hurting yourself and wasting time.

The easiest and best time to pull weeds is when the soil is damp—like a few hours after a rain, or after watering the garden well. Grab the pesky weed as close to soil level as you can and tug gently until you feel the roots loosening. If you can't feel that "looseness," scratch away as much soil as necessary from the sides of the stalk. Then slowly increase your "pulling pressure," ending in a good firm tug. If you're pulling an annual that has set seed, be especially careful that you don't scatter the seed all over the place.

Be sure to pick up pulled perennial weeds; don't leave these beasts lying in the garden. The tiniest piece might reroot and come back to life. Pick up the pulled weed, shake off the precious garden soil still clinging to its roots, then throw the weed into the compost pile. Long-rooted weeds will have collected lots of precious minerals from deep down below, and composting will get these minerals back to your plants.

Grow a Weed Bed

Weeds aren't always a gardener's enemy. Some weeds, including lamb's-quarters, yarrow, dandelion, and chicory, can be great soil builders and conditioners. (For example, dandelions have a taproot that pulls up minerals from deep in the soil.) If you have the space to spare, try including weeds in your crop rotation scheme. They may do wonders for your soil. One hint: To keep your garden under control, never allow *any* weeds to go to seed, even helpful weeds. If a bed is "resting" under a weed cover, cut the weeds back before they go to seed. Let the cuttings wilt before you turn under the weeds.

Weeds for Dinner: Sweet Revenge

Not only are many of the weeds that plague your garden edible, but they're also some of the best-tasting natural foods around. Add tender baby wild edible weeds to salads for a gourmet touch. Some of the best weeds to add to your menu include chickweed, dandelion, lamb's-quarters (you can also cook these young shoots as you'd cook spinach), pigweed, and purslane.

With baby wild edibles, you get two crops from one space. The weeds will grow right along with head lettuce, which takes 4 to 5 weeks to mature. You'll harvest the edible weeds both before and after the main crop of lettuce and other vegetables, then till the remaining weeds into the soil as green manure.

If you gather wild salad greens from anywhere other than your own organic garden or lawn, make sure they haven't been sprayed. Better to have a boring salad than one dressed with herbicides or fertilizers!

My Definition of Weeds

Some of the weeds in my lawn are excellent salad fodder, including oxalis and dandelions. I leave some clover, too, because it supplies nitrogen. My rule of thumb is: If a weed is competing with what I want growing there and looks like it might win, out it comes. Or if I just don't like the way it looks, I'll make the effort to pull it out. As for the others, I tend to be tolerant—it's all green once it's mowed!

Jerry F.
Howard Lake,
Minnesota

Cease Centipede Grass

Centipede grass, also called wire grass, can be a real pest when it invades a garden bed. It just won't go away. I stop centipede grass invasions before they start by using an edger regularly to keep a clean edge on my beds. I also watch for any runners that are headed where I don't want them and pull them out. It's a garden devil, but it is a good grass for southern lawns!

Vicki N.
Gaffney, South Carolina

Sorry, Charlie

Creeping Charlie can be a recurring nightmare if it catches hold in your lawn. To solve problems with this low-growing, yellow-flowered weed, try borax, the same laundry additive that makes your white socks whiter. Mix 5 teaspoons of borax in 1 quart of water. (Measure exactly: Too little and you won't get the job done; too much and you could kill your grass, too.) This amount of spray will cover a 25-square-foot area. Water and fertilize your turf after the treatment so it rapidly fills in the space left by the dead weeds. Borax is most effective as a weed killer in late spring or early summer, when weeds are growing actively. Be warned, though: Borax doesn't work on other weeds (such as dandelions), and it may cause a temporary yellowing of nearby grass. If you see some yellowing in surrounding grass, just mow frequently and it should green up within 6 weeks.

Quick Fixes for Lawn Weeds

Weeds in your lawn come bearing a message: They're telling you that you've fertilized the grass too much, for instance, or not enough. Or maybe you cut it too short, or your soil is too hard. Maybe they're simply pointing out that you are growing the wrong type of grass for your conditions. Address these underlying problems and your weed problems will eventually disappear. In the short term, here are some quick fixes for weed problems.

Annual bluegrass. Pull, hoe, or till out small bunches. For large patches, use solarization, as described on page 192. (Be aware that the trapped heat also will kill any turfgrass beneath the plastic.) Remove the plastic after several weeks, and rake out the dead grass. Corn gluten meal is also effective against it.

Broadleaf plantain. Use a pronged dandelion-type weeder to lift the plantain's rosette, then pull up the long taproot from the soil. The smaller the plantain, the easier it will be to do this.

Crabgrass. Dig out the plants completely from small patches of crabgrass because new crabgrass can grow from any remaining roots. Immediately sow grass seed where the weed grew. For a severe crabgrass problem, spread corn gluten meal on your lawn in spring—before overwintering seeds germinate.

Dandelion. Use a V-shape dandelion weeder to dig them out completely: If you don't get all of the root, try again when it re-sprouts. For large patches, spread corn gluten meal in early spring before seeds sprout.

Ground ivy. Rake it out—this weed has very shallow roots and comes out with a simple tug. Put the pulled ivy in direct sunlight or in a hot compost pile, where it will quickly shrivel and die.

Quackgrass. For small stands of quackgrass, use a weeder and your fingers to extract the weed's shallow but extensive root net-work. Every bit of quackgrass left behind can grow into a new stand. Kill a large area of quackgrass by solarization, as described on page 192. It's a good idea to re-cover the area with plastic for a couple more weeks to kill any surviving pieces. Resow the area densely with turfgrass.

White clover. Use a hoe or tiller to remove this shallow-rooted weed, then mix compost into the soil to increase its water-holding capacity and fertility. Reseed bare spots with grass.

Dandelions Deserve Respect

The lowly dandelion is as nutritious as it is relentless. Bursting with more than 74 nutrients, the dandelion is high in vitamin C and is a good source of both calcium and iron. Just 1 cup of raw greens has five times more vitamin A than the same amount of broccoli. You can eat wild dandelions from your yard (pick at least 75 feet from the road-side), but some people prefer the broader-leaved cultivated varieties, such as 'Dandelion Amelioré'.

Dandelions are perfect for gardeners eager for a quick payoff. Begin picking as soon as they sprout and continue to harvest the leaves only until 6 weeks after sowing to avoid bitterness. Once they have flowered, clip back to the soil surface, then gather the young greens that sprout. You can repeat this process all summer.

Block Weeds with Boards

Smother colonies of weeds that pop up around your garden during the summer by covering them with boards or sheets of plywood (you may be able to get discards from a local sawmill). The boards will keep sun-light from reaching the weeds so they won't go to seed and others won't start to grow.

Cooking Transforms Nettles

Nettles (*Urtica dioica*) in the garden can be a pain (literally), but when gathered at just the right stage and properly prepared, they are delicious to eat. Cooking completely destroys the nettle's stinging qualities and converts the toxins into wholesome food. You must gather the first tender shoots that arise as soon as the weather is warm. Later in the year, the plants contain gritty particles that are unpalatable.

Take only the tender tops of young, first-grown nettles, before they begin to bloom. Wear leather or plastic-coated work gloves while gathering because even these young plants can sting fiercely. Wash the greens by stirring them in water with a long-handled spoon, then use a pair of kitchen tongs to put them directly into a large saucepan with a tight lid. Cover and cook gently for 20 minutes and drain, but save the juice.

You can chop the greens right in the cooking pot with a pair of kitchen shears. Season with butter and spice to taste, and they are ready to serve. The juice, taken as hot as you can drink it, has a reputation of helping to prevent colds.

Tough Tree Weeds

Some trees, such as mulberries and some maples, drop prolific quantities of fruit that in turn produce tiny forests of tree seedlings. If these seedlings take hold, the result can be a tough weed problem. Hand pulling just won't do the job. If you can't mow to keep such saplings cut back, you can try using special tools that pull the plant out, roots and all. These tools have a special clamp or a claw-hammer-type base at the bottom of a very sturdy handle. The clamp or claw holds the seedlings firmly as the handle provides the leverage needed to uproot them easily. Check mail-order supply catalogs that specialize in tools to find weed tree pullers such as these.

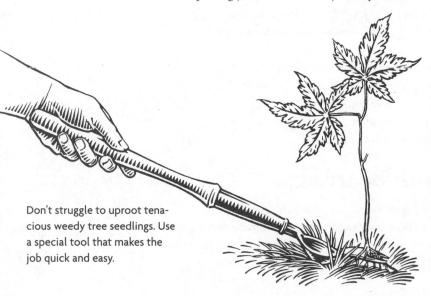

Don't struggle to uproot tenacious weedy tree seedlings. Use a special tool that makes the job quick and easy.

Gardener's Glossary

Acidic/Acid. Soil pH that's less than 7.0 (neutral); acid soils tend to be deficient in phosphorus and sometimes contain excess manganese and aluminum.

Aerate. To open channels in soil for air infiltration and movement.

Alkaline. Soil pH that's above 7.0 (neutral); alkaline soils tend to lack manganese and boron.

Annual. A plant that flowers, bears seed, and dies within one growing season.

Bacillus thuringiensis **(BT).** Naturally occurring pathogen that's toxic to insect larvae but not harmful to other organisms or humans; various strains are sold commercially.

Backfill. To fill in a planting hole around a plant's roots with soil.

Bareroot. Plants (usually woody ornamentals, such as roses, shrubs, or young trees) sold without soil on their roots.

Beneficials. Insects considered helpful in the garden because they prey on pest insects. Examples: lady beetles, ground beetles, tachinid flies.

Blanch. 1. To mound soil around stems or leaves of growing plants, especially leeks and asparagus, so that they become white and tender. **2.** In food preservation, the process of boiling vegetables for a specific time period in order to slow deterioration during storage.

Bolt. To produce flowers and seed prematurely (often due to hot weather).

Bottom water. To supply water to seedlings and plants growing in containers by adding water to a saucer or tray placed underneath the containers.

Broadcast. To scatter seed by hand in a random pattern.

Capillary mat. A mat made of absorbent material that is placed under seedling flats or other containers.

Cell pack. Thin plastic or peat containers that have several compartments; used for starting individual seedlings.

Clay. Soil type that absorbs and drains water very slowly due to lack of air space between particles.

Coldframe. Low, enclosed structure for protecting plants from cold; clear cover lets in sunlight.

Compost. A humus-rich, organic material formed by the decomposition of leaves, grass clippings, and other organic materials. Used to improve soil.

Corm. A swollen underground stem that looks similar to a bulb. Irises are one example of a plant that produces corms.

Cover crop. Plant grown and then turned under to improve soil texture and fertility. Examples: clover, rye, buckwheat, vetch.

Cross-pollinated. Fertilized by transfer of pollen from the flower of one plant to the female flower parts of another plant.

Crown. The point where a plant's roots and stem meet, usually at soil level.

Cultivar. A cultivated variety of a plant, usually selected for a special trait, such as compact growth or disease resistance.

Cutting. A piece of stem, leaf, or root taken from a parent plant in order to start a new plant.

Cutting (hardwood). Mature wood (deciduous or evergreen) taken at the end of the growing season or during dormancy in order to start new plants.

Damping-off. A fungal disease that causes seedlings to rot at the soil line.

Deadhead. To remove faded flowers.

Determinate tomatoes. Tomatoes that have vines that grow to a given height and then stop. Most of the fruit is produced and ripens at one time.

Diatomaceous earth. The fossilized remains of ancient marine organisms, sold as a control for soft-bodied insect pests, such as aphids and slugs.

Direct seed. To sow seeds outdoors in garden soil (as opposed to starting seed indoors for transplanting at a later date).

Double-dig. To work soil to a depth that is twice the usual by digging a trench, loosening the soil at the bottom of the trench, then returning the top layer of soil to the trench. This produces a raised bed that contains a deep layer of very loose, fluffy soil.

Drip irrigation. A type of irrigation in which water seeps slowly into the soil via hoses or pipe systems. There is less evaporation and more control than with overhead watering.

Drip line. Imaginary line on the soil marking the outside circumference of a tree's canopy.

Essential oil. A plant oil that conveys the characteristic fragrance of the plant.

Exchangeable sodium percentage (ESP). The ratio of sodium in the soil to the total amount of certain nutrients in the soil that are available for uptake by plant roots.

Flat. Shallow tray for starting seeds indoors; does not have individual compartments.

Force. To bring dormant plants (especially bulbs and cut branches) into bloom by manipulating temperature.

Frass. Insect excrement; can be used to help identify garden pests.

Friable. Having a crumbly texture. Desirable for soil.

Frost heaving. Alternate freezing and thawing of the soil, which causes the crowns of plants to be pushed up out of the ground.

Graft. To cause two plants to join by putting their growing tissues in contact under favorable conditions.

Green manure. A fast-maturing leafy crop—such as buckwheat, rye, or clover—that adds organic matter to the soil when it's turned under.

Harden off. To gradually expose a plant to outdoor conditions before transplanting it to the garden.

Hardiness. Ability to survive the winter without protection from the cold.

Humus. The complex, organic residue of decayed plant matter in soil.

Hybrid. The offspring of genetically different plants.

Indeterminate tomatoes. Tomato varieties that produce vines that continue to grow for the life of the plant.

Infusion. A liquid that results from steeping plant parts in water.

Inoculant. A substance that contains bacteria that aid in plant growth by stimulating nitrogen fixation in the soil in association with plant roots.

Interplanting. Combining plants that have different bloom times or growth habits so that bloom lasts longer and chance of disease is lower.

Landscape fabric. Synthetic fabric that allows water to pass through but resists penetration by plant stems or roots.

Layering. Propagating a plant by causing a stem to form roots along its length. After roots have formed, the rooted stem is cut free from the parent plant.

Leaf mold. Decomposed leaves. An excellent winter mulch, attractive to earthworms.

Legume. A plant that can fix nitrogen, i.e., cause atmospheric nitrogen in the soil to be transformed into nitrogen compounds that can be absorbed by plant roots. Legumes may be annuals, perennials, shrubs, or trees.

Loam. An ideal garden soil; contains plenty of organic matter and a balanced mix of small and large particles.

Medium. Soil mix or potting mixture.

Mesclun. A mix of salad greens.

Microclimate. Local conditions of shade, exposure, wind, drainage, and other factors that affect plant growth at a given site.

Miticide. A substance that kills mites.

Mulch. Material layered over the soil's surface to hold in moisture, suppress weeds, and (if organic) improve soil.

Nematodes. Threadlike microscopic organisms. There are types of nematodes that injure plants, types that parasitize plant pests, and types that play a beneficial role in breaking down organic matter.

Nitrogen fixation. A process by which atmospheric nitrogen in the soil is converted into nitrates.

Open-pollinated. Varieties whose seeds come from plants pollinated naturally.

Organic matter. Materials derived from plants and animals, such as leaves, grass clippings, and manure.

Overwinter. To keep a plant living through the winter so that it can continue growing the next year; may require the use of coldframes, row covers, or hoop houses.

Pathogen. Disease-causing microorganism.

Peat pot. Commercially available seedling container made from compressed peat moss. Gradually breaks down, so both pot and seedling can be planted without disturbing roots.

Perennial. Any plant that lives for at least three seasons; can be woody (trees and shrubs) or herbaceous (those that die back to the ground in winter).

Perlite. Lightweight expanded minerals added to potting mixes to improve aeration.

pH. Measure of soil acidity or alkalinity; 7.0 is neutral.

Pinching. Periodically removing the newest growth of a leafy plant to encourage a more "bushy" form.

Potbound. A containerized plant whose roots have completely filled the potting soil inside the container, making it difficult to remove the plant from the container. Potbound plants may have stunted growth.

Pot up. To plant in a container or to move a containerized plant into a larger container.

Primocane. A first-year cane or shoot of a bramble fruit such as a raspberry.

Proliferations. Buds or shoots that formed in an unusual way or location, such as on a leaf or from a flower.

Rhizome. A creeping horizontal stem that forms on or just below ground level.

Rogue. To remove unwanted individual plants from a garden or other site.

Rootstock. A plant onto which another plant is grafted.

Row cover. Translucent polyester fabric placed over garden plants or beds to protect them from pests. Heavier types also used to protect plants from cold. Lets in water and light.

Self-pollinated. Fertilized by transfer of pollen from the anthers of a flower to the stigma of the same flower or other flowers on the same plant.

Side-dress. To spread a layer of compost or other fertilizer on the soil surface, next to growing plants.

Soil amendment. Material added to a soil to improve its structure or fertility.

Soluble salts. The concentration of certain mineral elements present in the water in the soil.

Spore. A small reproductive unit, usually a single cell, produced by bacteria, fungi, and some types of plants.

Standard. A tree or shrub trained to a single bare trunk with a round "head" of foliage.

Stratification. Exposing seeds to certain cool conditions in order to break seed dormancy.

Succession crop. To follow early-maturing crops with other plantings so that beds continue to produce throughout the growing season.

Succulents. Plants that have thick, fleshy leaves and stems.

Thatch. A layer of partially decomposed leaves and other plant material at the base of grass plants in a lawn.

Thin. To remove excess seedlings or fruits to ensure best spacing for plant health, yield, and size.

Tilth. Soil texture and workability.

Top-dress. To apply a layer of fertilizer to the soil surface (not working it in).

Umbel-shaped. Plants with flower heads shaped like an umbrella, including dill, fennel, anise, yarrow, and coriander. Attractive to beneficial insects.

Underplant. To plant short plants, such as groundcovers, below taller plants, such as shrubs.

Vermicompost. Compost created by raising certain types of earthworms in a closed container and harvesting the worm castings (excrement).

Vermiculite. Lightweight mineral added to soil mix to improve aeration.

Wallo'Water. A product sold to protect plants from cold; water-filled plastic walls retain heat around plants.

Zones. Geographic regions; hardiness zones marked by a range of lowest temperatures in an average winter for a given area. Example: 0° to −10°F.

Resources

Use the listings below to find companies that sell seeds, plants, and organic gardening supplies, as well as companies that provide soil testing. When you contact associations or specialty nurseries by mail, please enclose a self-addressed, stamped envelope with your inquiry.

Vegetable and Flower Seeds

Bountiful Gardens
18001 Shafer Ranch Road
Willits, CA 95490
Phone: (707) 459-6410
Fax: (707) 459-1925
Web site: www.bountifulgardens.org

W. Atlee Burpee
300 Park Avenue
Warminster, PA 18974
Phone: (800) 888-1447
Fax: (215) 674-4170
Web site: www.burpee.com

The Cook's Garden
P.O. Box 535
Londonderry, VT 05148
Phone: (800) 457-9703
Fax: (800) 457-9705
Web site: www.cooksgarden.com

Fedco Seeds
P.O. Box 250
Waterville, ME 04903
Phone: (207) 873-7333
Fax: (207) 872-8317

Garden City Seeds
778 Highway 93 North, #3
Hamilton, MT 59840
Phone: (406) 961-4837
Fax: (406) 961-4877
Web site: www.gardencityseeds.com

Johnny's Selected Seeds
1 Foss Hill Road
RR 1, Box 2580
Albion, ME 04910
Phone: (207) 437-4301
Fax: (207) 437-2165
Web site: www.johnnyseeds.com

Nichols Garden Nursery
1190 Old Salem Road NE
Albany, OR 97321
Phone: (541) 928-9280
Fax: (800) 231-5306
Web site: www.nicholsgardennursery.com

Park Seed Co.
1 Parkton Avenue
Greenwood SC 29647
Phone: (800) 845-3369
Fax: (864) 941-4206
Web site: www.parkseed.com

Pinetree Garden Seeds
P.O. Box 300
New Gloucester, ME 04260
Phone: (207) 926-3400
Fax: (888) 527-3337
Web site: www.superseeds.com

Seeds of Change
P.O. Box 15700
Santa Fe, NM 87506
Phone: (888) 762-7333
Web site: www.seedsofchange.com

Southern Exposure Seed Exchange
P.O. Box 460
Mineral, VA 23117
Phone: (540) 894-9480
Fax: (804) 894-9481
Web site: www.southernexposure.com

Stokes Seed, Inc.
Box 548
Buffalo, NY 14240
Phone: (716) 695-6980
Fax: (888) 834-3334
Web site: www.stokeseeds.com

Territorial Seed Company
P.O. Box 158
Cottage Grove, OR 97424
Phone: (541) 942-9547
Fax: (888) 657-3131
Web site: www.territorial-seed.com

Tomato Growers Supply Co.
P.O. Box 2237
Fort Myers, FL 33902
Phone: (888) 478-7333
Fax: (888) 768-3476
Web site: www.tomatogrowers.com

Fruit

Bear Creek Nursery
P.O. Box 411
Bear Creek Road
Northport, WA 99157
Phone: (509) 732-6219
Fax: (509) 732-4417

Johnson Nursery, Inc.
5273 Highway 52 East
Ellijay, GA 30540
Phone: (888) 276-3187
Fax: (706) 276-3186
Web site: www.johnsonnursery.com

Lewis Nursery & Farms, Inc.
3500 NC Highway 133 West
Rocky Point, NC 28457
Phone: (910) 675-2394
Fax: (910) 602-3106

Raintree Nursery
391 Butts Road
Morton, WA 98356
Phone: (360) 496-6400
Fax: (888) 770-8358
Web site: www.raintreenursery.com

Strawberry Tyme Farms
RR 2 #1250, Street Johns Road
Simcoe, ON N3Y 4K1
Canada
Phone: (519) 426-3009
Fax: (519) 426-2573
Web site: www.strawberrytyme.com

Street Lawrence Nurseries
325 State Highway 345
Potsdam, NY 13676
Phone: (315) 265-6739
Web site: www.sln.Potsdam.ny.us

Perennials

André Viette Farm & Nursery
P.O. Box 1109
Fishersville, VA 22939
Phone: (540) 943-2315
Fax: (540) 943-0782
Web site: www.viette.com

Bluestone Perennials
7211 Middle Ridge Road
Madison, OH 44057
Phone: (800) 852-5243
Fax: (440) 428-7535
Web site: www.bluestoneperennials.com

Busse Gardens
17160 245th Avenue
Big Lake, MN 55309
Phone: (800) 544-3192
Fax: (612) 263-1473
Web site: www.bussegardens.com

Canyon Creek Nursery
3527 Dry Creek Road
Oroville, CA 95965
Phone: (530) 533-2166
Web site: www.canyoncreeknursery.com

Carroll Gardens
444 East Main Street
Westminster, MD 21157
Phone: (800) 638-6334
Fax: (410) 857-4112
Web site: www.carrollgardens.com

Forestfarm
990 Tetherow Road
Williams, OR 97544
Phone: (541) 846-7269
Fax: (541) 846-6963
Web site: www.forestfarm.com

Gardens North
5984 Third Line Road North
North Gower, ON K0A 2T0
Canada
Phone: (613) 489-0065
Fax: (613) 489-1208
Web site: www.gardensnorth.com

Heronswood Nursery Ltd.
7530 NE 288th Street
Kingston, WA 98346
Phone: (360) 297-4172
Fax: (360) 297-8321
Web site: www.heronswood.com

Kurt Bluemel, Inc.
2740 Greene Lane
Baldwin, MD 21013
Phone: (800) 248-7584
Fax: (410) 557-9785
Web site: www.bluemel.com

Niche Gardens
1111 Dawson Road
Chapel Hill, NC 27516
Phone: (919) 967-0078
Fax: (919) 967-4026
Web site: www.nichegdn.com

The Perennial Gardens
13139 224th Street
Maple Ridge, BC V4R 2P6
Canada
Phone: (604) 467-4218
Fax: (604) 467-3181
Web site: www.perennialgardener.com

Plant Delights Nursery
9241 Sauls Road
Raleigh, NC 27603
Phone: (919) 772-4794
Fax: (919) 662-0370
Web site: www.plantdel.com

Plants of the Southwest
Agua Fria, Route 6, Box 11A
Santa Fe, NM 87501
Phone: (800) 788-7333
Fax: (505) 438-8800
Web site: www.plantsofthesouthwest.com

Shady Oaks Nursery
P.O. Box 708
Waseca, MN 56093
Phone: (800) 504-8006
Fax: (888) 735-4531
Web site: www.shadyoaks.com

Siskiyou Rare Plant Nursery
2825 Cummings Road
Medford, OR 97501
Phone: (541) 772-6846
Fax: (541) 772-4917
Web site: www.wave.net/upg/srpn

Wayside Gardens
1 Garden Lane
Hodges, SC 29695
Phone/Fax: (800) 845-1124
Web site: www.waysidegardens.com

White Flower Farm
P.O. Box 50
Litchfield, CT 06759-0050
Phone: (800) 503-9624
Fax: (860) 496-1418
Web site: www.whiteflowerfarm.com

Gardening Supplies/Soil Testing

Arbico
18701 North Lago Del Oro Pkwy
Tucson, AZ 85739
Phone: (800) 827-2847
Web site: www.goodearthmarketplace.com

Gardener's Supply Co.
128 Intervale Road
Burlington, VT 05401
Phone: (888) 833-1412
Fax: (800) 551-6712
Web site: www.gardeners.com

Gardens Alive!
5100 Schenley Place
Lawrenceburg, IN 47025
Phone: (812) 537-8650
Fax: (812) 537-5108
Web site: www.gardensalive.com

Green Spot Ltd.
93 Priest Road
Nottingham, NH 03290
Phone: (603) 942-8925
Fax: (603) 942-8932
Web site: www.greenmethods.com

Harmony Farm Supply
3244 Highway 116 North
Sebastopol, CA 95742
Phone: (707) 823-9125
Fax: (707) 823-1734
Web site: www.harmonyfarm.com

Peaceful Valley Farm Supply
P.O. Box 2209
Grass Valley, CA 95945
Phone: (530) 272-4769
Fax: (530) 272-4794
Web site: www.groworganic.com

Snow Pond Farm Supply
P.O. Box 70
Salem, MA 01970
Phone: (978) 745-0716
Fax: (978) 745-0905
Web site: www.snow-pond.com

Woods End Research Laboratory
P.O. Box 297
Mt. Vernon, ME 04352
Phone: (800) 451-0337
Fax: (207) 293-2488
Web site: www.solvita.com

Worm's Way
7850 North Highway 37
Bloomington, IN 47404
Phone: (800) 274-9676
Web site: www.wormsway.net

Seed-Saving Organizations

Maine Seed-Saving Network
P.O. Box 126
Penobscot, ME 04476
Phone: (207) 326-0751

Seed Savers Exchange
3076 North Winn Road
Decorah, IA 52101
Phone: (319) 382-5990
Fax: (319) 382-5872
Web site: www.seedsavers.org

Seeds of Diversity Canada
P.O. Box 36, Station Q
Toronto, ON M4T 2L7
Canada
Phone: (905) 623-0353
Web site: www.seeds.ca

Recommended Reading

Ashworth, Suzanne. *Seed to Seed: Seed Saving Techniques for the Home Gardener.* Decorah, IA: Seed Saver Publications, 1991.

Bradley, Fern Marshall, and Barbara W. Ellis, eds. *Rodale's All-New Encyclopedia of Organic Gardening.* Emmaus, PA: Rodale, 1992.

Coleman, Eliot. *Four-Season Harvest: Organic Vegetables from Your Home Garden All Year Around.* White River Junction, VT: Chelsea Green, 1999.

DiSabato-Aust, Tracy. *The Well-Tended Perennial Garden.* Portland, OR: Timber Press, 1998.

Druse, Ken. *Making More Plants: The Science, Art, and Joy of Propagation.* New York: Clarkson Potter, 2000.

Editors, Rodale Organic Gardening Books. *Rodale Organic Gardening Basics: Roses.* Emmaus, PA: Rodale, 2000.

Gilkeson, Linda, Pam Peirce, and Miranda Smith. *Rodale's Pest & Disease Problem Solver: A Chemical-Free Guide to Keeping Your Garden Healthy.* Emmaus, PA: Rodale, 1996.

Jeavons, John. *How to Grow More Vegetables Than You Ever Thought Possible on Less Land Than You Can Imagine: A Primer on the Life-Giving Biointensive Method of Organic Horticulture.* Berkeley, CA: Ten Speed Press, 1991.

Martin, Deborah, and Grace Gershuny, eds. *The Rodale Book of Composting.* Emmaus, PA: Rodale, 1992.

Moyer, Anne Halpin. *Foolproof Planting: How to Successfully Start and Propagate More Than 250 Vegetables, Flowers, Trees, and Shrubs.* Emmaus, PA: Rodale, 1990

Nick, Jean M. A., and Fern Marshall Bradley. *Growing Fruits & Vegetables Organically.* Emmaus, PA: Rodale, 1994.

Ondra, Nancy J. *Soil and Composting.* (Taylor's Weekend Gardening Guides.) Boston: Houghton Mifflin, 1998.

OG magazine, Rodale Inc., Emmaus, PA 18098.

Phillips, Ellen, and C. Colston Burrell. *Rodale's Illustrated Encyclopedia of Perennials.* Emmaus, PA: Rodale, 1993.

Powell, Eileen. *From Seed to Bloom.* Pownal, VT: Storey, 1995.

Sombke, Laurence. *Beautiful Easy Flower Gardens.* Emmaus, PA: Rodale, 1995.

Index

Note: Pages references in **boldface** indicate illustrations.

USDA Plant Hardiness Zone Map

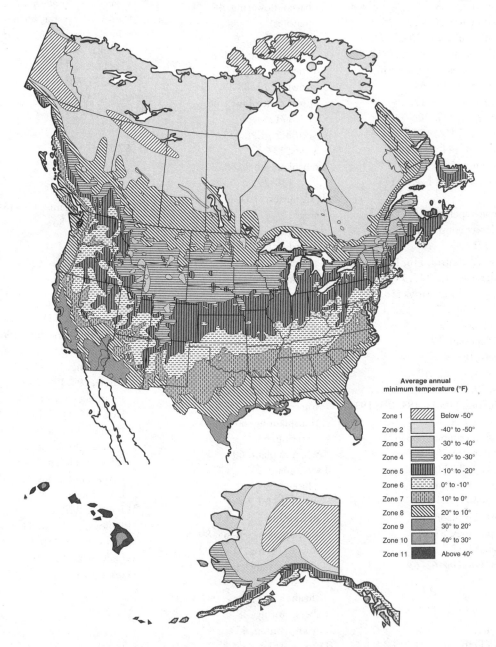

Average annual minimum temperature (°F)

Zone 1	Below -50°
Zone 2	-40° to -50°
Zone 3	-30° to -40°
Zone 4	-20° to -30°
Zone 5	-10° to -20°
Zone 6	0° to -10°
Zone 7	10° to 0°
Zone 8	20° to 10°
Zone 9	30° to 20°
Zone 10	40° to 30°
Zone 11	Above 40°

Revised in 1990, this map is recognized as the best indicator of minimum temperatures available. Look at the map to find your area, then match its color to the key at the right. When you've found your color, the key will tell you what hardiness zone you live in. Remember that the map is a general guide; your particular conditions may vary.